EXAMINATIONS

AND

LETTERS

OF THE

REV. JOHN PHILPOT,

ARCHDEACON OF WINCHESTER, AND MARTYR, 1555.

Wipf & Stock
PUBLISHERS
Eugene, Oregon

Wipf and Stock Publishers
199 W 8th Ave, Suite 3
Eugene, OR 97401

Examinations and Letters of the Rev. John Philpot
By Philpot, John
ISBN: 1-59752-202-3
Publication date 5/17/2005
Previously published by The Religious Tract Society

CONTENTS

	Page
INTRODUCTORY REMARKS	3

EXAMINATIONS.

THE process and history of John Philpot	5
The first examination before the queen's commissioners, 2nd October, 1555	6
The second examination, 24th October, 1555	11
The manner of his calling first before the bishop of London	15
The fourth examination before several bishops	19
The fifth examination, before several bishops and others	31
The sixth examination before several noblemen and the bishop of London, 6th November	46
The seventh examination before the bishop of London and others	64
A private conference between Philpot and bishop Bonner	73
Another conference between the same and other prisoners	74
A private conference between Philpot and the bishop in the Coalhouse	78
The eighth examination before the bishop of London and others	81
The ninth examination before the bishop and his chaplains	83
The tenth examination before the same	92
The eleventh examination before several bishops	95
The twelfth examination before the bishop of London and others	115
The thirteenth examination before the same	122
Another talk the same day	130
The last examinations	132
A letter concerning the handling of Master Green	139
A letter written by lady Vane	140
Philpot's supplication to the Parliament	141
The condemnation of Philpot	143
A prayer to be said at the stake	147

CONTENTS.

LETTERS.

	Page
1. A letter to the christian congregation	150
2. To Mistress Ann Hartpole	158
3. To certain godly Women	160
4. To Robert Glover, prisoner in Coventry	162
5. To certain godly Brethren	163
6. To lady Vane	170
7. To his own dear Sister	172
8. To lady Vane	175
9. To certain of his faithful Friends	178
0. To the Wife of one of the late bishops	182
11. To John Careless, prisoner in the King's Bench	ib.
12. To lady Vane, a letter full of spiritual consolation	184
13. To John Careless	186
14. To Robert Harrington	188
15. To Mistress Heath	190
16. To lady Vane, encouraging her under the evil times	192
17. To the same, complaining of the dissimulation and perjury of Englishmen falling again to the Pope	196
18. To John Careless, profitable to be read by all who mourn in repentance for their sins	198
19. To lady Vane	202

THE

EXAMINATIONS

OF

THE CONSTANT MARTYR OF CHRIST

JOHN PHILPOT,

ARCHDEACON OF WINCHESTER,

AT SUNDRY SEASONS IN THE TIME OF HIS SORE IMPRISONMENT

INTRODUCTORY REMARKS.

The examinations of John Philpot are among the most important of the writings of the British Reformers. His rank and learning made the papists very desirous that he should be brought to adopt their doctrines, and induced them to treat him with more forbearance than most of his fellow martyrs. His undaunted courage and ardent zeal also prompted him to pursue such a course as would be most likely to expose their cruel and illegal proceedings. With this view, he availed himself of his rights as one of the clergy of the diocese of Winchester, and refused to acknowledge Bonner's authority, or to submit to the brief course which that prelate could not venture to adopt towards a well known individual of family without his own concurrence.

Thus, Philpot's examinations were numerous, and before the principal Romanists, both ecclesiastics and laymen. He was enabled to record the particulars; and the greater part having been preserved and conveyed to Fox, were published by him even before the death of queen Mary. Their truth is undoubted, and they present an affecting picture, written by the martyr himself, of the sufferings he was called to undergo, and a lively portraiture of the illegal proceedings of the papists even in this country, and at a time when they were compelled to observe some outward show of respect to the laws of the land.

Nor are these examinations less valuable for the doctrinal points they exhibit. They contain a summary view of the leading errors of popery, and the sophistries by which they were supported, and also present a brief recapitulation of the arguments by which these sophistries were exposed. In this respect they will always be useful, so long as the church of Rome continues (as it still does) to advance the very same arguments in behalf of its usurped authority.

INTRODUCTORY REMARKS.

The reader will not fail to observe, that after all, the great question was the setting up of *other mediators*, and other means of salvation, than Jesus Christ our Lord. However this may appear at times to have been lost sight of amidst the discussion of subordinate topics, still it was the *real* point on which the whole difference turned, and nothing but a full and firm reliance thereon could have supported Philpot under his trials. If we are for a moment inclined to think that he sometimes betrayed more warmth than was desirable, let us remember that at the period in question coarser expressions were commonly used than at the present day, and also that a less ardent mind would probably have shrunk from the contest; while, like the prophet Elijah, Philpot was enabled to stand undaunted before the assembled priests of **Baal**, to plead for the Lord of hosts, who has promised, that " **as thy days, so shall thy strength be.**"

THE EXAMINATIONS

OF

JOHN PHILPOT.

FROM ACTS AND MONUMENTS, BY JOHN FOX. Ed. 1576.

The process and history of John Philpot, examined, condemned, and martyred, for the maintenance and defence of the gospel's cause, against the antichristian see of Rome.

MASTER JOHN PHILPOT was of a worshipful house, a knight's son, born in Hampshire, about A. D. 1521, and brought up in New College, Oxford, where he studied the civil law for six or seven years, besides the study of other liberal arts, especially of languages, wherein he profited much, namely, in the knowledge of the Hebrew tongue, &c. He was of good understanding, of singular courage, fervent in spirit, zealous in religion, and also well practised and exercised therein, (which is no small matter in a true divine,) of nature and condition plain and open, far from all flattery, further from all hypocrisy and deceitful dissimulation. What his learning was, his own examinations, penned by his own hand, can declare.

From Oxford he went into Italy, and places thereabouts, where coming from Venice to Padua, he was in danger through a Franciscan friar, who accompanying him in his journey, who when they came to Padua, sought to accuse him of heresy. At length returning again into England, his country, as the times ministered more boldness to him in the days of king Edward, he had divers conflicts with Gardiner, the bishop in the city of Winchester, as appears by Winchester's letters, and his examinations.

After that, having an advowson given him by the said bishop, he was made archdeacon of Winchester, under Doctor Poinet, who succeeded Gardiner in that bishopric.

Thus, during the time of king Edward, he continued to the no small profit of those parties thereabout. When that blessed king was taken away, and Mary his sister came in his place, whose study was wholly bent to alter the state of religion in the woeful realm of England, first she caused a convocation of the prelates and learned men to be assembled, to accomplish her desire.

In which convocation, Master Philpot being present according to his room and degree, with a few others, sustained the cause of the gospel manfully against the adversaries; for which cause, notwithstanding free liberty of speech and debate was promised by authority, he was called to account before bishop Gardiner, the chancellor, then restored to the see of Winchester, and being his ordinary, by whom he was first examined, although that examination came not to our hands. From thence again he was removed to Bonner and other commissioners, with whom he had divers conflicts, as in his examinations here following may appear.

The first Examination of M. John Philpot, before the queen's commissioners, M. Cholmley, M. Roper, and Dr. Story, and one of the scribes of the Arches, at Newgate Sessions' Hall, 2nd of October, 1555.

BEFORE I was called into an inner parlour where they sat, doctor Story came out into the hall where I was, to view me among others that were there, and passing by me, said, "Ha! Master Philpot," and returning immediately again, stayed against me, beholding me, and saying that I was well fed indeed.

Philpot. If I am fat and in good liking, Master doctor, it is no marvel, since I have been stalled up in prison this twelve months and a half, in a close corner. I am come to know your pleasure wherefore you have sent for me.

Story. We hear that you are a suspected person, and of heretical opinions, and therefore we have sent for you.

Phil. I have been in prison thus long only for the disputation made in the convocation-house, and upon suspicion of setting forth the report thereof.

Story. If you will revoke the same, and become an honest man, you shall be set at liberty, and do right well; or else you shall be committed to the bishop of London How sayest thou, wilt thou revoke it or no?

Phil. I have already answered in this behalf to mine ordinary.

Story. If thou answerest thus when thou comest before us anon, thou shalt hear more of our minds.

With this he went into the parlour, and a little while after I was called in.

The Scribe. Sir, what is your name?

Phil. My name is John Philpot.

Story. This man was archdeacon of Winchester, of doctor Poinet's presentment.

Phil. I was archdeacon indeed, but none of his presentment, but by virtue of a former advowson, given by my lord chancellor that now is.

Story. You may be sure that my lord chancellor would not make any such as he is, archdeacon.

Roper. Come hither to me, Master Philpot. We hear say that you are out of the Catholic church, and have been a disturber of the same; out of the which whoso is, he cannot be the child of salvation. Wherefore if you will come into the same, you shall be received and find favour.

Phil. I am come before your worshipful masterships at your appointment, understanding that you are magistrates authorized by the queen's majesty, to whom I owe and will do my due obedience to the uttermost. Wherefore I desire to know what cause I have offended in, wherefore I am now called before you. And if I cannot be charged with any particular matter done contrary to the laws of this realm, I desire your masterships that I may have the benefit of a subject, and be delivered out of my long wrongful imprisonment, where I have laid this year and a half, without being called to answer before now, and my living taken from me without any lawful cause.

Roper. Though we have no particular matter to charge you with, yet we may by our commission and by the law drive you to answer to the suspicion of a slander going on you; and besides this, we have statutes to charge you herein withal.

Phil. If I have offended any statute, charge me therewith, and if I have incurred the penalty thereof, punish me accordingly. And because you are magistrates and executors of the queen's majesty's laws, by force whereof you now sit, I desire that if I am found no notorious transgressor of any of them, I may not be burdened with more than I have done.

Chol. If the justice suspect a felon, he may examine him upon suspicion thereof, and commit him to prison though there is no fault done.

Story. I perceive whereabout this man goeth. He is plainly in Cardmaker's case, for he made the self-same allegations. But they will not serve thee, for thou art a heretic, and holdest against the blessed mass: how sayest thou to that?

Phil. I am no heretic.

Story. I will prove thee a heretic. Whosoever hath holden against the blessed mass, is a heretic; but thou has holden against the same, therefore thou art a heretic.

Phil. That which I spake, and which you charge me with, was in the convocation, where by the queen's majesty's will and her whole council, liberty was given to every man of that house to utter his conscience, and to say his mind freely, of such questions in religion as there were propounded by the prolocutor, for which I ought not to be molested and imprisoned as I have been, neither now be compelled by you to answer to the same.

Story. Thou shalt go to the Lollards' Tower, and be handled there like a heretic as thou art, and answer to the same that thou there didst speak, and be judged by the bishop of London.

Phil. I have already been convented of this matter before my lord chancellor, mine ordinary, who this long time hath kept me in prison. If his lordship will take my life away, as he has done my liberty and living, he may, which I think he cannot do of his conscience,[*] and therefore he has let me lie thus long in prison: wherefore I am content to abide the end of him that is mine ordinary, and do refuse the auditory of the bishop of London, because he is an incompetent judge for me, and not mine ordinary.

Story. But, sir, thou spakest words in the convocation-house, which is in the bishop of London's diocese, and therefore thou shall be carried to the Lollards' Tower, to be judged by him for the words thou spakest in his diocese against the blessed mass.

Phil. Sir, you know by the law, that I may have

[*] Gardiner did not personally interfere in the condemnation of the Protestants after the month of February, 1555, and he seems to have had particular reasons for not openly proceeding against Philpot.

Exceptionem fori;* and it is against all equity, that I should be twice vexed for one cause, and that by such as by the law have nothing to do with me.

Roper. You cannot deny, but that you spake against the mass in the convocation-house.

Story. Dost thou deny that which thou spakest there or no?

Phil. I cannot deny that I have spoken there, and if by the law you may put me to death therefore, I am here ready to suffer whatsoever I shall be adjudged unto.

The Scribe. This man is fed† of vain-glory.

Chol. Play the wise gentleman, and be conformable, and be not stubborn in your opinions, neither cast yourself away: I should be glad to do you good.

Phil. I desire you, sir, with the rest here, that I be not charged further at your hands than the law charges me, for what I have done; since there was no law directly against that wherewith I am now charg'd. And you, Master doctor, of old acquaintance in Oxford, I trust you will show me some friendship, and not extremity.

Story. I tell thee, if thou wouldest be a good Catholic man, I would be thy friend, and spend my gown to do thee good; but I will be no friend to a heretic, as thou art, but will spend both my gown and my coat but I will burn thee. How sayest thou to the sacrament of the altar?‡

Phil. Sir, I am not come now to dispute with your mastership, and the time now serves not thereto, but to answer to what I may be lawfully charged with.

Story. Well, since thou wilt not revoke what thou hast done, thou shalt be had into the Lollards' Tower.

Phil. Sir, since you will needs show me this extremity, and charge me with my conscience, I do desire to see your commission, whether you have this authority so to do, and after the view thereof I shall, according to my duty, make you further answer, if you may by virtue thereof burden me with my conscience.

Rop. Let him see the commission: is it here?

Story. Shall we let every vile person see our commission?

* An exception to the jurisdiction.
† Puffed up.
‡ This was the "neck question," as it was called, whereby protestants were distinguished from papists, and compelled to furnish ground of accusation against themselves.

Chol. Let him go from whence he came, and on Thursday he shall see our commission.

Story. No, let him lie in the meanwhile in the Lollards' Tower; for I will sweep the King's Bench and all other prisons also of these heretics: they shall not have that resort as they have had, to scatter their heresies.*

Phil. You have power to transfer my body from place to place at your pleasure; but you have no power over my soul. And I pass not † whither you commit me, for I cannot be worse treated than I am, kept all day in a close chamber: wherefore it is no marvel that my flesh is puffed up, wherewith Master doctor is offended.

Story. Marshal, take him home with you again, and see that you bring him again on Thursday, and then we shall rid your fingers of him, and afterwards of your other heretics.

Phil. God hath appointed a day shortly to come, in which he will judge us with righteousness, howsoever you judge of us now.

Rop. Be content to be ruled by Master doctor, and show yourself a Catholic man.

Phil. Sir, if I should speak otherwise than my conscience is, I should but dissemble with you; and why are you so earnest to have me show myself a dissembler both to God and you, which I cannot do?

Rop. We do not require you to dissemble with us, but to be a Catholic man.

Phil. If I stand in anything against that wherein any man is able to burden me with one jot of the scripture, I shall be content to be counted no Catholic man, or a heretic, as you please.

Story. Have we scripture, scripture?—And with that he rose up, saying, "Who shall be judge, I pray you? This man is like his fellow, Woodman, who the other day would have nothing else but scripture."—And this is the beginning of this tragedy.

---

* The imprisonment in the King's Bench was not so strict as that in the prisons of the popish bishops.
† **Care not.**

The second Examination of John Philpot, before the queen's commissioners, M. Cholmley, Roper, D. Story, Doctor Cooke, and the Scribe, the 24th day of October, 1555, at Newgate Sessions' Hall.

AT my coming, a man of Aldgate of my acquaintance said unto me, "God have mercy on you! for you are already condemned in this world; for doctor Story said, that my lord chancellor* has commanded to do you away." After a little consultation between them, Master Cholmley called me to him, saying,

Cholm. Master Philpot, show yourself a wise man, and be not stubborn in your own opinion, but be conformable to the queen's proceedings, and live, and you shall be well assured of great favour and reputation.

Phil. I shall do as becomes a Christian man.

Story. This man is the rankest heretic in all my lord chancellor's diocese, and has done more hurt than any man else there; and therefore his pleasure is, that the law do proceed against him, and I have spoken with my lord herein, and he desireth him to be committed to the bishop of London, and there to recant, or else be burned. He howled and wept in the convocation-house, and made such ado as never man did, as all the heretics do when they lack learning to answer. He shall go after his fellows. How sayest thou, wilt thou recant?

Phil. I know nothing I have done that I ought to recant

Story. Well, then, I pray, let us commit him to the Lollards' Tower, there to remain until he is further examined before the bishop of London, for he is too fine fed in the King's Bench, and has too much favour there. For his keeper said at the door yesterday, that he was the finest fellow and one of the best learned in England.— Dr. Story then rose up and went his way.

Cooke. This man has most stoutly maintained heresies since the queen's coming in, as any that I have heard of; therefore it is most proper that he should be judged by the bishop of London, for the heresies he has maintained.

Phil. I have maintained no heresies.

Cooke. No? Did you not openly speak against the

* Bishop Gardiner.

sacrament of the altar in the convocation-house? Call you that no heresy? Wilt thou recant that or no?

Phil. It was the queen's majesty's pleasure that we should reason thereof, not by my seeking, but by other men's procuring, in the hearing of the council.

Cooke. Did the queen give you leave to be a heretic? You may be sure her grace will not do so. Well, we will not dispute the matter with you; my lord of London shall proceed by inquisition upon you, and if thou wilt not recant, thou shalt be burned.

Phil. My lord of London is not my ordinary in this business, and I have already answered to mine ordinary in this matter; and therefore, as I have said before, you would do me great wrong, to vex me twice for one matter, since I have sustained this long imprisonment, besides the loss of my living.

Rop. You were a very unfit man to be an archdeacon.

Phil. I know I was as fit a man as he that has it now.

Cooke. A fit man, quoth he? He troubled Master Roper and the whole country.

Phil. There was never poor archdeacon so handled at your hands as I am, and that without any just cause you are able to lay unto me.

Cooke. Thou art no archdeacon.

Phil. I am archdeacon still, although another is in possession of my living; for I was never deprived by any law.

Cooke. No, sir, that needed not; for a notorious heretic should have no ordinary proceeding about his deprivation; but the bishop may upon knowledge thereof proceed to deprivation.

Phil. Master doctor, you know that the common law is otherwise; and besides this, the statutes of this realm are otherwise, which give this benefit to every person though he is a heretic, to enjoy his living until he be put to death for the same.

Cholm. No, there thou art deceived.

Phil. About the living I care not. But the unjust dealing grieves me, that I should be thus troubled for my conscience, contrary to all law.

Cholm. Why, will you not agree that the queen's majesty may cause you to be examined of your faith?

Phil. Ask doctor Cooke, and he will tell you that the temporal magistrates have nothing to do with matters of faith, for determination thereof. And St. Ambrose saith, that the things of God are not subject to the power and authority of princes.

Cooke. No? May not the temporal power commit you to the bishop, to be examined of your faith?

Phil. Yea, sir, I deny not that; but you will not grant that the same may examine any of their own authority.

Cooke. Let him be had away.

Phil. Your mastership promised me the last time I was before you, I should see your commission, by what authority you call me, and whether I by the same am bound to answer to so much as you demand.

Rop. Let him see the commission.

Then the scribe exhibited it to Master Roper, and was about to open the same.

Cooke. No, what will you do? He shall not see it.

Phil. Then you do me wrong, to call me and vex me, not showing your authority.

Cooke. If we do you wrong, complain of us; and in the meanwhile thou shalt lie in the Lollards' Tower.

Phil. Sir, I am a poor gentleman; therefore I trust of your gentleness you will not commit me to so vile and strait a place, being found no heinous trespasser.

Cooke. Thou art no gentleman.

Phil. Yes, that I am.

Cooke. A heretic is no gentleman; for he is a gentleman that hath gentle conditions.

Phil. The offence cannot take away the state of a gentleman as long as he lives, although he were a traitor; but I mean not to boast of my gentlemanship, but will put it under my feet, since you no more esteem it.

Story came in again, and said, What, will you suffer this heretic to prate with you all this day?

Cooke. He saith he is a gentleman!

Story. A gentleman, quoth he? he is a vile heretic knave; for a heretic is no gentleman. Let the keeper of the Lollards' Tower come in, and have him away

The Keeper. Here, sir.

Story. Take this man with you to the Lollards' Tower, or else to the Bishop's Coalhouse.

Phil. Sir, if I were a dog you could not appoint me a worse and more vile place; but I must be content with whatever injury you offer me. God give you a more merciful heart: you are very cruel upon one that never has offended you. I pray you, Master Cholmley, show me some friendship, that I be not carried to so vile a place.

Cholmley called me aside, and said, I am not skilled as to their doings, neither of their laws: I cannot tell what they mean. I would I could do you good.

Phil. I am content to go whither you will have me. There was never man more cruelly handled than I am at your hands, that without just cause known should be thus treated.

Story. Shall we suffer this heretic thus to reprove us? Have him hence.

Phil. God forgive you, and give you more merciful hearts, and show you more mercy in the time of need. 'Do quickly that you have in hand.'

Story. Do you not hear how he makes us to be Judases?

Phil. That is after your own understanding.

After this, I with four more were brought to the keeper's house in Paternoster-row, where we supped, and after supper I was called up to a chamber by the archdeacon of London's servant, who in his master's name offered me a bed for that night. To whom I gave thanks, saying, that "it should be a grief to me to lie well one night, and the next worse; wherefore I will begin as I am like to continue, to take such part as my fellows." And with that we were brought through Paternoster-row to my lord of London's Coalhouse; unto which is joined a little blind* house, with a great pair of stocks appointed both for hand and foot; but, thanks be to God, we have not played on those organs yet, although some before us have tried them; and there we found a minister of Essex, a married priest, a man of godly zeal, with one other poor man. And this minister,† at my coming, desired to speak with me, and greatly lamented his own infirmity, for through extremity of imprisonment he was constrained by writing to yield to the bishop of London; whereupon he was once set at liberty, and afterward felt such a hell in his conscience, that he could scarcely refrain from destroying himself, and never could feel quiet until he had gone unto the bishop's register, desiring to see his bill again, which as soon as he had received, he tore it in pieces, **and**

* Dark place.
† His name was Thomas Whittle. He was burned shortly after.

afterwards he was as joyful as any man might be. Of which when my lord of London* was told, he sent for him, and fell upon him like a lion, and like a manly bishop buffeted him well, so that he made his face black and blue, and plucked away a great piece of his beard; but now, thanks be to God, he is as joyful under the cross as any of us, and very sorry for his former infirmity. I write this, because I would all men should take heed how they do contrary to their conscience; which is to fall under the pains of hell. And here an end.

The manner of my calling first before the bishop of London, the second night of mine imprisonment in his Coalhouse.†

THE bishop sent M. Johnson, his registrar, to me, with a mess of meat and a good pot of drink, and bread, saying that my lord had no knowledge till then of my being here, for which he was sorry; therefore he had sent me and my fellows that meat, not knowing whether I would receive the same.

I thanked God for my lord's charity, that it pleased

---

* Bishop Bonner.

† The palace of the bishop of London at that period was at the north-west corner of St. Paul's Churchyard, on the site of the houses and courts now called London House Yard. It was of considerable size, and extended quite to the old cathedral, which was longer and wider than the present building, so that it was easy to convey the protestants from one part of these large piles of building to another without passing through the streets. Along the north side of St. Paul's Churchyard were a cloister, a burying-ground, a library, a charnel-house, and several chapels, which had been partly demolished in the reign of Edward VI., and between Cannon Alley and Cheapside was St. Paul's Cross, about the spot where a tree now stands. At that time the whole of the churchyard was enclosed and entered by gates, like the cathedral close at Wells, and some other cities. The convocation-house stood on the south side, and Lollards' Tower was over St. Gregory's church, which was built against the cathedral at the south-west corner, about the spot where the clock tower now stands. The bishop's palace contained a great number of apartments; the Coalhouse, in which Philpot and many others were confined, was at the back of the building in Paternoster-row, near the narrow alley which now passes from that street to St. Paul's Churchyard. These particulars will render Philpot's narrative more intelligible to the reader; and when he passes by the places just mentioned, he will be reminded of the sufferings of THE BRITISH REFORMERS, and let him feel thankful that "the blood of the martyrs has indeed proved the seed of the church."

him to remember poor prisoners, desiring Almighty God to increase the same in him and in all others, and therefore I would not refuse his beneficence, and therewith I took the same unto my brethren, praising God for his providence towards his afflicted flock, that he stirred up our adversaries to help them in their necessity.

Johnson. My lord would know the cause of your being sent hither, for he knoweth nothing thereof, ano wondereth that he should be troubled with prisoners o other dioceses than his own.

I here declared unto him the whole cause. After which he said, that my lord's will was, that I should have any friendship I would desire, and so he departed.

Soon after, one of my lord's gentlemen came for me, and I was brought into his presence, where he sat at a table alone, with three or four of his chaplains waiting upon him, and his registrar.

Bonner. Master Philpot, you are welcome; give me your hand.

Because he so gently put forth his hand, I, to render courtesy for courtesy, kissed my hand, and gave him the same.

Bon. I am right sorry for your trouble, and I promise you till within these two hours, I knew not of your being here. I pray you tell me what was the cause of your sending hither; for I promise you I know nothing thereof as yet, neither would I you should think that I was the cause thereof; and I marvel that other men will trouble me with their matters, but I must be obedient to my betters, though men speak otherwise of me than I deserve.*

I showed him the sum of the matter; that it was for the disputation in the convocation-house, for which I was, against all right, molested.

Bon. I marvel that you should be troubled therefore, if there was no other cause but this. But peradventure you have maintained the same since, and some of your

---

* The reader will observe the artful manner in which Bonner speaks to Philpot at first. Bonner had undertaken to sit in judgment upon all who were sent to him, and Philpot's imprisonment for the debate in the convocation-house was well known to him. But Bonner's object, as the reader will see, was to induce Philpot to avow the same sentiments in his presence, that he might proceed against him as having spoken heresy in the diocese of London, and condemn him without any open or public examination.

friends of late have asked, whether you stand to the same, and you have said, Yea: and for this you might be committed to prison.

Phil. If it please your lordship, I am burdened no otherwise than I told you, by the commissioners, who have sent me hither, because I would not recant the same.

Bon. A man may speak in the parliament house though it is a place of free speech, so that he may be imprisoned for it, as in case he speak words of high treason against the king or queen: and so it might be that you spake otherwise than it became you as a member of the Church of Christ.

Phil. I spake nothing which was out of the articles which were called in question, and agreed upon to be disputed by the whole house, and by the queen's permission and the council.

Bon. What, may we dispute of our faith?

Phil. Yea, that we may.

Bon. Nay, I trow* not by the law.

Phil. Indeed by the civil law I know it is not lawful, but by God's law we may reason thereof. For St. Peter saith, "Be ye ready to render account unto all men of that hope which is in you who demand of you the same."

Bon. Indeed St. Peter saith so. Why, then, I ask of you, what your judgment is of the sacrament of the altar?

Phil. My lord, St. Ambrose saith that the disputation of faith ought to be in the congregation, in the hearing of the people, and that I am not bound to render account thereof to every man privately, unless it be to edify. But now I cannot show you my mind, but I must run upon the pikes in danger of my life by so doing. Wherefore, as the said doctor said unto Valentinian, the emperor, so say I to your lordship: Take away the law, and I will reason with you. And yet if I come into open judgment, where I am bound by the law to answer, I trust I shall utter my conscience as freely as any that has come before you.

Bon. I perceive you are learned, I would have such as you be about me. But you must come and be of the church, for there is but one church.

Phil. God forbid I should be out of the church, I am sure I am within the same: for I know, as I am taught

* Think.

by the Scripture, that there is but one catholic church, "One dove, one spouse, one beloved congregation," out of which there is no salvation.

Bon. How chances it then, that you go out of the same, and walk not with us?

Phil. My lord, I am sure I am within the bounds of the church whereupon she is builded, which is the word of God.

Bon. What age are you?

Phil. I am four and forty.

Bon. You are not now of the same faith your godfathers and godmothers promised for you, in which you were baptized.

Phil. Yes, that, I thank God, I am: for I was baptized into the faith of Christ which I now hold.

Bon. How can that be? there is but one faith.

Phil. I am assured of that by St. Paul, saying "'That there is but one God, one faith, and one baptism,' of which I am.

Bon. You were, twenty years ago, of another faith than you are now.

Phil. Indeed, my lord, to tell you plainly, I was then "of no faith," a neuter, a wicked liver, neither hot nor cold.

Bon. Why do you not think that we now have the true faith?

Phil. I desire your lordship to excuse my answering at this time. I am sure that God's word, with the primitive church and all the ancient writers, agrees throughly with this faith I am of.

Bon. Well, I promise you I mean you no more hurt than to my own person: I will not, therefore, burden you with your conscience. Now I marvel that you are so merry in prison as you are, singing and rejoicing, as the prophet saith: "rejoicing in your naughtiness." You do not well herein: you should rather lament and be sorry.

Phil. My lord, our mirth is only singing certain psalms, according as we are commanded by St. Paul, willing us "to be merry in the Lord, singing together in hymns and psalms." And I trust your lordship cannot be displeased with that.

Bon. We may say unto you as Christ said in the gospel "We have piped unto you and ye have not grieved."

Here my lord stumbled, and could not bring forth the

text, and required his chaplains to help, and put him in remembrance of the text better: but they were mum: and I recited the text unto him, which made nothing to his purpose, unless he would have us to mourn, because they, if they laugh, sing sorrowful things unto us, threatening fagots and fire.

Phil. We are, my lord, in a dark comfortless place, and therefore it behoves us to be merry, lest, as Solomon saith, " sorrowfulness eat up our heart." Therefore I trust your lordship will not be angry at our singing of psalms, since St. Paul saith, " If any man be of an upright mind, let him sing." And we, therefore, to testify that we are of an upright mind to God, though we are in misery, do sing.

Bon. I will trouble you no further as now. If I can do you any good, I shall be glad to do it for you. God be with you, good Master Philpot, and give you good night. Have him to the cellar, and let him drink a cup of wine.

Thus I departed, and by my lord's registrar I was brought to his cellar-door, where I drank a good cup of wine. And my lord's chaplain, Master Cousin, followed me, claiming acquaintance with me, saying, that I was welcome, and he wished that I would not be singular.

Phil. I am well taught the contrary by Solomon saying, " Wo be to him that is alone." After that, I was carried to my lord's Coalhouse again, where I, with my five fellows, do rouse together in the straw as chearfully, we thank God, as others do in their beds of down.

Thus for the third part.

The fourth Examination of Master Philpot in the archdeacon's house of London, in the month of October, before the bishops of London, Bath, Worcester, and Gloucester.*

Bon. MASTER PHILPOT, it has pleased my lords to-day to dine with my poor archdeacon, and in the dinner time it

* The popish bishops present at this and the subsequent examinations were, Bonner of London, Bourn of Bath, Pate of Worcester, Brooks of Gloucester, Griffith of Rochester, Bayne of Coventry, Goldwell of St. Asaph, Day of Chichester, Glynn of Bangor, Heath of York, Tonstall of Durham. With the exception of the last, they all had been appointed, or restored, to their sees by queen Mary.

chanced us to have communication about you, and you were pitied here by many that knew you in New College. in Oxford: and I also pity your case, because you seem unto me, by the talk I had with you the other night, to be learned; and, therefore, now I have sent for you to come before them, that it might not be said hereafter, that I had so many learned bishops at my house, and yet would not vouchsafe them* to talk with you, and at my request, I thank, they are content so to do. Now, therefore, utter your mind freely, and you shall, with all favour, be satisfied. I am sorry to see you lie in so evil a case as you do, and would fain you should do better, as you may, if you list.

Bath. My lords here have not sent for you to fawn upon you, but for charity's sake to exhort you to come into the right Catholic way of the church.

Wor. Before he begins to speak, it is best that he call to God for grace, and to pray that it might please God to open his heart that he may conceive the truth.

With that I fell down upon my knees before them, and made my prayer on this manner.

Phil. Almighty God, who art the giver of all wisdom and understanding, I beseech thee of thine infinite goodness and mercy in Jesus Christ, to give me, who am a most vile sinner in thy sight, the Spirit of wisdom to speak, and make answer in thy cause, that it may content the hearers before whom I stand, and also to my better understanding, if I am deceived in any thing.

Bon. Nay, my lord of Worcester, you did not well to exhort him to make a prayer. For this is what they have a singular pride in, that they can often make their vain prayers, in which they glory much. For, in this point, they are much like to certain arrant heretics,† of whom Pliny maketh mention, who daily sung *Antelucanos Hymnos*, Praise unto God before the dawn of the day.

Phil. My Lord God make me and all you here present such heretics as those were that sung those morning hymns. for they were right Christians, with whom the tyrants of the world were offended for their well doing.

Bath. Proceed to what he has to say. He has prayed I cannot tell for what.

* Allow them.
† The early Christians. A proof of Bonner's knowledge of church history!

Fourth Examination.

Bon. Say on, Master Philpot: my lords will gladly hear you.

Phil. I have, my lords, been this twelvemonth and a half in prison without any just cause, that I know of, and my living is taken from me without any lawful order; and now I am brought, contrary to right, from my own territory and ordinary into another man's jurisdiction, I know not why. Wherefore, if your lordships can burden me with any evil I have done, I stand here before you to clear myself. And if no such thing may be justly laid to my charge, I desire to be released from this wrongful trouble.

Bon. There is none here goeth about to trouble you, but to do you good, if we can. For I promise you, you were sent hither to me without my knowledge. Therefore speak your conscience without any fear.

Phil. My lord, I have learned to answer in matters of religion, in the congregation, being thereto lawfully called: but now I am not lawfully called, neither is here a congregation where I ought to answer.

Bon. Indeed this man told me the last time I spake with him, that he was a lawyer, and would not utter his conscience in matters of faith, unless it were in the hearing of the people, where he might speak to vain-glory.

Phil. My lord, I said not I was a lawyer, neither do I arrogate to myself that name, although I was once a novice in the same, where I learned something for my own defence when I am called in judgment to answer to any cause, and whereby I have been taught, not to put myself further in danger than I need, and so far am I a lawyer, and no further.

Bath. If you will not answer to my lord's request you seem to be a wilful man in your opinion.

Phil. My lord of London is not my ordinary, before whom I am bound to answer in this behalf, as Dr. Cole, who is a lawyer, can well tell you by the law. And I have not offended my lord of London, wherefore he should call me.

Bon. Yes, I have to lay to your charge, that you have offended in my diocese by speaking against the blessed sacrament of the altar, and therefore I may call you and proceed against you, to punish you by the law.

Phil. I have not offended in your diocese. For that which I spake of the sacrament was in Paul's church in the convocation-house, which, as I understand, is a peculiar jurisdiction, belonging to the dean of Paul's, and therefore is counted of your lordship's diocese, but not in your diocese.

Bon. Is not Paul's church in my diocese? Well I wot, it costs me a good deal of money by the year the leading* thereof.

Phil. That may be, and yet it may be exempted from your lordship's jurisdiction. And though I had so offended in your diocese, yet I ought, by the law, to be sent to my ordinary, if I require it, and not to be punished by you who are not my ordinary. And already, as I have told you, I have been convented before my ordinary for this cause, which you go about to inquire of me.

Bon. How say you, Dr. Cole, may not I proceed against him by the law for what he has done in my diocese?

Cole. I think Master Philpot need not stand so much with your lordship in that point as he does, since you seek not to hinder him, but to assist him: therefore I think it best that he go to the matter which is laid against him about the convocation, and make no longer delay.

Phil. I would willingly show my mind of that matter, but I am sure it will be laid against me to my prejudice when I come to judgment.

Col. Why then you may speak under protestation.†

Phil. But what will my protestation avail in a cause of heresy (as you call it) if I speak otherwise than you will have me, since what I spake in the convocation-house, though a place privileged, cannot now help me.

Bon. But, Master doctor Cole, may not I proceed against him for the offence he has done in my diocese?

Cole. You may call him before you, my lord, if he be found in your diocese.

Phil. But I have by force been brought out of my own diocese to my lords, and require to be judged by my own ordinary; and therefore I know Master doctor will not say of his knowledge, that your lordship ought to proceed against me. To this Dr. Cole would say nothing.

Wor. Do you not think to find before my lord here as good equity in your cause as before your own ordinary?

Phil. I cannot blame my lord of London's equity, with whom, I thank his lordship, I have found more gen-

---
* Repairing the roof.
† How these men hunt for innocent blood.—*Fox.*

tleness since I came, than of mine own ordinary this twelvemonth and this half before, (I speak it for no flattery,) who never would call me to answer, as his lordship has done now twice: but I ought not to be forestalled of my right, and therefore I challenge the same for divers other considerations.

Bon. Now you cannot say hereafter but that you have been gently communed with by my lords here, and yet you are wilful and obstinate in your error, and in your own opinions, and will not show any cause why you will not come into the unity of the church with us.

Phil. My lords, if I do not declare my mind according to your expectation, it is, as I have said, because I cannot speak without present danger of my life. But rather than you should report me by this either obstinate or self-willed, without any just ground whereupon I stand: I will open unto you somewhat of my mind, or rather the whole, desiring your lordships, who seem to be pillars of the Church of England, to satisfy me in the same: and I will refer all other causes in which I dissent from you unto one or two articles, or rather to one, which includes them both: in which if I can by the Scriptures be satisfied by you, I shall as willingly agree to you as any others in all points.

Bon. These heretics come always with their "ifs," as this man does now, saying, " if he can be satisfied by the scriptures:" so that he will always have this exception, " I am not satisfied," although the matter be ever so plainly proved against them. But will you promise to be satisfied if my lords take some pains about you.

Phil. I say, my lord, I will be satisfied by the Scriptures in that wherein I stand. And I protest here before God and his eternal Son Jesus Christ my Saviour, and the Holy Ghost and his angels, and you here present that are judges of what I speak, that I do not stand in any opinion out of wilfulness or singularity, but only upon my conscience, certainly informed by God's word; from which I dare not go for fear of damnation; and this is the cause of my earnestness in this behalf.

Bon. I will trouble my lords no longer, seeing that you will not declare your mind.

Phil. I am about so to do, if it please your lordship to near me speak.

Bath. Give him leave, my lords, to speak what he has to say.

Phil. My lords, it is not unknown to you, that the chief cause why you count me, and such as I am, as heretics, is because we are not at unity with your Church. You say you are of the true Church; and we say, we are of the true Church. You say, that whosoever is out of your Church, is damned: and we think verily, on the other side, that if we depart from the true Church, wherein we are grafted in God's word, we should stand in the state of damnation. Wherefore if your lordship can bring any better authorities for your Church, than we can do for ours, and prove by the Scriptures that the Church of Rome now, of which you are, is the true Catholic Church, as in all your sermons, writings, and arguments, you uphold, and that all Christian persons ought to be ruled by the same, under pain of damnation, as you say; and that the same Church, as you pretend, has authority to interpret the Scriptures, as it seems good to her, and that all men are bound to follow such interpretations only—then I shall be as conformable to the same Church as you may desire, which otherwise I dare not. Therefore I require you for God's sake to satisfy me in this.

Cole. If you stand upon this point only, you may soon be satisfied, if you list.

Phil. It is what I require, and to this I have said I will stand, and refer all other controversies wherein I stand now against you, and will put my hand thereto, if you mistrust my word.

Bon. I pray you, Master Philpot, what faith were you of twenty years ago? This man will have every year a new faith.

Phil. My lord, I tell you plainly, I think I was of no faith, for I was then a wicked liver, and knew not God then, as I ought to do; God forgive me.

Bon. No, that is not so. I am sure you were of some faith.

Phil. My lord, I have declared to you, on my conscience, what I then was and judge of myself. And what is that to the purpose of the thing I desire to be satisfied by you?

Bon. Master doctor Cole, I pray you say your mind to him.

Cole. What will you say, if I can prove that it was decreed by a universal council in Athanasius's time, that all the Christian Church should follow the determination of the Church of Rome: but I do not now remember where?

Phil. If you, Master doctor, can show me the same, granted to the see of Rome, by the authority of the Scripture, I will gladly hearken thereto. But I think you are not able to show any such thing. For Athanasius was president of the Nicene council, and there no such thing was decreed, I am sure.

Cole. Though it were not then, it might be at another time.

Phil. I desire to see the proof thereof.

Upon this, Master Harpsfield, chancellor to the bishop of London, brought in a book of Ireneus, with certain leaves turned down, and laid it before the bishops to help them in their perplexity, if it might be; which after the bishops of Bath and Gloucester had read together, the bishop of Gloucester gave me the book.

Glo. Take the book, Master Philpot, and look upon that place, and there may you see how the Church of Rome is to be followed by all men.

I took the book, and read the place, which after I had read, I said it made nothing against me, but against the Arians and other heretics, against whom Ireneus wrote, proving that "they were not to be credited, because they taught and followed after strange doctrine in Europe, and that the chief church of the same was founded by Peter and Paul, and had to his time continued by faithful succession of the faithful bishops in preaching the true gospel, as they had received of the apostles, and nothing like to the late sprung heretics," &c. Whereby he concludes against them, that they were not to be listened to, neither to be credited; which thing if you, my lords, be able to prove now of the Church of Rome, then had you as good authority against me in my cause now, as Ireneus had against those heretics. But the Church of Rome has swerved from the truth and simplicity of the gospel, which it maintained in Ireneus's time, and was uncorrupted compared with what it is now; wherefore your lordships cannot justly apply the authority of Ireneus to the Church of Rome now, which is so manifestly corrupted from the primitive church.

Bon. So will you still say it makes nothing for the

purpose, whatsoever authority we bring, and you will never be satisfied.

Phil. My lord, when I by just reason prove that the authorities which are brought against me do not make to the purpose, as I have already proved, I trust you will receive my answer.

Wor. It is to be proved most manifestly by all ancient writers, that the see of Rome hath always followed the truth, and never was deceived; but of late certain heretics have defaced the same.

Phil. Let that be proved, and I have done.

Wor. Nay, you are of such arrogancy, singularity, and vain-glory, that you will not see it, be it ever so well proved.

Phil. Ha, my lords, is it now time, think you, for me to follow singularity or vain-glory, since it is now upon danger of my life and death, not only at present, but also before God to come? and I know, if I die not in the true faith, I shall die everlastingly, and again I know, if I do not as you would have me, you will kill me and many thousands more. Yet had I rather perish at your hands, than perish eternally. And at this time I have lost all my commodities of this world, and now I lie in a coalhouse, where a man would not lay a dog; with which I am well contented.

Cole. Where are you able to prove that the Church of Rome hath erred at any time? and by what history? It is certain, by Eusebius, that the Church was established at Rome by Peter and Paul; and that Peter was bishop twenty-five years at Rome.

Phil. I know well that Eusebius writes so. But if we compare what St. Paul writes to the Galatians, it will manifestly appear to the contrary, that he was not half so long there. He lived not more than thirty-five years after he was called to be an apostle. And Paul makes mention of his abiding at Jerusalem after Christ's death more than eighteen years.

Cole. What, did Peter write to the Galatians?

Phil. No, I say Paul makes mention of Peter when writing to the Galatians, and of his abiding at Jerusalem. And further, I am able to prove, both by Eusebius, and other historians, that the Church of Rome has manifestly erred, and at this present time does err, because she agrees not with that which they wrote The primitive church did according to the gospel, and there needeth none other proof but to compare the one with the other.

Bon. I may compare this man to a certain man I read of, who fell into a desperation, and went into a wood to hang himself, and when he came there, he went viewing of every tree, and could find none on which he might vouchsafe to hang himself. But I will not apply it as I might. I pray you, Mr. Doctor, go on with him.

Cole. My lord, there are on every side of me those that are better able to answer him, and I love not to fall into disputation, for now a-days a man shall only sustain shame and obloquy thereby from the people. I had rather show my mind in writing.

Phil. And I had rather that you should do so than otherwise, for then a man may better judge of your words, than by argument, and I beseech you so to do. But if I were a rich man, I dare wager a hundred pounds, that you shall not be able to show what you have said was decreed by a general council in Athanasius's time. For this I am sure of, that it was concluded by a general council in Africa many years after, that none of Africa, under pain of excommunication, should appeal to Rome; which decree I am sure they would not have made, if by the Scriptures and by a universal council it had been decreed that all men should abide and follow the determination of the Church at Rome.

Cole. But I can show that they revoked that error again.

Phil. So you say, Master doctor, but I pray you show me where. I have hitherto heard nothing of you for my contentation, but bare words without any authority.

Bon. What, I pray you! Ought we to dispute with you of our faith? Justinian in the law hath a title, "De fide Catholica,"* to the contrary.

Phil. I am certain that the civil law has such a constitution: but our faith must not depend upon the civil law. For, as St. Ambrose saith, "Not the law but the gospel hath gathered the Church together."

Wor. Master Philpot, you have the spirit of pride wherewith you are led, which will not let you yield to the truth: leave it for shame.

Phil. Sir, I am sure I have the spirit of faith, by the which I speak at this present time; neither am I ashamed to stand in my faith.

* Concerning the Catholic faith.

Glo. What, do you think yourself better learned than so many notable learned men that are here?

Phil. Elias alone had the truth, when there were four hundred priests against him.

Wor. Oh, you would be counted now for Elias. And yet I tell you he was deceived: for he thought there had been none good but himself, and yet he was deceived, for there were seven thousand besides him.

Phil. Yea, but he was not deceived in doctrine, as the other four hundred were.

Wor. By my faith, you are greatly to blame · that you cannot be content to be of the Church which ever has been of that faithful antiquity.

Phil. My lord, I know Rome, and have been there, where I saw your lordship.

Wor. Indeed, I fled from hence thither,* and I remember not that I saw you there. But I am sorry that you have been there: for the wickedness which you have seen there, peradventure, causes you to do as you do.

Phil. No, my lord, I do not as I do, for that cause ; for I am taught otherwise by the gospel, not altogether to refuse the minister for his evil living, so that he bring sound doctrine out of God's book.

Wor. Do you think that the universal Church may be deceived?

Phil. Saint Paul to the Thessalonians prophesieth that there should come a universal departing from the faith in the latter days before the coming of Christ, saying, " Christ shall not come, till there come a departing first."

Cole. Yea, I pray you, how understand you the word departing there in St. Paul? It is not meant of faith, but of the departing from the empire: for it is in Greek APOSTASIA.

Phil. Indeed, Master doctor, you put me in good remembrance of the meaning of St. Paul in that place, for APOSTASIA is properly a departing from the faith, and thereof cometh APOSTATA, which properly signifies one that departs from his faith. And Saint Paul in the same place afterwards speaketh of the decay of the empire.

Cole. APOSTASIA does not only signify a departing from the faith, but also from the empire, as I am able to show.

Phil. I never read it as such, and when you shall be

---

* In the reign of Henry VIII,

Fourth Examination. 29

able to show it, as you say in words, I will believe it, and not before.

Wor. I am sorry that you should be against the Christian world.

Phil. The world commonly, and such as are called Christians, for the multitude hath hated the truth, and have been enemies to the same.

Glo. Why, Master Philpot, do you think that the universa' Church has erred, and you only are in the truth?

Phil. The Church that you are of, was never universal, for two parts of the world, Asia and Africa, never consented to the supremacy of the bishop of Rome, as at this day they do not, neither follow his decrees.

Glo. Yes, in the Florentine council* they did agree.

Phil. It was said so by false report, after they of Asia and Africa were gone home; but it was not so indeed, as the proceedings of them all hitherto doth prove the contrary.

Glo. I pray you by whom will you be judged in matters of controversy which happen daily?

Phil. By the word of God, for Christ saith in Saint John, " The word that he spake, shall be judge in the latter day."

Glo. What if you take the word one way, and I another way; who shall be judge then?

Phil. The primitive church.

Glo. I know you mean the doctors that wrote thereof.

Phil. I mean so.

Glo. What if you take the doctors in one sense, and I in another, who shall be judge then?

Phil. Then let that be taken which is most agreeable to God's word.

Cole. My lords, why do you trouble yourselves to answer him in this matter? This is not the thing which is laid to his charge, but his error of the Sacrament, and he to shift himself from that brought in another matter.

Phil. This is the matter, Master Cole, to which I have referred all other questions, and desire to be satisfied.

Wor. It is a wonder to see how he stands with a few against a great multitude.

Phil. We have almost as many as you. For we have Asia, Africa, Germany, Denmark, and a great part of France, and daily the number of the gospel increases; so

* About A. D. 1432.

that I am credibly informed, that for this religion in which I stand, and for which I am like to die, a great multitude daily come out of France, through persecution, so that the cities of Germany are scarcely able to receive them; and therefore your lordship may be sure the word of GOD will one day take place, do what you can to the contrary.

Wor. They were well occupied to bring you such news, and you have been well kept to have such resort unto you. Thou art the arrogantest fellow, and stoutest fond* fellow, that ever I knew.

Phil. I pray your lordship to bear with my hasty speech; for it is part of my corrupt nature to speak somewhat hastily; but for all that, I mean with humility to do my duty to your lordship.

Bon. Master Philpot, my lords will trouble you no further at this time, but you shall go from whence you came, and have such favour as in the mean while I can show you; and upon Wednesday next you shall be called again to be heard what you can say for maintenance of your error.

Phil. My lord, my desire is to be satisfied by you in that I have required; and your lordship shall find me, as I have said.

Wor. We wish you as well as ourselves.

Phil. I think the same, my lords, but I fear you are deceived, and have a zeal of yourselves, not according to knowledge.

Wor. God send you more grace.

Phil. And also God increase the same in you, and open your eyes that you may see to maintain his truth and his true Church.

Then the bishops rose up and consulted together, and caused a writing to be made, in which I think my blood by them was bought and sold,† and thereto they put their hands; and after this I was carried to my coalhouse again.

Thus ends the fourth part of this tragedy. God hasten the end thereof to his glory. Amen.

* Foolish. † My condemnation was settled.

Fifth Examination.

John Philpot to certain persons that required him to write his Examinations.

BECAUSE I have begun to write unto you of my examinations before the bishop and others, more to satisfy your desire than that it is worthy to be written; I have thought it good to write unto you also that which hath been done of late, that the same might come to light which they do in darkness and privy corners, and that the world now, and the posterity hereafter, might know how disorderly, unjustly, and unlearnedly these ravening wolves do proceed against the poor and faithful flock of Christ, and condemn and persecute the sincere doctrine of Christ in us, which they are not able by honest means to resist, but only by tyranny and violence.

The fifth Examination of John Philpot, had before the bishops of London, Rochester, Coventry, St. Asaph, (I believe,) and one other whose see I know not, Dr. Story, Dr. Curtop, Dr. Saverson, Dr. Pendleton, with divers other chaplains and gentlemen of the queen's chamber, and divers other gentlemen; in the gallery of my lord of London's palace.

Bon. Master Philpot, come hither, I have desired my lords here and other learned men, to take some pains once again, and to do you good; and because I mind to sit in judgment on you to-morrow, as I am commanded, I would you should have as much favour as I can show you, if you will be any thing conformable. Therefore play the wise man, and be not singular in your own opinion, but be ruled by these learned men.

Phil. My lord, you say you will sit on me in judgment to-morrow; I am glad thereof. For I was promised by them which sent me unto you, that I should have been judged the next day after; but promise hath not been kept with me, to my further grief. I look for no other but death at your hands, and I am as ready to yield my life in Christ's cause, as you are to require it.

Bon. Lo, what a wilful man is this! By my faith it is but folly to reason with him, or with any of these heretics. I am sorry that you will not be more tractable, and that I am compelled to show extremity against you.

Phil. My lord, you need not show extremity against me unless you list; neither by the law, as I have said, have you any thing to do with me, for you are not my ordinary, although I am, contrary to all right, in your prison.

Bon. Why, the queen's commissioners sent you hither unto me upon your examination had before them. I know not well the cause; but I am sure they would not have sent you hither to me, unless you had made some talk to them otherwise than became a Christian man.

Phil. My lord, indeed they sent me hither without any occasion then ministered by me. Only they laid unto me the disputation I made in the convocation-house, requiring me to answer the same, and to recant it; which because I would not do, they sent me hither to your lordship.

Bon. Why did you not answer them thereto?

Phil. Because they were temporal men, and ought not to be judges in spiritual causes whereof they demanded of me, without showing any authority whereby I was bound to answer them; and hereupon they committed me to your prison.

Bon. Indeed, I remember now, you maintained open heresy in my diocese, wherefore the commissioners sent you unto me that I should proceed against you, for you have spoken in my diocese.

Phil. My lord, I stand still upon my lawful plea in this matter, that though it were a great heresy as you suppose it, yet I ought not to be troubled therefore, in respect of the privilege of the parliament house, whereof the convocation-house is a member, where all men in matters propounded may frankly speak their minds. And here is present a gentleman of the queen's majesty's, who was present at the disputation, and can testify the questions which were then in controversy, were not set forth by me, but by the prolocutor, who required in the queen's majesty's name, all men to dispute their minds freely in the same, that were of the house.

The queen's gentleman. Though the parliament house is a place of privilege for men of the house to speak, yet may none speak any treason against the queen, or maintain treason against the crown.

Phil. But if there is any matter which otherwise it were treason to speak of, were it treason for any person to speak therein, specially the thing being proposed by the speaker? I think not.

Fifth Examination.

The queen's gentleman. You may make the matter easy enough to you yet, as I perceive, if you will revoke the same which you did there so stubbornly maintain.

St. Asaph. This man did not speak under reformation, as many there did, but earnestly and persuasibly, as ever I heard any.

Phil. My lords, since you will not cease to trouble me for that I have lawfully done, neither will admit my just defence for what was, spoken in the convocation-house by me, but act therein contrary to the laws and custom of the realm, I appeal to the whole parliament house, to be judged by the same, whether I ought thus to be molested for what I have there spoken.

Roch. But have you spoken and maintained the same since that time, or not?

Phil. If any man can charge me justly therewith, here I stand to make answer.

Roch. How say you to it now? will you stand to what you have spoken in the convocation-house, and do you think you said then well, or no?

Phil. My lord, you are not my ordinary to proceed ex officio* against me, and therefore I am not bound to tell you my belief of your demands.

St. A. What say you now? Is there not in the blessed Sacrament of the altar, (and with that they put off all their caps for reverence of the idol,) the presence of our Saviour Christ, really and substantially after the words of consecration?

Phil. I do believe that in the sacrament of Christ's body duly ministered, there is such manner of presence, as the word teacheth me to believe.

St. A. I pray you, how is that?

Phil. As for that, I will declare another time when I shall be lawfully called to dispute my mind of this matter; but I am not yet driven to that point. And the Scripture sayeth, " All things ought to be done after an order."

Another bishop. This is a froward and vain-glorious man.

Bon. It is not lawful for a man by the civil laws to dispute of his faith openly, as it appeareth in the title, " De summa trinitate et fide catholica."†

Phil. My lord, I have answered you this question before.

---
* By right of your office.
† Respecting the Trinity and the Catholic faith.

Bon. Why, I never asked thee of this before now.

Phil. Yes, that you did at my last examination, by that token I answered your lordship by St. Ambrose, that the church is congregated by the word, and not by man's law. Wherefore I add now further this saying: "That he who refuseth the word, and objecteth the law, is an unjust man, because the just shall live by faith." And moreover, my lord, the title which your lordship alleges out of the law, makes it not unlawful to dispute of all the articles of the faith, but only of the Trinity.

Bon. Thou liest, it is not so: and I will show you by the book how ignorant he is.

And with that he went with all haste to his study, and brought his book and openly read the text and the title of the law, and charged me with such words as seemed to make for his purpose, saying, "How sayest thou to this?"

Phil. My lord, I say as I said before, that the law means the catholic faith determined in the council of Chalcedon, where the articles of the creed were only concluded upon.*

Bon. Thou art the veriest beast that ever I heard, I must needs speak it, thou compellest me thereunto.

Phil. Your lordship may speak your pleasure of me. But what is this to the purpose, which your lordship is so earnest in? You know that our faith is not grounded upon the civil law; therefore it is not material to me whatever the law saith.

Bon. By what law wilt thou be judged? Wilt thou be judged by the common law?

Phil. No, my lord, our faith depends not upon the laws of man.

St. A. He will be judged by no law, but as he pleases himself.

Wor. The common laws are but abstracts of the Scriptures and doctors.

Phil. Whatsoever you account them, they are no ground of my faith, by which I ought to be judged.

Bon. I must needs proceed against thee to-morrow.

Phil. If your lordship do so, I shall have exceptionem fori,† for you are not my competent judge.

Bon. By what law canst thou refuse me to be thy judge?

Phil. By the civil law, De competente judice.‡

---

* Spoken of. † Exception to the jurisdiction.
‡ Concerning competent judges.

Bon. There is no such title in the law. In what book is it, cunning lawyer as you are?

Phil. My lord, I take upon me no great cunning in the law: but you drive me to my shifts for my defence, and I am sure if I had the books of the law, I were able to show what I say.

Bon. What? De competente judice? I will go and fetch thee my books. There is a title indeed, De officiis judicis ordinarii. "Of the duties of the ordinary judge."

Phil. Verily, that is the same De competente judice, which I have alleged.

With that he ran to his study, and brought the whole course of the law between his hands, which, as it might appear, he had well occupied, by the dust they were embrued withal.

Bon. There are the books; find it now if thou canst, and I will promise thee to release thee out of prison.

Phil. My lord, I stand not here to reason matters of the civil law, although I am not altogether ignorant of the same, for I have been a student in the same six or seven years; but to answer to the articles of faith with which you may lawfully burden me. And whereas you go about to proceed unlawfully, I challenge, according to my knowledge, the benefit of the law in my defence.

Bon. Why, thou wilt answer directly to nothing thou art charged with: therefore say not hereafter but you might have been satisfied here by learned men, if you would have declared your mind.

Phil. My lord, I have declared my mind unto you and to others of the bishops at my last being before you, desiring to be satisfied by you only as to one thing, whereunto I have referred all other controversies; which if your lordships now, or other learned men, can simply resolve me of, I am as contented to be conformable in all things, as you shall require; the which is to prove that the church of Rome (whereof you are) is the catholic church.

Cov. Why, do you not believe your creed, "I believe in the holy catholic church."

Phil. Yes, that I do; but I cannot understand Rome (wherewith you burden us) is the same, neither like it.

St. A. It is most evident that St. Peter built the catholic church at Rome. And Christ said, "Thou art Peter, and upon this rock I will build my church."*

* That Peter built the Church of Rome is false, for the

Moreover, the succession of bishops in the see of Rome can be proved from time to time, as cannot be of any other place so well, which is a manifest proof of the catholic church, as divers doctors write.

Phil. That which you would have to be undoubted, is most uncertain, and even by the authority which you allege of Christ, saying unto Peter: "Thou art Peter, and upon this rock I will build my church," unless you can prove the rock to signify Rome, as you would make me falsely believe. And although you could prove the succession of bishops from Peter, yet this is not sufficient to prove Rome the catholic church, unless you can prove the profession of Peter's faith, whereupon the Catholic church is built, has continued in his successors at Rome, and at this present time remains there.

Bon. Is there any more churches than one catholic church? and I pray you tell me, into what faith were you baptized?

Phil. I acknowledge one holy catholic and apostolic church, whereof I am a member, I praise God, and am of that catholic faith of Christ, whereinto I was baptized.

Cov. I pray you, can you tell what this word "catholic" signifies? show, if you can.

Phil. Yes, that I can, I thank God. The catholic faith, or the catholic church, is not as the people are taught now-a-days, that which is most universal, or received by the most part of men, whereby you do infer faith to hang upon the multitude, which is not so, but I esteem the catholic church to be as St. Austin defines the same. "We judge," saith he, "the catholic faith, of that which hath been, is, and shall be." So that if you can be able to prove that your faith and church hath been taught from the beginning, and is, and shall be, then may you count yourselves catholic, otherwise not. And catholic is a Greek word, compounded of KATA, which signifies after or according, and OLON, a sum, or principal, or whole. So that, catholic church, or catholic faith, is as much as to say, the first, whole, sound, or chief faith.

Bon. Does St. Austin say as he alleges, or does he mean as he taketh the same? how say you, Master Curtop?

scripture saith, that Peter was set over the circumcised, or Jews, and not over the Gentiles; and also it is proved by Orosius, Suetonius, Tertullian, and other histories, that the faith of Christ was in Rome in Tiberius's time, before Peter ever saw Rome.—*Fox.*

Curtop. Indeed, my lord, St. Augustine has such a saying, speaking against the Donatists, that the catholic faith ought to be esteemed of things in times past, and as they are practised according to the same, and ought to be through all ages, and not after a new manner, as the Donatists began to profess.

Phil. You have said well, Master Curtop, and after the meaning of St. Austin, and to confirm that which I have said for the signification of catholic.

Cov. Let the book be seen, my lord.

Bon. I pray you, my lord, be content, or in good faith I will break even off, and let all alone. Do you think the catholic church have erred, until within these few years, in which a few, from singularity, have swerved from the same?

Phil. I do not think that the catholic church can err in doctrine; but I require you to prove this church of Rome to be the catholic church.

Curtop. I can prove that Ireneus, who lived within a hundred years after Christ, came to Victor, then bishop of Rome, to ask his advice about the excommunication of certain heretics, which he would not have done, by all likelihood, if he had not taken him to be supreme head.*

Cov. Mark well this argument. How are you able to answer to it? Answer if you can.

Phil. It is soon answered, my lord, that it is of no force. This fact of Ireneus maketh no more for the supremacy of the bishop of Rome, than mine has done, who have been at Rome as well as he, and might have spoken with the pope if I had list; and yet I would that none in England did favour his supremacy more than I do.

St. A. You are the more to blame, by the faith of my body, for that you favour the same no better, since all the catholic church, until these few years, have taken him to be supreme head of the church, besides this good man Ireneus.

Phil. It is not likely that Ireneus, or the primitive church, so took him; for I am able to show seven general councils after Ireneus's time, wherein he was never so

---

* Where Master Curtop finds this I cannot say; but this I find, that Eusebius doth report that Ireneus did reprove Victor, bishop of Rome, for his rash sentence in excommunicating the churches of Greece, concerning the observation of the feast of Easter. Euseb lib. v. cap. 26.—*Fox.*

taken, which may be a sufficient proof that the catholic primitive church never took him for supreme head.

The other bishop. This man will never be satisfied, say what we can. It is but folly to reason any more with him.

Phil. O, my lords, would you have me satisfied with nothing? Judge, I pray you, who of us has the better authority, he who bringeth the example of one man going to Rome, or I that by these many general councils am able to prove, that he was never reckoned as head for many hundred years after Christ, as by the Nicene, the first and the second Ephesine, the Chalcedonian, the Constantinopolitane, the Carthaginian, and the Aquiliensean councils do appear.

Cov. Why will you not admit the church of Rome to be the catholic church?

Phil. Because it follows not the primitive catholic church, neither agrees with the same—no more than an apple is like a nut.

Cov. Wherein does it dissent?

Phil. It were too long to recite all, but two things I will name:—the supremacy, and transubstantiation.

Curtop. As for transubstantiation, although it was set forth and decreed for an article of faith not much above three hundred years ago, yet it was always believed in the church.

Bon. Yea, that it was. Very well said of you, Master Curtop.

Phil. You have said right, that transubstantiation is but a late plantation of the bishop of Rome, and you are not able to show by any ancient writer, that the primitive church believed any such thing. (With this Curtop shrunk away, and immediately after the ambassador of Spain came in, to whom my lord of London went, leaving the others with me, to whom I said,) My lords, if you can show me that this church of Rome, whereof you are members, is the true catholic church, I shall be content to be one thereof, and as conformable to the same as you can require me in all things; for I know there is no salvation but within the church.

Cov. Can you prove that the church of Rome is not the catholic church?

Phil. Yea, that I am able, but I desire rather to hear of you for the proof thereof. And seeing I cannot have my request at your hands, neither be satisfied with any probable authority, I will show you good proof why it is not. For if the primitive church were catholic, as it was indeed, and ought to be the rule and schoolmistress of the church to the world's end: then the church of Rome is not now the catholic church, which dissents so far from the same both in doctrine and the use of the sacraments.

Cov. How prove you that the church of Rome now dissents in doctrine and use of the sacraments from the primitive church?

Phil. Compare the one with the other, and it shall soon appear; as you may see both in Eusebius and other ecclesiastical and ancient writers.

Cov. What have you to say more, why it is not the catholic church?

Phil. Because it is not, by your interpretation of catholic, universal; neither ever was, although you falsely persuade the people that it is so. For the world being divided into three parts, Asia, Africa, and Europe; two parts thereof, Asia and Africa, professing Christ as well as we, never consented to the church of Rome, which is of Europe. This is a sufficient testimony that your faith never was universal.

Cov. How prove you that?

Phil. All the historians who write of the proceedings of the church, testify the same. Besides that, this present time declares that to be true which I say. For at this present time the churches of Asia and Africa do not consent to the church of Rome. Yea, and besides all this, most part of Europe does not agree, neither allow the church of Rome; as Germany, the kingdom of Denmark, the kingdom of Poland, a great part of France, England, and Zealand, which is a manifest proof that your church is not universal.

After this, the bishop of London called away the other bishops, and left with me divers gentlemen, and certain of his chaplains, as Doctor Saverson, an Englishman, who had proceeded doctor in Bologna, who began with me in this manner.

D. Sav. Master Philpot, I remember you beyond sea, since the time you reasoned with a friar, a notable learned man. coming from Venice to Padua in a barge.

Phil. I cannot forget that, for the friar threatened to accuse me of heresy as soon as he came to Padua, because I talked with him so boldly of the truth. He was no such learned man as you name him to be, but only in his school points a good purgatory friar.*

D. Sav. Well, he was a learned man for all that. And I am sorry to hear that you this day having communed with so many notable learned men, are not more conformable to them than you are.

Phil. I will be conformable to all that be conformable to Christ in his word. And I pray you, good Master doctor, be not so conformable to please men more than God, contrary to your learning, † for sake of worldly esteem.

D. Sav. No, that I am not. Why should you think thus of me?

Phil. Upon no evil that I know of you, Master doctor; but I speak as one wishing that you should not be led away from the truth for promotion's sake, as many doctors are now-a-days.

D. Sav. I have heard your arguments hitherto, and methinks that a great many of the old ancient writers are against you, in that you do not allow the church of Rome, neither the supremacy; for St. Cyprian, who is an old ancient writer, allows the bishop of Rome to be supreme head of the church.‡

Phil. That I am sure he does not. For he writing unto Cornelius, then bishop of Rome, calls him only his companion and fellow bishop, neither attributes to him the name either of pope, or any usurped terms which now are ascribed to the bishop of Rome, to the setting forth of his dignity.

D. Sav. You cannot be able to show that St. Cyprian calls Cornelius his fellow bishop.

Phil. I will wager with you what I am able, that I can show it you in Cyprian, as I have said.

D. Sav. I will lay no other wager with you, but book for book, that it is not so.

Phil. I agree thereto, and I pray you, one of my lord's chaplains, to fetch Cyprian hither for the trial hereof.

And with that one of them went to my lord's study and brought forth Cyprian, and he turned to the first book of

---

* One who could talk in favour of purgatory.
† Knowledge.
‡ For the further debating of this matter, that Cyprian doth allow no such thing, read the answer of Master Nowel to Master Dorman —*Fox.*

his epistles, the third epistle, and there would have seemed to have gathered a strong argument for the supremacy of the bishop of Rome, because he saith, "It goeth not well with the church when the high-priest is not obeyed, which supplieth the stead of Christ after God's word, and the consent of his fellow bishops, and the agreement of the people."

D. Sav. How can you do away this place which makes so plainly for the bishop of Rome's supremacy?

Phil. It makes not so plain, Master doctor, on your side, as you gather, as by and by I will give you to understand. But first I challenge the wager which we made, that your book is mine. For here you may see that he calleth Cornelius his fellow bishop, as he does also in other places. And now for the understanding of that place: you misconstrue it, to take the high-priest for the bishop of Rome only, and otherwise than it was in his time. For there were by the Nicene council four patriarchs appointed, the patriarch of Jerusalem, the patriarch of Constantinople, the patriarch of Alexandria, and the patriarch of Rome; of which four, the patriarch of Rome was placed lowest in the council, and so continued many years, for the time of seven or eight general councils, as I am able to show.* Therefore St. Cyprian, writing to Cornelius, patriarch of Rome, whom he calls his fellow bishop, finds himself offended, that certain heretics being justly excommunicated by him, as the Novatians were, fled from his diocese, who was their chief bishop, refusing to be obedient to him, and to be reformed, to the bishop of Rome and to the patriarch of Constantinople; and there were received in communion of congregation, in derogation of good order and discipline in the church, and to the maintaining of heresies and schisms; and that heresies did spring up and schisms daily rise hereof, so that obedience was not given to the priest of God, nor was he respected in the church. For as the priest, and the judge in Christ's stead, in the decree of

---

* In the Nicene Council three patriarchs only were named, to whom afterwards the patriarch of Constantinople was also joined. Cyprian hath also these words following in the same epistle. "It was declared amongst us, and it is according to justice and equity that every man's cause should be heard where the fault was committed; and to every several pastor there is a portion of the flock appointed to rule and govern, for the which he must make an account before God." Cyprian, lib. iv. epist. 2.—*Fox.*

Nicene council, not the bishop of Rome only, but every patriarch in his precinct was appointed; who had every one of them a college or cathedral church of learned priests, in hearing of whom, by a convocation of his fellow bishops, with the consent of the people, all heresies were determined by the word of God: and this is the meaning of St. Cyprian.

D. Sav. You take it so, but it seems to me otherwise.

Phil. Upon what ground it should seem otherwise unto you, I know not, but this meaning which I have declared, the general councils, seven or eight, one after another, confirmed, which did not allow one supreme head only.

Pend. There were not so many general councils, but four only allowed.

Phil. That is not so, Master Pendleton, although there are four specially allowed for the confirmation of the Trinity; but besides these four there were many other general councils, as you may learn by many writers.

A chaplain. Did not Christ build his church upon Peter? St. Cyprian saith so.

Phil. St. Cyprian, "De simplicitate prælatorum," in his treatise "Concerning the simplicity of the prelates," declares in what respect he so said: "God gave in the person of one man the keys to all, that he might signify the unity of all men." And also St. Augustine saith in the tenth treatise of St. John, "If in Peter had not been the mystery of the church, the Lord had not said unto him, I will give unto thee the keys. For if that were said unto Peter, the church hath them not; if the church have them, when Peter received them he signified the whole church." And also St. Jerome, a priest of Rome, writing to Nepotian, saith, "That all churches lean to their own pastors," where he speaks of the ecclesiastical hierarchy or regiment,* but he makes no mention of the bishop of Rome. And to Evagrius he says, "Wheresoever a bishop is, whether it is at Rome, or at Evagia, or at Rhegium, he is of one power and of one jurisdiction."

D. Sav. St. Jerome "Of the heavenly hierarchy?" It was Dionysius you mean.

Phil. I say not that Jerome wrote any book so intituled; but I say, that in the epistle by me alleged, he mentions the ecclesiastical regiment.

* Rule.

D. Sav. I wonder you will stand so steadfast in your error, to your own destruction.

Phil. I am sure we are in no error, by the promise of Christ made to the faithful once, which is, that he will give to his true church such a spirit of wisdom, that the adversaries thereof shall never be able to resist. And by this I know we are of the truth, for that neither by reasoning nor by writing, your synagogue of Rome is able to answer. Where is there one of you all that ever has been able to answer any of the godly learned ministers of Germany, who have disclosed your counterfeit religion? Which of you all, at this day, is able to answer Calvin's Institutions, who is minister of Geneva?

D. Sav. A godly minister indeed, of a receipt of cutpurses and runagate traitors. And of late I can tell you there is such contention fallen between him and his own sects, that he was fain to fly the town, about predestination. I tell you truth, for I came by Geneva hither.

Phil. I am sure you blaspheme that godly man, and that godly church where he is minister, as it is your church's plan when you cannot answer men by learning, to oppress them with blasphemies and false reports. For in the matter of predestination he is of no other opinion than all the doctors of the church are, agreeing to the scriptures.

D. Sav. Men are able to answer him if they list. And I pray you, which of you have answered bishop Fisher's book?

Phil. Yes, Master doctor, that book is answered and answered again, if you list to seek what has been written against him.

After this, Doctor Story came in. To whom I said, "Master doctor, you have done me great injury, and without law have straitly imprisoned me, more like a dog than a man And besides this, you have not kept promise with me, for you promised that I should be judged the next day."

Story. I am come now to keep promise with thee. Was there ever such a fantastical man as this? Nay, he is no man, he is a beast Yea, these heretics are worse than brute beasts; for they will from a vain singularity take upon them to be wiser than all men; being, indeed, very fools and assheads, not able to maintain that which of arrogant obstinacy they do stand in.

Phil. Master doctor, I am content to abide your railing judgment of me now. Say what you will, I am content, for I am under your feet to be trod on as you list. God forgive it you. Yet I am no heretic. Neither you nor any other shall be able to prove that I hold a jot against the word of God, or otherwise than a christian man ought.

Story. The word of God!—forsooth, the word of God! —It is but a folly to reason with these heretics, for they are incurable and desperate. But I may reason with thee, not that I have any hope to win thee. Whom wilt thou appoint to be judge of the word whereto thou standest?

Phil. Verily, the word itself.

Story. Do you not see the ignorance of this beastly heretic? He would have the word to be judged of the word. Can the word speak?

Phil. If I cannot prove that which I have said by good authority, I will be content to be counted a heretic and an ignorant person, and what you please further.

Story. Let us hear what wise authority you can bring?

Phil. It is the saying of Christ in St. John, "The word which I have spoken," saith Christ, "shall judge in the last day." If the word shall judge in the last day, much more it ought to judge our doings now; and I am sure I have my judge on my side, who shall absolve and justify me in another world. However now it shall please you by authority, unrighteously to judge of me and others, sure I am in another world to judge you.

Story. What! you purpose to be a stinking martyr, and to sit in judgment with Christ at the last day, to judge the twelve tribes of Israel.

Phil. Yea, sir, I doubt not thereof, having the promise of Christ, if I die for righteousness' sake, which you have begun to persecute in me.

Story. I told you it is but vain to argue with this heretic: he is drowned in his heresies without all learning.

Phil. Sir, I have brought you for that I have said good authority out of God's book, to which you answer nothing, but go about still to give railing judgment against me without any cause.

Story. I will come to you by and by. When the judge in Westminster-hall gives sentence, does the word give sentence, or the judge? tell me.

Phil. Civil matters are subject to civil men, and they have authority by the word, to be judge of them. But the word of God is not subject to man's judgment, but ought to judge all the wisdom, thoughts, and doings of men; and therefore your comparison disproves nothing that I have said, neither answers at all thereto.

Story. Wilt thou not allow the interpretation of the church upon the scriptures?

Phil. Yes, if it be according to the word of the true church; and this I say to you, as I have said heretofore, that if you can prove the church of Rome, whereof you are, to be the true catholic church which I ought to follow, I will be as ready to yield thereto, as long as it can be so proved, as you may desire me.

Story. What a fellow is this! He will believe nothing but what he himself pleases. Are we not in possession of the church? Have not our forefathers these many hundred years taken this church for the catholic church whereof we are now? And if we had no other proof but this, it were sufficient; for the prescription of time makes a good title in the law.

Phil. You do well, Master doctor, to allege prescription of many years, for it is all that you have to show for yourselves. But you must understand that prescription hath no place in matters belonging to God, as I am able to show by the testimony of many doctors.

Story. Well, sir, you are like to go after your father Latimer the sophister, and Ridley, who had nothing to allege for himself, but that he had learned his heresy of Cranmer. When I came to him with a poor bachelor of arts, he trembled as though he had the palsy, as these heretics have always some token of fear whereby a man may know them, as you may see this man's eyes do tremble in his head. But I despatched them; and I tell thee that there hath been yet never a one burned, but I have spoken with him, and have been a cause of his despatch.[*]

Phil. You have the more to answer for, Master doctor, as you shall feel in another world, how much soever you now triumph in your proceedings.

Story. I tell thee I will never be confessed thereof;[†] and, because I cannot now tarry to speak with my lord, I pray one of you tell my lord, that my coming was to

---

[*] Dr. Story confesses himself to be the chief despatcher of all God's saints that suffered in queen Mary's time.—*Fox.* For an account of this man, of whom it was emphatically said, "Story worse than Bonner," see *Strype's Annals*, vol. i. p. 78. 572

[†] Confess it as a sin.

signify to his lordship, that he must out of hand rid this heretic away. (And, going away, he said unto me,) I certify thee that thou mayest thank no other man but me.

Phil. I thank you therefore with all my heart, and God forgive it you.

Story. What! dost thou thank me? If I had thee in my study half an hour, I think I should make thee sing another song.

Phil. No, Master doctor; I stand upon too sure a ground to be overthrown by you now.

And thus they departed all away from me one after another, until I was left all alone. And afterwards with my keeper going to my coalhouse, as I went, I met with my lord of London, who spake unto me gently, as he hath hitherto in words, saying, " Philpot, if there be any pleasure I may show you in my house; I pray you require it, and you shall have it."

Phil. My lord, the pleasure that I will require of your lordship is to hasten my judgment which is committed unto you; and so despatch me forth from this miserable world, unto my eternal rest.

For all this fair speech I can attain for this fortnight space, neither fire, nor candle, nor yet good lodging. But it is good for a man to be brought low in this world, and to be counted among the vilest, that he may in time of reward receive exaltation and glory. Therefore, praised be God, who hath humbled me, and given me grace with gladness to be content therewith.

Let all that love the truth say, Amen.
Thus endeth the fifth tragedy.

The sixth Examination of John Philpot, before the right honourable lords, the lord chamberlain to the king's majesty, the Viscount Hereford, commonly called Lord Ferrars, the Lord Rich, the Lord St. Johns, the Lord Windsor, the Lord Chandos, Sir John Bridges, lieutenant of the tower, and two others whose names I know not, with Bonner the Bishop of London and Dr. Chadsey, the sixth day of November, anno 1555.

BEFORE that I was called to the lords, and whilst they were in sitting down, the bishop of London came aside

Sixth Examination. 47

to me and whispered in my ear, willing me to conduct myself prudently before the lords of the queen's majesty's council, and to take heed what I said; and he pretended thus to give me counsel because he wished me to do well, as I might now do if I list. And after the lords and other worshipful gentlemen of the queen's majesty's servants were set, my lord of London placed himself at the end of the table, and called me to him, and by the lords I was placed at the upper end against him; where I kneeling down, the lords commanded me to stand up; and in this manner the bishop began to speak.

London. Master Philpot, I have heretofore both privately myself, and openly before the lords of the clergy more times than once caused you to be talked with, to reform you of your errors, but I have not found you yet so tractable as I would wish; wherefore now I have desired these honourable lords of the temporality and of the queen's majesty's council, who have taken pains with me this day, I thank them therefore, to hear you what you can say, that they may be judges whether I have sought all means to do you good or no. And I dare be bold to say in their behalf, that if you show yourself conformable to the queen's majesty's proceedings, you shall find as much favour for your deliverance as you can wish. I speak not this to fawn upon you, but to bring you home into the church. Now let them hear what you can say.

Phil. My lord, I thank God of this day, that I have such an honourable audience to declare my mind before. And I cannot but commend your lordship's equity in this behalf, which agrees with the order of the primitive church, which was, if any body had been suspected of heresy, as I am now, he should be called first before the archbishop or bishop of the diocese where he was suspected; secondly, in the presence of others his fellow bishops and learned elders; and, thirdly, in hearing of the laity: where, after the judgment of God's word declared, and with the assent of other bishops and consent of the people, he was condemned to exile as a heretic, or absolved. And the second point of that good order I have found at your ordship's hands already, in being called before you and your fellow bishops, and now have the third sort of men, at whose hands I trust to find more righteousness* in my cause than I have found with my lords of the clergy God

* Justice.

grant I may at last have the judgment of God's word concerning the same.

Lon. Master Philpot, I pray you before you go any further, tell my lords here plainly whether you were by me or by my procurement committed to prison or not, and whether I have showed you any cruelty since you have been committed to my prison.

Phil. If it shall please your lordship to give me leave to declare forth my matter, I will touch that afterward.

Rich. Answer first of all to my lords two questions, and then proceed forth to the matter. How say you? Were you imprisoned by my lord, or no? Can you find any fault since with his cruel using of you?

Phil. I cannot lay to my lord's charge the cause of my imprisonment, neither may I say that he has used me cruelly; but rather for my part, I might say that I have found more gentleness at his lordship's hands than I did from my own ordinary, for the time I have been within his prison, for he has called me three or four times to mine answer, to which I was not called in a twelvemonth and a half before.

Rich. Well, now go to your matter.

Phil. The matter is, that I am imprisoned for the disputations had by me in the convocation-house against the Sacrament of the altar; which matter was not moved principally by me, but by the prolocutor, with the consent of the queen's majesty and of the whole house; and that house being a member of the parliament house, ought to be a place of free speech for all men of the house, by the ancient and laudable custom of this realm. Wherefore I think myself to have sustained hitherto great injury for speaking my conscience freely in such a place as I might lawfully do it; and I desire your honourable lordships' judgment, who are of the parliament house, whether of right I ought to be impeached therefore, and sustain the loss of my living, as I have done, and moreover of my life, as it is sought for.

Rich. You are deceived herein; for the convocation-house is no part of the parliament house.

Phil. My lord, I have always understood the contrary by such as are more expert men in things of this realm than I am. And again, the title of every act leads me to think otherwise, which alleges the agreement of the spirituality and temporality when assembled together.

Sixth Examination.

Rich. Yea, that is meant of the spiritual lords of the upper house.

Windsor. Indeed the convocation-house is called together by one writ of the summons of the parliament of an old custom; notwithstanding that house is no part of the parliament house.*

Phil. My lords, I must be contented to abide your judgments in this behalf.

Rich. We have told you the truth. Yet we would not that you should be troubled for any thing that was spoken there: so that you, having spoken amiss, declare now that you are sorry therefore.

Lon. My lords, he spoke there manifest heresy, yea and there stoutly maintained the same against the blessed sacrament of the altar, (and with that he put off his cap that all the lords might reverence and vail their bonnets at that idol, as they did,) and would not allow the real presence of the body and blood of Christ in the same; yet, my lords, God forbid that I should show him extremity† for so doing, in case he will repent and revoke his wicked sayings; and, in faith, if he will so do, with your lordships' consent he shall be released directly. If he will not, he shall look for the extremity of the law, and that shortly.

Chamb. My lord of London speaks reasonably unto you, take it whilst it is offered you.

Rich. How say you? Will you acknowledge the real presence of the blood and body of Christ in the mass, as all the learned men of this realm do, and as I do, and will believe as long as I live, I do protest it.

Phil. My lord, I acknowledge in the sacrament of the body and blood of Christ such a presence, as the word of God doth allow and teach me.

Rich. That shall be no otherwise than you please.

Lon. A sacrament is the sign of a holy thing; so that there is both the sign, which is the accident, as the whiteness, roundness, and shape of bread; and there is also the thing itself, as very Christ both God and man. But these heretics will have the sacraments to be but bare signs. How say you? Declare unto my lords here

---

* Whether the convocation be part of the parliament house or not, yet free liberty was given by the queen to every man to speak according to his conscience.—*Fox.*

† Severity.

whether you allow the thing itself in the sacrament or no?

Phil. I confess, that in the Lord's supper there is in due respects both the sign and the thing signified, when it is duly ministered after the institution of Christ.

Lon. You may see how he goes about the bush, as he hath done before, with my lords of the clergy, and dare not utter his mind plainly.

Rich. Show us what manner of presence you allow in the sacrament.

Phil. If it shall please you, my lord of London, to give me leave to proceed orderly thereunto, and to let me declare my mind without interruption, I will throughly open my mind therein.

L. Chand. I pray you, my lord, let him speak his mind.

Phil. My lords, that at the first I have not plainly declared my judgment unto you is, because I cannot speak hereof without the danger of my life.

Rich. There is none of us here that seeks thy life, or means to take any advantage of what thou shalt speak.

Phil. Although I mistrust not your honourable lordships that are here of the temporality; yet here is one that sitteth against me (pointing to my lord of London) that will lay it to my charge, even to the death.* Notwithstanding, seeing your honours require me to declare my mind respecting the presence of Christ in the sacrament, that ye may perceive that I am not ashamed of the gospel of Christ, neither maintain any opinion without probable and sufficient authority of the scripture, I will show you frankly my mind without any concealment, whatsoever shall ensue unto me therefore, so that my lord of London will not hinder me from uttering my mind.

Rich. My lord, permit him to say what he can, seeing he is willing to show his mind.

Lon. I am content, my lords, let him say what he can, I will hear him.

Phil. That which I intend to speak unto you (right honourable lords) I protest here, first before God and his angels, that I speak it not of vain-glory, neither of singularity, neither of wilful stubbornness; but truly upon a good conscience, grounded on God's word, against which

---

* They say they seek not his life, and yet they know to answer to that they ask will be his death.—*Fox*.

I dare not act for fear of damnation, which will follow that which is done contrary to knowledge. Neither do I disagree to the proceedings of this realm in religion because I love not the queen, whom I love from the bottom of my heart; but because I ought to love and fear God in his word more than man in his laws, though I stand as I seem to do in this consideration, and for none other, as I call God to witness.

There are two things, principally, by which the clergy at this day deceive the whole realm; that is, the sacrament of the body and blood of Christ, and the name of the catholic church; both which they usurp, having indeed neither of them. And as touching their sacrament, which they term of the altar, I say now, as I said in the convocation-house, that it is not the sacrament of Christ, neither in the same is there any manner of Christ's presence. Wherefore they deceive the queen's majesty, and you of the nobility of this realm, in making you believe that to be a sacrament which is none; and they cause you to commit manifest idolatry in worshipping that for God, which is not God. And in testimony of the truth of this, besides manifest proof which I am able to make to the queen's majesty, and to all you of her nobility, I will yield my life. To do which, if it were not upon a sure ground, it were to my utter damnation.

And though they take on them the name of the catholic church, whereby they blind many folks eyes, they are not at all so, calling you from the true religion which was revealed and taught in king Edward's time, unto vain superstition. And this I will say for the trial hereof, that if they can prove themselves to be the catholic church, as they shall never be able to do, I will never be against their doings, but revoke all that I have said. And I shall desire you, my lords, to speak for me to the queen's majesty, that I may be brought to the just trial hereof. Yea, I will not refuse to stand against ten of the best of them in this realm. And if they are able to prove otherwise than I have said, either by writing or by reasoning, with good and lawful authority, I here promise to recant whatsoever I have said, and to consent to them in all points. (And in the declaration of these things more at large, which now I write in sum, the bishop of London soon would have interrupted me; but the lords procured me liberty to make out my tale, to the great grief of the lord bishop of London, as it appeared by the dumps* he was in.) . . . . .

Lon. I pray you, how will you join these two scriptures together, "*Pater major me est, et pater et ego unum sumus.*" I must interpret the same, because my lords here understand not the Latin; that is to say, "The Father is greater than I, and I and the Father are one."† But I cry you mercy, my lords; I have mis-spoken, in saying you understand no Latin: for the most part of you understand Latin as well as I. But I spake in consideration of my lord Chandos and Master Bridges his brother, whom I take to be no great Latin men. Now show your skill and join these two scriptures by the word if you can.

Phil. Yes, that I can right well; for we must understand that in Christ there are two natures, the divinity and humanity;‡ and in respect of his humanity it is spoken of Christ, "The Father is greater than I," but in respect of his Deity he said again, "The Father and I are one."

Lon. But what scriptures have you?

Phil. I have sufficient scripture for the proof of what I have said. For the first, it is written of Christ in the Psalms, "Thou hast made him a little lesser than angels." It is the Psalm beginning "Cœli enarrant." And there I misreckoned, wherewithal my lord took me.

Lon. It is in Domine Dominus noster. You may see, my lords, how well this man is used to say his matins.

Phil. Though I say not matins in such order as your lordship meaneth, yet I remember of old that Domine Dominus noster, and Cœli enarrant, the eighth and nineteenth Psalms, are not far asunder; and although I misnamed the psalm, it is no prejudice to the truth which I have proved.

Lon. What say you then to the second scripture? How couple you that to the other by the word?

Phil. The text itself declares, that notwithstanding Christ abased himself in our human nature, yet he is still one in Deity with the Father. And this St. Paul to the Hebrews more at large sets forth. And as I have by the scriptures joined these two scriptures together, so am I

---

* Displeasure.
† Most of the quotations of scripture, both by Philpot and the Romish clergy, were made from the Latin Vulgate.
‡ Divine nature and human nature.

able to do in all other articles of faith which we ought to believe, and expound them by the manifest word of God.

Lon. How can that be, seeing St. Paul saith, " That the letter killeth, but it is the Spirit that giveth life."

Phil. St. Paul means not that the written word of God, in itself killeth, which is the word of life, and the faithful testimony of the Lord; but that the word is unprofitable and killeth him that is void of the Spirit of God, although he be the wisest man of the world; and therefore St. Paul said, " That the gospel to some was a savour of life unto life, and to some other a savour of death unto death." Also an example hereof we have in the sixth of John, of them who hearing the word of God, without the Spirit, were offended thereby; wherefore Christ said, " The flesh profiteth nothing, it is the Spirit that quickeneth."

Lon. What! do you understand that of St. Paul and of St. John so?

Phil. It is not mine own interpretation, it is agreeable to the word in other places; and I have learned the same from ancient fathers interpreting it likewise. And to the Corinthians it is written, " The natural man perceiveth not the things that be of the Spirit of God; but the spiritual man which is indued with the Spirit, judgeth all things."

Lon. You see, my lords, that this man will have his own mind, and will wilfully cast away himself. I am sorry for him.

Phil. The words that I have spoken are none of mine but of the gospel, whereon I ought to stand. And if you, my lord of London, can bring better authority for the faith you would draw me unto, than that which I stand upon, I will gladly hear the same by you or by any other in this realm.

Wherefore I, kneeling down, besought the lords to be good unto me a poor gentleman, who would fain live in the world if I might, and to testify, as you have heard me to say this day, that if any man can prove that I ought to be of another manner of faith than that of which I now am, and can prove the same sufficiently, I will neither be wilful nor desperate, as my lord of London would make you believe me to be.

Rich. What countryman are you? Are you of the Philpots of Hampshire?

Phil. Yea, my lord, I was Sir Peter Philpot's son of Hampshire.

Rich. He is my near kinsman; wherefore I am the more sorry for him.

Phil. I thank your lordship that you claim kindred with oor prisoner.

Rich. In faith I would go a hundred miles on my bare t to do you good.

Chamb. He may do well enough if he list.

St. John. Master Philpot, you are my countryman, and I would be glad you should do well.

Rich. You said even now, that you would desire to maintain your belief before ten of the best in the realm. You did not well to compare with the nobility of the realm. But what if you have ten of the best in the realm to hear you, will you be tried by them?

Phil. My lord, your lordship mistakes me if you think that I challenge ten of the best of the nobility in this realm. It was no part of my mind, but I meant of the best learned on the contrary side.

Rich. Well, I take your meaning. What if means be made to the queen's majesty, that you shall have your request, will you be judged by them?

Phil. My lord, it is not meet that a man should be judged by his adversaries.

Rich. By whom then would you be judged?

Phil. I will make your honours judges, that shall be hearers of us.

Rich. I dare be bold to procure for you of the queen's majesty that you shall have ten learned men to reason with you, and twenty or forty of the nobility to hear; if you will promise to abide their judgment. How say you? Will you promise here before my lords so to do?

Phil. I will be contented to be judged by them.

Rich. Yea, but will you promise to agree to their judgment?

Phil. There are causes why I may not so do, unless I were sure they would judge according to the word of God.

Rich. O, I perceive you will have no man judge but yourself, and think yourself wiser than all the learned men of this realm.

Phil. My lord, I seek not to be my own judge, but am

content to be judged by others; so that the order of judgment in matters of religion be kept that was in the primitive church, which is, first, that God's will by his word was sought, and thereunto both the spirituality and temporality were gathered together, and gave their consent and judgment, and such kind of judgment I will stand to.

Lon. My lords, he would make you believe that he were profoundly seen* in ancient writers of the judgments of the primitive church, and there was never any such manner of judgment used as he now talks of.

Phil. In the epistles of St. Cyprian I am able to show it.

Lon. Ha! I tell you there is no such thing; bring me Cyprian hither.

Phil. You shall find it otherwise, when the book comes.

And doctor Chedsey, his chaplain, whom he appointed to fetch his book, whispered the bishop in his ear, and brought not the book, lest he should have sustained the reproach thereof if the book had been brought. Well, my lord, said I, Master doctor knows it is so, or else he would have brought the book ere this.

Rich. You would have no other judge, I see, but the word.

Phil. Yes, my lord; I will be tried by the word, and by such as will judge according to the word. As, for an example, if there were a controversy between your lordship and another upon the words of a statute, must not the words of the statute judge and determine the controversy.

Rich. No, truly, the judges of the law may determine the meaning thereof.

Lon. He hath brought as good an example against himself as can be.

And here the bishop thought he had a good hold against me, and therefore enlarged it with many words as to the judgment of the church.

The Lords. He has overthrown himself by his own argument.

Phil. My lords, it seems to your honours that you have great advantage of me by the example I brought in, to express my cause. But if it is pondered thoroughly, it makes wholly with me, and nothing against me, as my lord of London has pretended. For I will ask of my lord Rich here, whom I know to have good knowledge in the

* Learned.

laws and statutes of this realm, albeit a judge may discern the meaning of a statute agreeably to the words, whether he may judge a meaning contrary to the express words or no?*

Rich. He cannot do so.

Phil. Even so say I, that no man ought to judge the word of God to have a meaning contrary to the express words thereof, as this false church of Rome doth in many things. With this the lords seemed to be satisfied, and made no further reply therein.

Rich. I marvel then why you deny the express words of Christ in the sacrament, he said, " This is my body," and yet you do not hesitate to say it is not his body. Is not God omnipotent; and is not he able as well by his omnipotency to make it his body, as he was to make man flesh of a piece of clay? Did not he say, "This is my body which shall be betrayed for you?" and was not his very body betrayed for us? Therefore it must needs be his body.

Lon. My lord Rich, you have said wonderful well and learnedly. But you might have begun with him before also, in the sixth of John, where Christ promised to give his body in the sacrament of the altar, saying, " The bread which I will give is my flesh." How can you answer to that?

Phil. If it please you to give me leave to answer first my lord Rich, I will also answer this objection.

Rich. Answer my lord of London first, and after come to me.

Phil. My lord of London may be soon answered, that the saying of St. John is, that the humanity† of Christ which he took upon him for the redemption of man, is the bread of life, whereby our bodies and souls are sustained to eternal life, of which the sacramental bread is a lively representation and an effectual coaptation,‡ to all such as believe on his passion. And as Christ saith in the same sixth of John, " I am the bread that came down from heaven;" but yet he is not material, neither natural bread: so likewise the bread is his flesh, not naturally or sub-

---

* As a judge of the law may not discern the meaning of a statute otherwise than agreeably to the words, so hath the church no power to judge the meaning of God's word contrary to itself.—*Fox.*

† Human nature.

‡ Adjustment of parts one to another.

stantially, but by signification, and by grace in a sacrament.

And now to my lord Rich's argument. I do not deny the express words of Christ in the sacrament, "This is my body," but I deny that they are to be taken naturally and corporeally: they must be taken sacramentally and spiritually, according to the express declaration of Christ, saying, that the words of the sacrament which the Capernaites took carnally, as the papists now do, ought to be taken spiritually, and not carnally, as they falsely imagine, not considering what interpretation Christ has made in this respect; neither following the institution of Christ, nor the practice of the apostles and of the primitive church, who never taught nor declared any such carnal manner of presence as is now exacted of us violently, without any ground of scripture or antiquity. They used only to put out of the church such as did not receive the sacrament with the rest, and also to burn that which was left after the receiving, as by the canon of the apostles, and by the decree of the council of Antioch, may appear.

Lon. No, that is not so: they were only catechumens who went out of the church at the celebration of the communion, and no others.

Phil. It was not only such as were novices in faith, but all others that did not receive.

Lon. What say you to the omnipotence of God? Is not he able to perform that which he spake, as my lord Rich hath very well said? I tell thee that God, by his omnipotence, may make himself to be this carpet if he will.

Phil. As concerning the omnipotence of God, I say that God is able to do, as the prophet David saith, whatsoever he willeth, but he willeth nothing that is not agreeable to his word; as that is blasphemy which my lord of London has spoken, that God may become a carpet. For as I have learned of ancient writers, "God cannot do that which is contrary to his nature," and it is contrary to the nature of God to be a carpet. A carpet is a creature, and God is the Creator, and the creator cannot be the creature; wherefore, unless you can declare by the word, that Christ is otherwise present with us than spiritually and sacramentally by grace, as he hath taught us, you allege the omnipotence of God in vain.

Lon. Why, wilt thou not say that Christ is really present in the sacrament?—or do you deny it?

Phil I deny not that Christ is really present in the sacrament to the receiver thereof according to Christ's institution.

Lon. What mean you by really present?

Phil. I mean by really present, present indeed.

Lon. Is God really present everywhere?

Phil. He is so.

Lon. How prove you that?

Phil. The prophet Isaiah saith, "That God filleth all places:" and it is said, "Wheresoever there are two or three gathered together in Christ's name, there is he in the midst of them."

Lon. What! in his human nature?

Phil. No, my lord, I mean the Deity, according to what you demanded.

Rich. My lord of London, I pray you let Master Doctor Chadsey reason with him, and let us see how he can answer him; for I tell thee, he is a learned man indeed, and one that I credit before a great many of you, whose doctrine the queen's majesty and the whole realm doth well allow, therefore hear him.

Lon. My lords, I pray you, will it please you to drink? You have talked a great while, and much talk is thirsty. I will leave Master doctor and him reasoning together awhile, with your leave, and will come to you by and by.

Rich. My lord Rich said to the lords, I pray you let the poor man drink, for he is thirsty; and with that he called for a cup of drink, and gave it to me, and I drank before them all. God requite it him! for I was athirst indeed. Afterwards Doctor Chadsey began thus, making a great process, of which this is the effect.

Chad. Master Philpot finds fault with the convocation-house before your lordships, that he has lain thus long in prison, and that he had there a dozen arguments, whereof he could not be suffered to prosecute one thoroughly; which is not so, for he had leave to say what he could, and was answered to as much as he was able to bring; and when he had nothing else to say, he fell to weeping. I was there present, and can testify thereof: although there is a book abroad of the report of the disputation to the contrary, in the which there is never a true word.* And

* Four untruths of Doctor Chadsey at once.—*Fox.*

as you require to be satisfied respecting the sacrament. I will show you the truth thereof, both by the scriptures and by the doctors.

Phil. It is very likely, indeed, that you will conclude with any truth, since you have begun with so many untruths, as to say that I was answered whilst I had anything to say, and that I wept for lack of matter to say, and that the book of the report of the disputation is not true. God be praised, there were a good many noblemen, gentlemen, and worshipful men that heard and saw the doings thereof, who can testify that you here have made an unjust report before these honourable lords. And that I wept, was not for lack of matter, as you slander me; for I thank God, I have more matter than the best of you all shall ever be able to answer, as little learning as I have; but my weeping was, as Christ's was over Jerusalem, seeing the destruction that should fall upon her. And I foreseeing then the destruction which you, through violence and unrighteousness, which you there declared, would work against the true church of Christ and his faithful members, as this day beareth witness, was compelled to weep in remembrance of that which I with many more have felt and shall feel.

All these words I then had spoken, but was interrupted by my lord King, saying that I should suffer Doctor Chadsey to proceed out in his matter, and afterwards I should have leisure to answer him in every article. But he promised more than he could perform, as the end declared, for he had not the consent of the spirituality to his promise, who now rule the roast. God shorten their cruel days, for his elect's sake. And therefore I add this, which I had purposed to have spoken, if then I might have been suffered, lest any that know not perfectly the things done in the convocation-house, and now laid to my charge, if they should not be answered by me, might reckon Doctor Chadsey's sayings to be true. And as concerning the book of the report of the disputations, I wrote the same, and it is true in every argument, as the dean of Rochester, and Master Cheyney, archdeacon of Hereford, yet alive, and within the realm, can testify.

Chad. You have of scriptures the four evangelists, proving that Christ's real presence is in the sacrament after the words of consecration, and St. Paul to the Corinthians; which all say, "This is my body." They say not as you would have me believe, This is not the body. But especially the sixth of John proves the same most manifestly, where Christ promised to give his body, which he performed in his last supper, as it appears by these words, "The bread which I will give is my flesh, which I will give for the life of the world."

Phil. My lord Rich, with your leave, I must needs interrupt him a little, because he speaks open blasphemy against the death of Christ; for if that promise brought in by St. John was performed by Christ in his last supper, then needed he not to have died after he had given the sacrament.

Rich. Let Master doctor make an end of his arguments, and afterward object to him what you can.

Chad. You must note that, "I will give," is said twice in this saying of St. John. The first refers to the sacrament of the altar; and the second to the sacrifice upon the cross; and besides these manifest scriptures, there are many ancient doctors proving the same, as Ignatius, Ireneus, and St. Cyprian—whose authority he recited at large, which I omit, because I was not permitted to answer the same.

Rich. Now answer, and object to him what you can, and you shall be heard.

Phil. My lord, the chief ground where he, with the rest of his side, ground themselves against us, are these words, "This is my body," by a false pretence of the omnipotence of God. And before I come to the particular answers of all that he has alleged, that your lordships may the better understand what I mean and whereupon I stand, I will require Master doctor to answer me one question. But first of all, I do protest to your honours that I think as reverently of the sacrament as a christian man ought to do, and that I acknowledge the sacrament of the body and blood of Christ, ministered after Christ's institution, is one of the greatest treasures and comforts that he left us on the earth; and contrariwise, it is the greatest discomfort, and abominable, not being ministered as it ought to be, as it is used now-a-days. And now to my question, which is this: whether these words only, "Hoc est corpus meum," "This is my body," spoken by a priest over the bread and wine, may make the body and blood of Christ, as you suppose, or not?

Chadsey staggered what he should say, at last he said, that these words alone pronounced by the priest, are sufficient to make the bread and the wine the very body and blood of Christ really.

Phil. That is blasphemy to say, and against all the scriptures and doctors, who affirm that the form and substance in consecration must be observed which Christ used and instituted, as St. Cyprian saith, "In the sacrifice which is Christ, Christ only is to be followed." And by the law it is forbidden to add or take away from God's word. And St. Peter saith, "If any man speak, let him speak as the word of God." Wherefore, whosoever saith that these words only, "This is my body," make a presence of Christ, without "bless, take, and eat," which are three as substantial points of the sacrament, as "This is my body" is,—he is highly deceived.

Therefore, St. Austin saith, "Let the word be joined to the element, and it becometh a sacrament." So that if the entire words of Christ's institution are not observed in the ministration of a sacrament, it is no sacrament: as the sacrifices which the ten tribes offered at Bethel to God, were not acceptable, because they were not in all points done according to God's word. Wherefore, except blessing be made according to the word, which is a due thanksgiving for our redemption in Christ, and also a showing forth of the Lord's death in such a manner that the congregation may be edified; and moreover a taking and eating after Christ's commandment : except, I say, these three parts are first performed, which is not done in the mass, these words, "This is my body," which are last placed in the institution of the Lord's supper, cannot be verified. For Christ commanded, "Take ye, eat ye," as well as "This is my body."

Chad. Christ said : "Take, eat, this is my body," and not, Take ye, eat ye.

Phil. No, Master doctor, are not these the words of Christ, "Accipite, manducate?" and do not these words in the plural number signify, "Take ye, eat ye;" and not, take thou, eat thou, as you would suppose?

Chad. I grant it is as you say.

Phil. Likewise of consequence, you, Master doctor, must needs deny what you have said ; that these words, "This is my body" only being spoken, are sufficient to make the body and blood of Christ in the sacrament, as you have untruly said.

Then came in the bishop of London again, and said, What is it that you would have Master doctor deny?

Phil. My lord, Master doctor hath affirmed, that these words, "This is my body," spoken by the priest, alone do make the sacrament.

Lon. Indeed if Master Bridges should speak these words over the bread and wine, they would be of no effect: but if a priest speak them after a due manner, they are effectual, and make a real body.

Phil. Master doctor has said otherwise.

Lon. I think you mistake him; for he means the words duly pronounced.

Phil. Let him revoke what he hath granted, and then will I begin again with that which before was said: that, "This is my body," hath no place, except "bless, take, and eat," duly go before. And therefore because the same words do not go before "This is my body," but preposterously follow in your sacrament of the mass, it is not the sacrament of Christ, neither hath it Christ present in it.

Chad. If "This is my body," alone, do not make the sacrament, no more do, "bless, take, and eat."

Phil. I grant that the one without the other cannot make the sacrament. And it can be no sacrament unless the whole action of Christ concur together according to the first institution.

Chad. Why, then you will not have it to be the body of Christ, unless it is received?

Phil. No verily, it is not the very body of Christ to any, but to such as worthily receive the same according to his institution.

Lon. Is not a loaf a loaf, being set on the table, though nobody eat thereof?

Phil. It is not a like case, my lord. For a loaf is a loaf before it is set on the table: but the sacrament is not a perfect sacrament before it is duly ministered at the table of the Lord.

Lon. I pray you, what is it in the mean while before it is received after the words of consecration are spoken? Answer me.

Phil. It is, my lord, the sign begun of a holy thing, and yet no perfect sacrament until it is received. For in the sacrament there are two things to be considered, the sign and the thing itself, which is Christ and his whole passion; and it is that to none but such as worthily receive

Sixth Examination. 63

the holy signs of bread and wine according to Christ's institution.

Wind. There never were any that denied the words of Christ as you do. Did he not say, " This is my body."

Phil. My lord, I pray you be not deceived. We do not deny the words of Christ; but we say, these words are of no effect if spoken otherwise than Christ instituted them in his last supper. For an example, Christ bade the church " to baptize in the name of the Father, the Son, and the Holy Ghost." If a priest say those words over the water, and there is no child to be baptized, those words only pronounced do not make baptism. And again, baptism is only baptism to such as are baptized, and to none other standing by.

L. Chamb. I pray you my lord, let me ask him one question. What kind of presence in the sacrament duly ministered according to Christ's ordinance do you allow?

Phil. If any come worthily to receive, then do I confess the presence of Christ to be wholly, with all the fruits of his passion, unto the said worthy receiver, by the Spirit of God, and that Christ is thereby joined to him and he to Christ.

L. Chamb. I am answered.

Lon. My lords, take no heed of him, for he goeth about to deceive you. His similitude that he brings in of baptism, is nothing like to the sacrament of the altar. For if I should say to sir John Bridges being with me at supper, and having a fat capon, Take, eat, this is a fat capon, although he eat not thereof, is it not a capon still? And likewise of a piece of beef, or of a cup of wine, if I say: Drink, this is a good cup of wine, is it not so, because he drink not thereof?

Phil. My lord, your similitudes are too gross for such high mysteries as we have in hand, as, if I were your equal, I could more plainly declare; and there is much more dissimilitude between common meats and drinks than there is between Baptism and the Sacrament of the body and blood of Christ. Like must be compared to like, and spiritual things with spiritual, and not spiritual things with corporeal things. And meats and drinks are of their own natures good or evil, and your words commending or discommending, do but declare what they are. But the sacraments are to be considered, according to the word which Christ spake of them, of which, " Take ye, and eat ye," are some of the chief, concurrent to the making of the same, without which there can be no sacraments: and therefore in Greek, the sacrament of the body and blood of Christ is called KOINOONIA, that is, "Communion," and likewise in the gospel Christ commanded, saying, " Divide it among you."

Chad. St. Paul calls it a communication.

Phil. That still more expressly shows that there must be a participation of the sacrament together.

Lon. My lords, I am sorry I have troubled you so long with this obstinate man, with whom we can do no good: I will trouble you no longer now. The lords then rose up, none of them saying any evil word unto me but, half amazed, in my judgment. May God work it to good.

Thus endeth the sixth part of this tragedy: the seventh look for with joy.

The seventh Examination of John Philpot, had the 19th of November, before the bishops of London and Rochester, the chancellor of Litchfield, and Doctor Chadsey.

Lon. SIRRAH, come hither: how chance you come no sooner? Is it well done of you to make Master chancellor and me tarry for you this hour? by the faith of my body, half an hour before mass, and half an hour at mass, looking for your coming?

Phil. My lord, it is not unknown to you that I am a prisoner, and that the doors are shut upon me, and I cannot come when I list: but as soon as the doors of my prison were open I came immediately.

Lon. We sent for thee, that thou shouldst come to mass. How say you, would you have come to mass or not if the doors had been opened sooner.

Phil. My lord, that is another manner of question.

Lon. Lo, Master chancellor, I told you we should have a froward fellow of him: he will answer directly to nothing. I have had him before both the spiritual lords and the temporal, and thus he doeth still: yet he reckons himself better learned than all the realm. Yea, before the temporal lords the other day, he was so foolish as to challenge the best: he would make himself learned, but is a very ignorant fool indeed.

Seventh Examination. 65

Phil. I reckon I answered your lordship before the lords plain enough.

Lon. Why answerest thou not directly, whether thou wouldst have gone to mass with us or no, if thou hadst come in time?

Phil. Mine answer shall be thus, that if your lordship can prove your mass, whereunto you would have me to come, to be the true service of God, whereunto a christian ought to come, I will afterward come with a good will.

Lon. Look I pray you: the king and queen, and all the nobility of the realm come to mass, and yet he will not. By my faith, thou art too well handled: thou shalt be worse handled hereafter, I warrant thee.

Phil. If to lie in a blind coalhouse without fire and candle, may be counted good handling, then may it be said, I am well handled. Your lordship hath power to treat my body as you please.

Lon. Thou art a fool, and a very ignorant fool. Master chancellor, in good faith I have handled him and his fellows with as much gentleness as they can desire. I let their friends come to them to relieve them. And the other day they had got up to the top of the leads with a many prentices, gazing abroad as though they had been at liberty. But I shall cut off your resort: and as for the prentices, they were as good not to come to you, if I take them.

Phil. My lord, we have no such resort to us as your lordship imagines, and there come very few unto us. And of prentices I know not one, neither have we any leads to walk on over our coalhouse that I know of: wherefore your lordship hath mistaken your mark.

Lon. Nay: now you think because my lord chancellor is gone,[*] that we will burn no more: yes, I warrant you, I will despatch you shortly, unless you recant.

Phil. My lord, I had not thought that I should have been alive now, neither so raw as I am, but well roasted to ashes.

Chan. Cast not yourself wilfully away, Master Philpot. Be content to be ruled by my lord here, and by other learned men of this realm, and you may do well enough.

---

[*] Gardiner, bishop of Winchester, died a few days before.

Phil. My conscience bears me record that I seek to please God, and that the love and fear of God cause me to do as I do: and I were of all other creatures most miserable, if for mine own will I lost all the commodities I might have in this life, and afterwards were cast to damnation. But I am sure, it is not my will whereon I stand, but God's will, who will not suffer me to be cast away, I am sure.

Chan. You are not so sure, but you may be deceived.

Lon. Well, since thou wilt not be conformable by any fair means, I will proceed against thee ex officio,* and therefore hearken here to such articles as I have written, and I charge thee to make answer to them. And with that he read a libel† which he had in his hand of divers articles, and when he had done, he bade me answer.

Phil. Your libel, my lord, contains in sum two special points: the first pretends, that I am of your diocese, and therefore that your lordship upon divers suspicions and reports of heresy going upon me, is moved to proceed against me by your ordinary office. This first is not true, for I am not of your lordship's diocese, as the libel pretends. And the second is, that I being baptized in the catholic church, and in the catholic faith, am gone from them, which is not so, for I am of that catholic faith and church I was baptized unto.

Lon. What, art thou not of my diocese, where are you now, I pray you?

Phil. My lord, I cannot deny but I am in your coal-house, which is your diocese: yet I am not of your diocese.

Lon. Thou wert sent to me by the queen's majesty's commissioners, and thou art now in my diocese: wherefore I will proceed against thee as thy ordinary.

Phil. I was brought hither through violence, and therefore my being at present in your diocese, is not enough to abridge me of my own ordinary jurisdiction, neither does it make me unwillingly subject to your jurisdiction, since it comes by force, and by such men as had no just authority so to do, any more than a sanctuary man being by force brought forth from his place of privilege, thereby oses his privilege, but he always may challenge the same wheresoever he be brought.

* By my office. † An accusation in writing.

Seventh Examination.

Chad. Hath not the queen's majesty authority by her commissioners, to remove your body whither she will, and ought you not to obey herein?

Phil. I grant that the queen's majesty, of her just power, may transpose my body whither it shall please her grace to command the same. But yet by your laws, " spiritual causes are not subject to the temporal power." As for example, you, Master doctor, if the queen's majesty appointed two temporal men to be judges over you in certain spiritual matters, might not you allege the privilege of a clerk,* and demand competent spiritual judges in your cause?

Lon. Does not a man, I pray you, " lose his privilege by his crimes."

Phil. My lord, your rule is true in temporal matters, but in spiritual causes, which are otherwise privileged, it is not so.

Lon. What sayest thou then to the second article, and to the other?

Phil. My lord, I say that I am not bound to answer the second, neither the rest, unless the first is proved.

Lon. Well, suppose the first may be proved, as it will be, what will you say then to the second, that you are not of the same catholic faith, neither of the same church now, as you were baptized in?

Phil. I am of the same catholic faith, and of the same catholic church which is of Christ, the pillar and establishment of truth.

Lon. Nay, that you are not.

Phil. Yes, that I am.

Lon. Your godfathers and godmothers were of another faith than you are now.

Phil. I was not baptized into my godfather's faith nor my godmother's, but into the faith and into the church of Christ.

Lon. How know you that?

Phil. By the word of God, which is the touchstone of faith and the limits of the church.

Lon. How long has your church stood, I pray you?

Phil. Even from the beginning, from Christ, and from his apostles, and from their immediate successors.

Chan. He will prove his church to be before Christ.

* A person in holy orders.

Phil. If I did so, I did not amiss: for there was a church before the coming of Christ, which makes one catholic church.

Chan. It is so indeed.

Phil. I will desire no better rules than what are oftentimes brought of your side, to prove both my faith and the catholic church: that is, antiquity, universality, and unity.

Lon. Do you not see what a bragging, foolish fellow this is? He would seem to be very well read in the doctors, and yet he is but a fool. By what doctor art thou able to prove thy church? Name him, and thou shalt have him.

Phil. My lord, let me have all your ancient writers, with pen, and ink, and paper, and I will prove both my faith and my church out of every one of them.

Lon. No, that thou shalt not have. You shall see how he lieth. St. Cyprian saith, "There must be one high-priest, to the which the residue must obey," and they will have no head, neither vicar-general.

Phil. St. Cyprian saith not, that there should be a vicar-general over all. For in his book, " De simplicitate prælatorum," I am sure he saith the contrary: "There is but one bishopric, which is wholly possessed of every bishop in part."

Lon. Bring hither the book, thou shalt see the manifest place against thee.

Dr. Chadsey brought the book, and turned to the place in an epistle written unto Cornelius, then bishop of Rome, and recited these words to this effect: "That it went not well with the church, where the high-priest was not obeyed," and so would have concluded for the confirmation of the bishop's saying.

Phil. Master doctor, you misconstrue the place of St. Cyprian: for he means not there by the high-priest, the bishop of Rome: but every patriarch in his precinct, of whom there were four appointed in his time. And in writing unto Cornelius he meaneth by the high-priest, himself, who was then chief bishop of Africa, whose authority the heretics began to despise. Whereof he complains to Cornelius, and saith: "The church cannot be well ordered, where the chief minister by order, after the judgment of the scriptures, after the agreement of the people, and the consent of his fellow bishops, is not obeyed."

Lon. Has not the bishop of Rome always been supreme head of the church, and Christ's vicar in earth, even from Peter?

Phil. No, that he has not. For by the word of God he has no more authority than the bishop of London has.

Lon. Was not Peter head of the church? and has not the bishop of Rome, who is his successor, the same authority?

Phil. I grant that the bishop of Rome, as the successor of Peter, has the same authority as Peter had: but Peter had no more authority than every one of the apostles had.

Chan. Yes, that St. Peter had: for Christ said specially unto him, " I will give thee the keys of the kingdom of heaven." Which he spake to none other of his disciples but to him.

Phil. St. Augustine answers otherwise to the objection, and saith: " That if in Peter there had not been the figure of the church, the Lord had not said to him, To thee I will give the keys of the kingdom of heaven. Which if Peter received not, the church hath them not. If the church hath them not, then Peter hath them not."

Lon. What if I can prove and show you out of the civil law, that all Christendom ought to follow the holy catholic church of Rome, as there is a special title thereof, " De catholica fide et sancta Romana Ecclesia?"*

Phil. That is nothing material, seeing the things of God are not subject to man's laws: and the divine matters must be ordered by the word of God, and not of man.

A doctor. What will you say, if I can prove that Christ built his church upon Peter, and that out of St. Cyprian? Will you then believe that the bishop of Rome ought to be supreme head of the church?

Phil. I know what St. Cyprian writes in that behalf: but he means nothing as you take it.

A doctor. St. Cyprian hath these words: " That upon Peter was builded the church, as upon the first beginning of unity."

Phil. He declares in an example, that unity must be in the church: and grounded on Peter's church alone, and not upon men. Which he does more manifestly declare in the book " De simplicitate prælatorum," saying: " In the person of one man Christ gave the keys to all, that he

---

* Of the catholic faith and the holy Roman church

in signification thereby might declare the unity of all men."

A doctor. What? will you understand St. Cyprian so? That were good indeed.

Phil. I think you cannot understand St. Cyprian better than he declares himself.

Lon. I will desire you, Master chancellor, to take some pains with Master Doctor Chadsey, about his examination, for I must go to the parliament house. And I will desire you to dine with me.

Then the doctor took again his former authority in hand for want of another, and would have made a further circumstance, digressing from his purpose. To whom I said, "he knew not where about he went," and therewith he laughed. And I said, "his divinity was nothing but scoffing."

Doctor. Yea, then I have done with you.—And so he went away.

Phil. You are too young in divinity to teach me in the matters of my faith. Though you are learned in other things more than I, yet in divinity I have been longer practised than you, for any thing I can hear of you; therefore be not too hasty to judge what you do not perfectly know.

Chan. Peter and his successors from the beginning have been allowed to be the supreme head of the church, and that by the scriptures, for Christ said unto him in St. John thrice: "Feed my sheep."

Phil. That is no otherwise to be taken, than "Go ye and preach," which was spoken to all the apostles, as well as unto Peter. And that Christ said thrice, "Feed my sheep," signifies nothing but the earnest study that the ministers of God ought to have in preaching the word. God grant that you of the clergy would weigh your duty in this behalf more than you do. Is this a just interpretation of the scriptures, to take "Feed my sheep," for "to be lord of the whole world."—In the mean while came in a bachelor of divinity, who is a reader of Greek in Oxford, belonging to the bishop, and he took upon him to help Master chancellor.

Schol. What will you say if I show you a Greek author called Theophilact, who interprets it so? Will you believe his interpretation?

Phil. Theophilact is a late writer, and one that was a

favourer of the bishop of Rome; and therefore not to be credited, since his interpretation is contrary to the manifest words of the scripture, and contrary to the determination of many general councils.

Schol. In what general council was not the bishop of Rome supreme head over all?

Phil. In the Nicene council I am sure it was otherwise; for Athanasius was there the chief bishop and president of the council, and not the bishop of Rome.

Schol. Nay, that is not so.

Phil. Then I perceive you are better skilled in words than in the knowledge of things; and I will gage with you what you will, that it is so; as you may see in the Epitome of the Councils.

Schol. I will bring Eusebius and show the contrary, and the book of general councils.—He went into my lord's closet, and brought Eusebius; but the general councils he brought not, saying (to save his honesty) that he could not find them; then he would have proved that it was otherwise in Eusebius, but was not able to show the same, and so he shrank away confounded.

Chan. The church of Rome hath been always taken for the whole catholic church: therefore I would advise you to come into the same with us. You see all the men of this realm condemn you. And why will you be so singular?

Phil. I have said, and still do say, that if you are able to prove it to me, that I will be of the same. But I am sure that the church which you make so much of, is a false church, and a synagogue of satan. And you with the learned men of the realm persecute the true church, and condemn such as are more righteous than yourselves.

Chan. Do you hear, Master doctor, what he saith, that the church of Rome is the devil?

Chad. I wish you thought more reverently of the church of Rome. What will you say if I can show you out of St. Austin in his epistle written to pope Innocent, that the whole general council of Carthage allowed the church of Rome to be chief over all other?

Phil. I am sure you can show no such thing.—And with that he fetched the book of St. Austin, and turned to the epistle; but he could not prove his allegation manifestly, but by conjectures as thus:

Chad. Here you may see, that the council of Carthage,

writing to Innocent, the bishop calls the see of Rome the apostolic see. And besides this they write unto him, certifying him of things done in the council for the condemnation of the Donatists, requiring his approbation, which they would not have done, if they had not taken the church of Rome for the supreme head of others. And moreover you may see how St. Austin proves the church of Rome to be the catholic church by continual succession of the bishops until his time, which succession we can prove until our days: therefore by the same reasoning of St. Augustine we say now, that the church of Rome is the catholic church.

Phil. Master doctor, I have considered how you weigh St. Augustine: and contrary to his meaning and words, you would infer your false conclusion. As to its being called by him the apostolical see, that is not material to prove that the church of Rome now is the catholic church. I will grant that it is the apostolic see, in respect that Paul and Peter once preached the gospel there, and abode there for a certain season. And I would you could prove it to be the apostolical see of the true religion, and of the same sincerity as when the apostle left it, and had taught there. If you could do this, you might boast of Rome as the apostolical see; otherwise it is now of no more force, than if the Turks at Antioch and at Jerusalem should boast of them as apostolic sees, because the apostles once abode there, and founded the church of Christ.

And whereas that the whole council of Carthage wrote to pope Innocent, certifying him of what was done in the general council, and desiring him to set his helping hand to suppress the Donatists, as they had done, that fact of the council proves nothing as to the supremacy of the bishop of Rome, no more than if the whole convocation-house now gathered together, and agreeing upon certain articles, sent the same to some bishop, who from certain impediments is not present, willing him to agree thereto, and to set them forth in his diocese; which would not make any such bishop of greater authority than the rest, because his consent is brotherly required.

And touching the succession of the bishops of Rome, brought in by St. Augustine, it makes nothing now to prove the same catholic church, unless you can conclude with the same reason as St. Augustine does. And the rehearsal of the succession of the bishops tends to this only—to prove the Donatists to be heretics, because they began at Rome and in Africa, to found a different church of their own setting up than was grounded by Peter and Paul, and by their successors, whose names he recites unto his time, all of whom taught no such doctrine, neither any such church as the Donatists. And if presently you are able to prove by the bishops of Rome, (whereof you glory) that such doctrine hath been taught by any of the successors of Peter's see, as is now taught and believed concerning us, you have good reason against us: otherwise it is of no force, as I am able to declare.

Chan. Well, Master doctor, you see we can do no good in persuading him. Let us minister unto him the articles which my lord has left us. How say you, Master Philpot, to these articles; Master Johnson, I pray you write his answers.

Phil. Master chancellor, you have no authority to inquire of me my belief in such articles, for I am not of my ord of London's diocese: and, to be brief with you, I will make no further answer herein, than I have already made to the bishop.

Chan. Why, then let us go our ways, and let his keeper take him away.

Thus endeth the seventh part of this tragedy.

The summary of a private Conference or talk between Master Philpot and the bishop.

THE next day, in the morning betimes, the bishop sent one of his men unto me,* to call me up into his chapel to hear mass.

Bishop's man. Master Philpot, where are you?

Phil. Who is it that calleth me?

Bishop's man. My lord's will is, you should rise and come to hear mass: will you come or not?

Phil. My stomach is not very good this morning: you may tell my lord I am sick.—After this the keeper was sent to bring me to my lord.

The Keeper. Master Philpot, you must rise and come to my lord.

Phil. I am at your commandment, master keeper, as

* In the dark coalhouse

soon as I can.—And going out of the prison, he asked me, saying, "Will you go to mass?"

Phil. My stomach is too weak to digest such raw meats of flesh, blood, and bone this morning.*—After this my keeper presented me to the bishop in his hall.

Lon. Master Philpot, I charge you to answer to such articles as my chaplain and my registrar have from me to object against you: go and answer them.

Phil. My lord, all judgments ought to be public. Therefore if your lordship have any thing to charge me with lawfully, let me be lawfully and openly called into judgment, and I will answer according to my duty; but in corners I will not.

Lon. Thou art a foolish knave, I see well enough. Thou shalt answer whether thou wilt or not. Go thy ways with them I say.

Phil. I may well go with them at your lordship's pleasure; but I will make them no further answer than I have said already.

Lon. Wilt thou not, thou knave? Have him away, and set him in the stocks. What a foolish knave!

Phil. Indeed, my lord, you handle me with others like fools; and we must be content to be made fools at your hands; stocks and violence are your bishop-like alms. You go about by force in corners to oppress, and are ashamed that your doings should come to light: God shorten your cruel kingdom for his mercy's sake.

And I was put by and by into the stocks, in a house alone, separate from my fellows. God be praised that he hath thought me worthy to suffer any thing for his name's sake. BETTER IT IS TO SIT IN THE STOCKS OF THIS WORLD, THAN TO SIT IN THE STOCKS OF A DAMNABLE CONSCIENCE.

Another Conference between the bishop and Master Philpot, and other prisoners.

THE next day after, an hour before day, the bishop sent for me again by the keeper.

The Keeper. Master Philpot, arise, you must come to my lord.

* According to the Romish church the wafer or sacramental bread when consecrated, is said to be wholly changed into the body of Christ, and to contain his flesh, blood, and bones; and the mass or sacramental service must always be performed fasting.

Phil. I wonder what my lord means, that he sends for me thus early. I fear he will use some violence towards me, wherefore, I pray you, make him this answer, that if he send for me by an order of law, I will come and answer : otherwise, since I am not of his diocese, neither is he my ordinary, I will not come unto him without I am violently constrained.

Keeper. I will go tell my lord what answer you make.— And so he went away to the bishop, and immediately returned with two of the bishop's men, saying that I must come whether I would or not.

Phil. If by violence any of you will enforce me to go, then must I go, otherwise I will not.—And therewith one of them took me with force by the arm, and led me up into the bishop's gallery.

Lon. What? thou art a foolish knave indeed: thou wilt not come without thou be fetched.

Phil. I am brought indeed, my lord, by violence unto you, and your cruelty is such, that I am afraid to come before you. I would your lordship would proceed against me gently by the law.

Lon. I am blamed by the lords the bishops, that I have not despatched thee ere this. And in faith I made suit to my lord cardinal,* and to all the convocation-house, that they would hear thee? And my lord of Lincoln† stood up, and said that thou wert a frantic fellow, and a man that will have the last word. And they all have blamed me, because I have brought thee so often before the lords openly: and they say it is meat and drink to you to speak in an open audience, you glory so of yourself. Wherefore I am commanded to take a further order with thee; and, in good faith, if thou wilt not relent, I will make no farther delay. But if thou wilt be conformable, I will yet forgive thee all that is past, and thou shalt have no hurt for any thing that is already said or done.

Phil. My lord, I have answered you already in this matter, what I will do. And as for the report of Master White, bishop of Lincoln, I wonder not. He is known to be mine enemy, for that I, being archdeacon, did excommunicate him for preaching false doctrine. If Christ my master were called a mad man, it is no marvel though you count me frantic.

Lon. Hadst not thou a pig brought thee the other day

* Cardinal Pole. † Dr. White.

with a knife in it? Wherefore was it, I pray thee, but to kill thyself? Or as it is told me (I am counselled to take heed of thee) to kill me? But I fear thee not. I think I am able to tread thee under my feet: do the best thou canst.

Phil. My lord, I cannot deny but that there was a knife in the pig's belly that was brought me. But who put it in, or for what purpose I know not, unless it were because he that sent the meat, thought I was without a knife, and so put it in. But other things your lordship need not fear; for I was never without a knife since I came to prison. And touching your own person, you should live long, if you should live until I go about to kill you. And I confess, that by violence your lordship is well able to overcome me.

Lon. I charge thee to answer to mine articles. Hold him a book. Thou shalt swear to answer truly to all such articles as I shall demand of thee.

Phil. I will first know your lordship to be mine ordinary, before I swear herein.

Lon. What, we shall have an anabaptist of thee, who thinks it not lawful to swear before a judge.

Phil. My lord, I am no anabaptist, I think it lawful to swear before a competent judge, being lawfully required. But I refuse to swear in these causes before your lordship, because you are not my ordinary.

Lon. I am thine ordinary, and here pronounce by sentence peremptorily, that I am thine ordinary, and that thou art of my diocese.—(And here he bade call in more to bear witness.)—And I make thee, (said he, taking one of his servants by the arm,) to be my notary. And now hearken to my articles.

When he had read them he admonished me to make answer, and said to the keeper, Bring me his fellows, and I shall make them to be witnesses against him.

In the meanwhile came in one of the sheriffs of London, whom the bishop, calling for two chairs, placed by him, saying, "Master sheriff, I would you should understand how I proceed against this man. Master sheriff, you shall hear what articles this man maintains;" and so read a rabblement of feigned articles: as that I denied baptism to be necessary to them that were born of Christian parents, that I denied fasting and prayer, and all other good deeds, and that I maintained bare faith alone to be sufficient to salvation, whatsoever a man did besides, and that

I maintained God to be the author of all sin and wickedness!

Phil. Nay, my lord, have you nothing of truth to charge me with, but you must imagine these blasphemous lies against me? You might as well have said I had killed your father. The Scriptures say, " That God will destroy all them that speak lies." And is not your lordship ashamed to say before this worshipful gentleman, (who is unknown to me,) that I maintain these abominable blasphemies which you have rehearsed ; which if I maintained, I were well worthy to be counted a heretic, and to be burned a hundred times if it were possible.

Lon. I object them unto thee, to hear what thou wilt say in them, and how thou canst clear thyself of them.

Phil. Then it was not justly said by your lordship in the beginning, that I did maintain them, since I hold scarcely one of these articles you have read, in form as they are written.

Lon. How sayest thou? Wilt thou answer to them or not?

Phil. I will first know that you are my ordinary, and that you may lawfully charge me with such things, and then afterwards, being lawfully called into judgment, I will show my mind fully thereof, and not otherwise.

Lon. Well, then I will make thy fellows to be witnesses against thee. Where are they? Come.

Keeper. They are here, my lord.

Lon. Come hither, sirs, hold them a book, you shall swear by the contents of that book, that you shall, all manner of affections laid apart, say the truth of all such articles as you shall be demanded of, concerning this man here present, who is a very naughty man, and take you heed of him that he does not deceive you ; as I am afraid he does you much hurt, and strengthens you in your errors.

Prisoners. My lord, we will not swear, except we know whereto. We can accuse him of no evil, we have been but a little while acquainted with him.

Phil. I wonder that your lordship, knowing the law, will go about contrary to the same, to have infamous [*] persons to be witnesses ; for your lordship takes them to be heretics, and by the law a heretic cannot be a witness.

[*] Persons whom the law regards as of bad fame, and not competent witnesses.

Lon. Yes, one heretic against another may be well enough. And, master sheriff, I will make one of them be witness against another.

Phil. You have the law in your hand, and you will do what you list.

Prisoners. No, my lord.

Lon. Will you not? I will make you swear, whether you will or not. I think they are anabaptists, master sheriff, they think it not lawful to swear before a judge.

Phil. We think it lawful for a man to swear when judicially called, as we are not now, but in a blind corner.

Lon. Why then, seeing you will not swear against your fellow, you shall swear for yourselves; and I do here, in the presence of master sheriff, object the same articles unto you as I have done unto him, and require you, under the pain of excommunication, to answer particularly unto every one of them when you shall be examined, as you shall be examined presently by my registrar and some of my chaplains.

Prisoners. My lord, we will not accuse ourselves. If any man can lay any thing against us, we are here ready to answer thereto: otherwise we pray your lordship not to burden us; for some of us are here before you we know no just cause why.

Lon. Master sheriff, I will trouble you no longer with these froward men.—And so he rose up and was going away, talking with master sheriff.

Phil. Master sheriff, I pray you record how my lord proceeds against us in corners, without order of law, having no just cause to lay against us.

And after this we were all commanded to be put in the stocks, where I sat from morning until night; and the keeper at night, upon favour, let me out.

Another private Conference between the bishop and Master Philpot in the Coalhouse.

THE Sunday after, the bishop came into the coalhouse at night with the keeper, and viewed the house, saying that he was never there before; whereby a man may guess how he has kept God's commandment in visiting the prisoners, seeing he was never with them that have been so nigh him. And he came not then for any good zeal, but to view the place, and thought it too good for me, and therefore after supper, between eight and nine, he sent for me, saying,

Lon. Sir, I have great displeasure of the queen and the council for keeping you so long, and letting you have so much liberty; and besides that, you are yonder, and strengthen the other prisoners in their errors, as I have laid wait for your doings, and am certified about you well enough. I will separate you therefore from them, and you shall hurt no more as you have done, and I will out of hand despatch you, as I am commanded, unless you will be a conformable man.

Phil. My lord, you have my body in your custody; you may transport it whither it please you: I am content. And I would you would make quick expedition in judging me, as you say. I long therefore: and as for conformity, I am ready to yield to all truth, if any can bring better than I can.

Lon. Why, you will believe no man but yourself, whatever they say.

Phil. My belief must not hang upon men's sayings, without sure authority of God's word, which if any can show me, I will be pliant to the same; otherwise I cannot go from my certain faith to that which is uncertain.

Lon. Have you then the truth only?

Phil. My lord, I will speak my mind freely unto you, and upon no malice I bear to you, before God. You have not the truth, neither are you of the church of God; but you persecute both the truth and the true church of God, for which cause you cannot prosper long. You see God does not prosper your doings according to your expectations. He has of late showed his just judgment against one of your greatest doers, who, by report, died miserably.* I envy not the authority you possess. You that have learning should know best how to rule. And seeing that God has restored you to your dignity and living again, use the same to God's glory, and to the setting forth of his true religion; otherwise it will not continue, do what you can.—With this saying he was apaused,† and said at length:—

Lon. That good man was punished for such as thou art. Where is the keeper? Come, have him to the place that is provided for him. Go your way before

* Gardiner bishop of Winchester.   † Struck.

And he followed me, calling the keeper aside, commanding him to keep all men from me, and to search me narrowly, as the sequel did declare, and brought me to his private door that goes into the church, and commanded two of his men to accompany the keeper, and to see me placed.

And afterwards I passed through Paul's church up to Lollards' tower, and after that turned along all the west side of Paul's through the wall, and passing through six or seven doors, came to my lodging through many straits; where I called to remembrance, that strait is the way to heaven. And it is in a tower right on the other side of Lollards' tower, as high almost as the battlements of Paul's, eight feet wide, and thirteen long, and almost over the prison where I was before, having a window opening towards the east, by which I may look over the tops of a great many houses, but see no man passing into them; and whoso walks in the bishop's outer gallery going to his chapel, may see my window and me standing in the same.

And when I was come to my place, the keeper plucked off my gown, and searched me very narrowly, and took away penner, inkhorn, girdle, and knife, but, as God would, I had an inkling * a little before I was called, of my being removed, and thereupon, full sore against my will, I cast away many a sweet and friendly letter. But what I had written of my last examination, I thrust into my hose, thinking the next day to have made an end thereof, and with walking, it was fallen down to my leg, which the keeper by feeling did soon discover, and asked what that was. I said they were certain letters; and with that he was very busy to have them out. "Let me alone," said I, "I will pluck them out." With that I put my hand, having two other letters therein, and brought up the same writing to my body, and there left it, giving him the other two letters that were not of any great importance; while, to make a show as if they had been weighty, I began to tear them as well as I could, till they snatched them from me; and so I deluded him, I thank God, of his purpose.

After this he went his way, and as he was going, one of them that came with him, said that I did not deliver the writings I had in my hose, but two other letters which I had in my hand before. "Did he?" quoth he; "I will

* A hint given.

go search him better." Which I hearing, conveyed mine examination I had written into a place beside my bed, and took all the letters I had in my purse, and was tearing of them when he came again, and as he came I threw the same out of my window, saying that I heard what he said; wherefore I prevented his searching again, whereof I was right glad. God be praised, that gave me that present shift to blind their eyes from the knowledge of my writings, which if they had known, it would have been an occasion for straiter keeping and looking unto, although they look as narrowly as they can.

The eighth Examination of John Philpot, before the bishop of London, the bishop of St. David's, Master Mordant, and others, in the bishop's chapel.

THE next day after, my keeper came before day in the morning to call me down, and so I was brought down into his wardrobe, where I was left with a keeper, and there continued all the day. But after dinner I was called down into the chapel, before the bishop of London, the bishop of St. David's, Master Mordant, one of the queen's council, master archdeacon of London, and before a great many more: and the bishop spake unto me in this manner.

Lon. Sir, here I object and lay unto you in the presence of my lord of St. David's, and of Master Mordant, and of these worshipful men, these articles here in this libel contained.—And he read them openly.

When I would particularly have answered to some of his blasphemies, he would not permit me, but said, I should have leisure enough to say what I would, when he had said all, adding, "and to these I add another schedule. Also I require thee to answer as to the catechism set forth in the schismatical time of king Edward. Also I will thee to answer to certain conclusions agreed upon both in Oxford and Cambridge. And I here bring forth these witnesses against thee, in thine own presence, namely my lord of St. David's, Master Mordant, and Master Harpsfield, with as many of you as were present in the disputation he made in the convocation-house, willing you to testify (by your oaths taken upon a book) his stubborn and irreverent behaviour he there used against the blessed sacrament of the altar. Give me a book," and receiving one, he opened the same, saying, "I will teach him here one trick in our law, which he knows not; that is, my lord of St. David's, because you are a bishop, you have this privilege, that you may swear by looking on the gospel book without touching the same." And so he opened the book in his sight, and shut it again, and caused the others to put their hands on the book, and take their oaths, and willed them to resort to his registrar, to make their depositions when they might be best at leisure; and afterwards he turned to me, and said, "Now, sir, you shall answer but two words, whether you will answer to these articles which I have laid unto you, directly, yea, or nay?"

Phil. My lord, you have told a long tale against me, containing many lying blasphemies, which cannot be answered in two words. Besides this, you promised me at the beginning, that I should say what I could for my defence, and now you will not give me leave to speak. What law is this?

Lon. Speak, yea or nay; for you shall say no more at this time.—The cause was, as I guess, that he saw so many there gathered to hear.

Phil. Then my two words you would have me speak, shall be that I have appealed from you, and take you not for my sufficient judge.

Lon. Indeed, Master Mordant, he has appealed to the king and to the queen; but I will be so bold with her majesty, as to stay that appeal in mine own hands.

Phil. You will do what you list, my lord; you have the law in your hands.

Lon. Wilt thou answer, or no?

Phil. I will not answer otherwise than I have said.

Lon. Registrar, note his answer.

Phil. Knock me on the head with a hatchet, or set up a stake and burn me out of hand, without further law. You may do so as well as do what you do, for all is without order of law; such tyranny was never seen, as you use now-a-days. May God of his mercy destroy your cruel kingdom.—And whilst I spake this, the bishop went away in haste.

St. David's. Master Philpot, I pray you be quiet, and have patience.

Phil. My lord, I thank God I have patience to bear and abide all your cruel intents against me: notwithstanding I speak this earnestly, being moved thereto justly to notify your unjust and cruel dealing with men in corners, without due order of law.

After this, at night I was conducted again by three or four into the coalhouse.

The ninth Examination of Master Philpot, before Bonner and his chaplains.

IN the morning of the next day I was called betimes by my keeper, and brought again into the wardrobe, where I remained until the bishop had heard his mass, and afterwards he sent up for me into his inward parlour, and there he called for a chair to sit down, and brought his infamous libel of his forged articles in his hand, and sat down, willing me to draw near unto him, and said:

Lon. I am this day appointed to tarry at home from the parliament house, to examine you and your fellows upon these articles, and you stand dallying with me, and will neither answer to nor from. All your exceptions will not serve you. Will it be a fair honesty for you, think you, that when thou comest before my lord mayor and the sheriffs, and other worshipful audience, when I shall say before them all, that I have had thee these many times before me, and before so many learned men, and thou couldest say nothing that thou standest in, notwithstanding all thy brags of learning, neither wouldest answer directly to anything?

Phil. My lord, I have told you my mind plain enough; but yet I do not intend to lose the privilege the law gives me. Which is free choice to answer where I am not bound, and this privilege will I cleave unto, until I be compelled otherwise.

Lon. Well, I perceive you will play the obstinate fool. Lay thine appellation when thou comest into judgment and answer in the meanwhile to these articles.

Phil. No, my lord, by your leave, I will not answer to them until my lawful appeal is tried.

Lon. Well, thou shalt hear them.—And with that he began to read them.

I shrunk back into the window, and looked on a book; and after he had read them over, he said unto me:

Lon. I have read them over, although it has not pleased

you to hear me. I marvel, in good faith, what thou meanest to be so wilful and stubborn, seeing thou mayest do well enough if thou list. It is but a singularity. Dost thou not see all the realm against thee?

Phil. My lord, I speak unto you in the witness of God, before whom I stand, that I am neither wedded to my own will, neither stand upon my own stubbornness or singularity, but upon my conscience instructed by the word of God; and if your lordship can show better evidence than I have, for a good faith, I will follow the same.

Lon. What, thou wilt not for all that! Well, all that is past shall be forgotten, if you be conformable unto us. Thou mightest find as much favour as thou wouldest desire.

Then I perceiving that he fawned so much upon me, thought it good to give him some hope of my relenting, to the intent I might give him and his hypocritical generation openly a further foil, perceiving that they dare reason openly with none, but with such as are unlearned, and for lack of knowledge not able to answer, or else with such as they have a hope that for fear or love of the world will recant. I said, "My lord, it is not unknown to you, that I have openly, in the audience of a great number, stood to the maintenance of these opinions I am in, and by learning offered to defend them; therefore, my lord, I would it might openly appear to the world, that I am won by learning, or else what will they say, but that either for fear or love of the world, without any ground, I am turned from the truth. But if I hear any kind of learning openly showed, I shall be as conformable as you may require me."

Lon. Yea, marry, now you speak somewhat like a reasonable man. You might have had a great deal more favour and liberty in my house than you have had; and you shall lack nothing that is within my house; call for it and you shall have it. And what is it that you would openly be satisfied in by learning, tell me?

Phil. My lord, I have openly said, and believe it also, that your sacrifice of the mass is no sacrament.

Lon. What, do you deny the presence of Christ in the sacrament?

Phil. No, my lord, I deny not the presence of Christ in the sacrament, but I have denied the sacrament of the altar, as it is used in your mass, to be the true sacrament

Ninth examination.

of Christ's institution; and first it must be proved a sacrament, ere any kind of presence can be granted.

Lon. Why, do you deny the mass to be a sacrament? I pray you, what is a sacrament? Is it not a sign of a holy thing, as St. Augustine doth define it?

Phil. Yes, verily, that it is.

Lon. Then I make this argument unto you. A sacrament is the sign of a holy thing—But the mass is a sign of a holy thing—Therefore it is a sacrament.

Phil. You must add this to your major or first proposition, as St. Augustine means, that a sacrament is the sign of a holy thing instituted of God and commanded; for otherwise it can be no sacrament, for all men cannot make a sacrament.

Lon. I grant that, and such a sign of a holy thing is the mass of Christ's institution.

Phil. I deny that, my lord.

Lon. I will prove this by St. Augustine by and by. I will go show you the book, and you shall have any book I have that you will demand. Ho! who is without there? Call me Master Doctor Chadsey, Master archdeacon, Master Cosins, and other chaplains, hither.

One answered, Here, my lord.. Master Doctor Chadsey is gone to Westminster, and Master archdeacon was here even now.

Lon. Master Cosins, I pray you examine him upon these articles, and write the answer he makes to every one of them. I will go and examine his fellows, and send you St. Augustine by and by. I find this man more conformable than he was before.

Cosins. I trust, my lord, you shall find him at length a good catholic man. Why here are a sight of heresies. I dare say you will hold none of them, neither stand to any of them. How say you to the first?

Phil. Master Cosins, I have told my lord already, that I will answer to none of these articles which he has objected against me; but if you will with learning answer that which is in question between my lord and me, I will gladly hear and commune with you.

Cosins. Will you? Why, what is it then which is in question between my lord and you?

Phil. Whether your mass is a sacrament or no.

Cosins. What, whether the mass is a sacrament? Who ever doubted thereof?

Phil. If it is an undoubted truth, you may the sooner prove it; for I doubt much thereof.

Cosins. Why, I will prove it. It is the sign of a holy thing; therefore it is a sacrament.

Phil. I deny your antecedent.*

Cosins. What, will you so? Then there is no reasoning with you.

Thus Master Cosins gave over in the plain field† for want of further proof. And then the morrow-mass chaplain ‡ began to speak for his occupation, and Master Harpsfield came out from my lord with St. Augustine's epistles, saying:

Harps. My lord has sent you here St. Augustine to look upon, and I pray you look what he says in a certain epistle which he writes. I will read over the whole. Here may you hear of the celebration of the mass, and how he reproves them that went a-hawking and hunting before the celebration of the same, on the Sabbath and holy days.

Phil. I perceive the contents of this epistle, and I see nothing herein against me, neither anything that makes for the proof of your sacrament of the mass.

Harps. No! Does he not make mention of the mass, and the celebration thereof? What can be spoken more plain?

Phil. St. Augustine means the celebration of the communion, and of the true use of the sacrament of the body and blood of Christ, and not your private masses which you of late years have erected instead thereof. For this word mass has been an old term attributed to the communion, even from the primitive church. And I pray you tell me what Missa signifies; I think not many that say mass, can well tell.

Cosins. No? That is marvel.

Phil. Then tell, if you can.—But Master Cosins and the morrow-mass chaplain were dumb, looking upon Master Harpsfield for help, and at length he spake.

Harps. You think it comes of the Hebrew word Massah, as though none were seen§ in the Hebrew but you.

Phil. I have not gone so long to school, to derive the signification of Missa, which is a Latin word, out of Hebrew; but I have learned to interpret Greek words by

---

* The first proposition.
† At once, before he came to any difficult places.
‡ A priest who said early mass. § Learned

Greek, and Latin by Latin, and Hebrew by Hebrew. I take the communion to be called Missa, à mittendo, from such things as at the celebration of the communion were sent by such as were of ability, for the relief of the poor, where the rich brought of their devotion and ability, and required the minister, in the celebration of the communion, to pray unto God for them, and to accept their common alms, which they at such times sent for the help of their poor brethren and sisters; and for this cause was it called Missa, as learned men do witness. At which celebration of the mass, all that were present communicated in both kinds,* according to Christ's institution, as they did in St. Augustine's time. But unless you can show that your mass is used as it then was, you shall never by the name of mass, which St. Augustine attributed to the true use of the communion, prove your private mass to be a sacrament, unless you can prove the same is done now in your masses as it was then, which are quite contrary.

Harps. What, deny you the mass to be a sacrament? For shame speak it not.

Phil. I will not be ashamed to deny it, if you cannot prove it.

Harps. Why, it is a sacrifice, which is more than a sacrament.

Phil. You may make of it as much as you list; but you shall never make it a sacrifice, as you imagine, but first it must be a sacrament, for of the sacrament you deduce your sacrifice.

Harps. Why, did not Christ say, "This is my body?" and does not the priest pronounce the same words that Christ did?

Phil. The pronunciation is not enough, unless the words are therewith applied to the use which Christ spake them to. For though you speak the words of baptism over water ever so many times, yet there is no baptism unless there is a christian person to be baptized.

Harps. Nay, that is not the same; for "Hoc est corpus meum"† is an indicative proposition, showing a working of God in the substance of bread and wine.

Phil. It is not only an indicative proposition, but also

---

* The bread and the wine.—The reader will recollect that the church of Rome withholds the cup from the people.

† This is my body.

an imperative or commanding. For he that said, "Hoc est corpus meum," "This is my body," said also, "Accipite, manducate," "Take ye, eat ye." And except the former part of the institution of Christ's sacrament is accomplished according to the communion, the latter, "This is my body," cannot be verified, take it which way you will, and how you will.

Morrow-mass Chaplain. Why, then you will make the sacrament to stand in the receiving, and that receiving makes it a sacrament.

Phil. I do not say, that the receiving alone makes it the sacrament; but I say, that a common receiving must needs be concurrent with the true sacrament, as a necessary part, without which it cannot be a sacrament, because Christ made this a principal part of the sacrament, "Take ye, eat ye," which you do not in your mass according to Christ's institution. Therefore it can be no sacrament, for it wants somewhat of Christ's institution.

Cosins. We forbid none to come to it, but as many as list may be partakers with us at the mass, if they require it.

Phil. Nay, that they shall not, though they require it. You will minister but one kind unto them, which is not according to Christ's institution. Besides that, you ought, before you go to mass, to exhort all that are present to make a sacrifice of thanksgiving for Christ's passion with you, and to exhort them to be partakers with you, according to Christ's commandment, saying unto all that are present, "Take ye, eat ye;" and likewise by preaching show forth the Lord's death, which you do not.

Cosins. And if all things are done even as you would have it, and whilst the minister is about to minister the sacrament, before any other have received it there rise a sudden hurly-burly, so that the communicants are compelled to go away, is it not a sacrament although none hath communicated besides the priest?

Phil. In this case where all things are appointed to be done according to God's word, if incident or necessity had not hindered, I cannot say, but that it is a sacrament, and that he who has received, has received the true sacrament.

After this, the morrow-mass priest made this apish reason: If the sacrament of the mass is no sacrament unless all receive it, because Christ said, "Take ye, eat ye," then the sacrament of baptism is no sacrament where there is but one baptized, because Christ said to his apostles, "Gc preach the gospel to all creatures, baptizing all nations in the name of the Father," &c.

Phil. In that saying of Christ, " Baptizing all nations," is a commandment to the apostles, to baptize all sorts of men, and to exclude none that believe, be he Gentile or Jew, not meaning all at once, for that were impossible. And there are many examples, that baptism may be ministered to one person alone, as we have example in Christ baptized of John, and in the eunuch baptized of Philip, with many more such; but so have you not of the sacrament of the body and blood of Christ, but contrariwise by the express words of St. Paul you are commanded to use it in a communion and participation of many together, see the second epistle to the Corinthians, "As oft as ye come together to eat,(meaning the Lord's supper,) tarry one for another." And also the minister in the celebration of the sacrament, spoke to all that were present, in Christ's behalf, to communicate with him, saying, "Take ye, and eat ye." Wherefore, as many as are present and do not communicate, break God's commandment in not receiving the same, and the minister is no just minister that does not distribute the sacrament as Christ did, to all that are present; and where God's word is transgressed, there Christ is not present, and consequently it is no sacrament.

Harps. What, would you have it no sacrament without it is a communion?

Phil. I make it not so, but God's express word teaches me so. Yea, also, all the ancient writers; as St. Chrysostome writing upon the epistle to the Ephesians saith, "That the oblation is in vain, where none doth communicate with the priest." If by his judgment the action of the priest, alone, is in vain, where there is no communion, how can that be a sacrament which he calls a vain oblation, and a vain standing at the altar?*

Cosins. You are such a fellow as I have not heard before, that will not have the mass to be a sacrament; you are no man for me to reason withal. Come, let us go, (pointing to the morrow-mass chaplain,) we will leave you, master archdeacon and him together; and so they went away. Afterwards the archdeacon fell into earnest persuasion with me, saying:

Harps. Master Philpot, you and I have old acquaintance a long time; we were school-fellows both in Winchester

In the Romish daily mass the priest alone communicates.

and in Oxford many years. Wherefore I must wish you as well to do as myself, and I pray you so think of me.

Phil. I thank you for your good-will towards me. But if you are deceived, as I am sure you are, I shall desire you not to wish me deceived with you. For I tell you plainly, before God, you are highly deceived, and maintain false religion, and are not what you take yourselves for; and if you do not repent, and leave off your persecuting Christ's truth, you will go to the devil for it. Therefore consider it in time, I give you warning; for in the day of judgment I shall else be a witness against you, that I told you this while here talking together.

Harps. Fie! that is but your own vain singular opinion. I perceive you are still the man you were in Oxford.

Phil. I trust you can report no notorious evil that ever you knew of me there.

Harps. I can say no evil of your conversation, but I knew you to be a studious man. But if you remember when we met in disputation in Parvis,* you would not lightly give over, and for that cause I speak that I have said.

Phil. Master Harpsfield, you know that in the schools at Oxford, when we were young men, we strove much for vain-glory and contention—more than for the truth. But now our years and our riper learning teach us to look to the truth, which must be our portion for ever. And if I was then, in my time of ignorance, earnest in my own cause, I ought now to be earnest in my master Christ's cause, and in his truth. I know now that nothing done from vain-glory and singularity can please God, though it has ever so goodly a show; wherefore I pray you judge not so of me now.

Harps. What, will you think yourself better learned than all the learned men in this realm?

Phil. My faith hangeth not upon the learned of the world, but upon the learned of God's word.

Harps. Well, I will talk with you no more now, but I will pray to God to open your heart.

Phil. I pray God to open both our hearts, to do his will more than we have done in times past.

Harps. Ho! keeper, take him away with you.

Phil. I pray you, Master Harpsfield, tell me what this pronoun "Hoc" demonstrates and shows in this indicative

* A scholastic disputation at the university.

proposition, as you call it. "Hoc est corpus meum." "This is my body?"

Harps. It demonstrates the substance of bread, which by the words spoken by the priest, and by the omnipotency of God, is turned into the substance of Christ's very body.

Phil. Is the substance of the bread, as you say, turned into Christ's body?

Harps. Yea, that it is.

Phil. Why, then Christ's body receives daily a great increase of many thousand pieces of bread into his body, and that is become his body now, which was not so before, and by this you would seem to make out that there is an alteration in Christ's glorified body, which is a wicked thing to think.

Then he tried again, and remembering himself better, and seeing the inconvenience of his first assertion of the transubstantiation of bread into Christ's body, he said, that the substance of bread after the words spoken by the priest, was evacuated or vanished away by the omnipotence of God.

Phil. This is another song than you sang first. And here you may see how contrary you are to yourselves. For indeed your schoolmen do hold, that the very substance of bread is really turned into the substance of Christ's body. And now, you perceiving of late the inconvenience which is objected against you in that opinion, you are driven to imagine a new shift, and to say, the substance of bread is evacuated, contrary to what your church at first believed and taught. O what contrariety is there among you, and all to deface the sincere truth!

Harps. Is not God omnipotent? and cannot he do as he has said?

Phil. But his omnipotence will not do as you say, contrary to his word and his honour. It is not for God's honour to include him bodily into a piece of bread, and of necessity to tie him thereto. It is not to God's honour for you to make into God and man a piece of bread, which you see before your face doth putrefy after a certain time. Is not God's omnipotence as able to give his body with the sacramental bread, as to make so many turnings away of the bread, as you do, and that directly against the scriptures, which call it bread many times after the consecration? Are you not ashamed to make so many alterations of the Lord's holy institution as you do, and to take away the substantial parts of the sacrament, as "Take ye, eat ye, drink ye all of this: do ye this in remembrance of me;" and to place in their stead, "Hear ye, gaze ye, knock ye, worship ye, offer ye, sacrifice ye, for the quick and the dead." If this is not blasphemy to God and his sacrament—to add and to pluck away in this sort, and that contrary to the mind of all ancient writers, and contrary to the example of Christ and all his apostles, tell me.

Harps. I know you have gathered the sayings of the doctors together which make for your purpose: I will talk no longer with you.

Phil. I pray God open both our hearts, to do more his will than we have done in times past.

Harps. Ho, keeper, take him away with you.

The tenth Examination of John Philpot, before bishop Bonner, his registrar, and others.

THE next day after dinner, I was brought into my lord's upper hall, and there he called me before him and his registrar, and before doctor Chadsey, in the presence of two homely gentlemen, and a priest whom I knew not. The bishop said:

Lon. I do here lay unto this man in your presence, requiring you to be witness against him, these articles, this book of the catechism, made in king Edward's days, also these conclusions, agreed upon both in Oxford and Cambridge. Also I lay unto him, that he has despised the censures of the church, and has stood accursed more than this twelvemonth, and never required absolution thereof. How say you, wast thou not accursed by my lord chancellor?

Phil. I was excommunicated by him wrongfully, and without any just cause, and without order of law, being never personally cited.

Lon. Didst thou not tell me the other day, when I required thee to come to the mass, that thou wast excommunicated, and therefore by the law couldst not hear mass? How long hast thou been thus excommunicate?

Phil. More than a twelvemonth and a half.

Lon. Lo! you may hear what he saith. Write it.

Phil. But as you would have written that I have said,

Tenth examination.

I have been thus long excommunicated, so also let him write that I required my absolution of my lord chancellor, who excommunicated me, but he would not give it me; saying that because I was a heretic, as it pleased him to call me, therefore I was accursed by your law, and so he commanded me to prison, where I remain still.

Gent. Why do you not require absolution at my lord's hands here now?

Phil. Because he is not my ordinary, neither has he by the law anything to do with me of right.

Lon. What an obstinate fool is this! I tell thee I will be thine ordinary whether thou wilt or no.

Phil. And because of this your unrighteous force towards me, I have appealed from you, and require you, master registrar, that my appeal may be entered in writing.

Lon. Have you heard such a froward fellow as this? He seemed yesterday to be very tractable, and I had a good hope in him. I tell thee thou art of my diocese.

Phil. I am of Winchester diocese, and not of London diocese.

Lon. I pray you, may not a man be of two dioceses at once?

Phil. No, that he cannot.

Lon. Lo! will you see what an ignorant fool this is in the law, in which he would seem to be skilled! I tell thee a man may be of three dioceses at once; as if thou wert born in London, by reason thereof thou shouldest be of my diocese; or else, if thou wert not born here, but hadst a dignity, also thou art to be counted of my diocese; or else by reason of thy habitation in my diocese.

Phil. In none of these respects am I of your lordship's diocese.—But for all that, this will not follow, that I dwelling at Winchester am at present of London diocese.

Lon. What wilt thou lay thereof? Wilt thou recant if I prove it?

Phil. But what shall I win if you do not.

Lon. I will give thee my bishopric if I prove it not.

Phil. Yea, but who shall deliver it me if I win?

Lon. Thou art an arrogant fool. Enter their oaths, and take these witnesses' depositions. I must be gone to the parliament house.

After this spake unto me a priest standing by, asking me whether I was kin to my lord Rich or no.

Phil. He said so himself unto me the other day, but how I know not.

Chad. I heard him say, that he was his very nigh kinsman.

Priest. Why then you and I must be of kin, for he is my nigh kinsman. How chance it that you and I are of contrary judgments?

Phil. It is no marvel, for Christ prophesied, "That the father shall be divided against the son, and the son against the father, for my truth's sake."

Priest. You hold, as I understand, against the blessed sacrament of the altar, and against the holy mass.

Phil. If you can prove it a sacrament, I will not hold against you.

Priest. What, prove it a sacrament! Does not St. Paul say, "That such things as the eye hath not seen, neither ear heard, hath God prepared for them that love him?"

Phil. That saying of St. Paul concerns not your sacrament, but is meant of the heavenly joys that are prepared for all faithful believers.

Priest. Why then I perceive you understand not St. Paul. By God, you are deceived.

Phil. You ought not to swear, kinsman, if you will that I shall so call you. And without disworship* of our kindred, I understand St. Paul as well as you, and know what I say.—And with that I showed him a Greek testament with Erasmus's translation, and with the Old also, demanding him which text he was best acquainted withal.

Priest. I knew Greek too once, as well as you. I care not which you read.

Phil. You know them then all alike: you understand the one as well as the other.—With this my kinsman departed in a fury.

The next day I was brought down again after dinner to the chapel, and there my kinsman, to verify the scriptures, that a man's own kinsfolks shall be his enemies, came in with the bishop, as a witness against me; and there the bishop caused another that came to him about other matters, to swear also to be a witness against me.—He was a priest also.

Lon. You shall swear to depose all the truth of certain

* Disrespect to.

articles you shall be inquired of concerning this man; and here I, according to the law, do bring them forth in thy presence.*

Phil. My lord, I do not agree to the production of them, but do appeal from all these and your other proceedings against me; and require you, master registrar, that my appeal may be entered, and I will pay you for your labour.

Reg. Your appeal shall be entered at leisure. Whom do you appeal unto? tell me.

Phil. I appeal to a higher judge, as to the lieutenant of the archbishopric of Canterbury; for I know not who is bishop thereof at this present.—With that the bishop went away, and my kinsman, looking big upon me, but saying never a word.

Thus have I in haste scribbled out all mine examinations hitherto, that the same which has been done unto me in darkness may come to light, and that the papists' unjust proceedings and shamelessness in their false religion might be known to their confusion. Jesus is Immanuel, that is, God with us, Amen. 1555.

The eleventh Examination of John Philpot, had on St. Andrew's day, before the bishop of Durham, the bishop of Chichester, the bishop of Bath, the bishop of London, the prolocutor, Master Christopherson, and doctor Chadsey, Master Morgan of Oxford, Master Hussey of the Arches, doctor Weston, doctor Harpsfield, archdeacon Master Cosins, and Master Johnson, registrar to the bishop of London—in his palace.

I was coming, being sent for with my keeper, and the bishop of London met me at his hall door, and full mannerly he played the gentleman-usher to bring me before the lords, saying:

Lon. My lords, I shall desire you to take some pains with this man; he is a gentleman, and I would he should do well; but he will cast himself wilfully away.

Dur. Come hither, sir; what is your name?

Phil. My name is Philpot.

Dur. I have heard of that name, that it is of a worshipful

* As witnesses.—An evasion to comply with the letter of the law

stock, and since you are a gentleman, do so that you may live worshipfully among other gentlemen. What is the cause of your trouble now?

I told him the cause, as in my former examinations is expressed.

Dur. Well, all causes set apart, will you now be a conformable man to the catholic faith, and leave all new-fangled opinions and heresies? I was in Germany with Luther at the beginning of these opinions, and can tell how they began. Leave them, and follow the catholic church throughout the whole world, as the whole realm now doth.

Phil. My lord, I am of the catholic faith, and desire to live and die in the same; but it is not unknown to your lordship, that I with others, for the last twenty years, have been taught another manner of faith than that which you now go about to compel us unto; wherefore it is requisite that we have time to weigh the same, and to hear how it agrees with God's word. For faith is not suddenly either to be won or removed, but as St. Paul saith, "Faith cometh by hearing, and hearing by the word."

Chich. If you will give me leave, my lord, I will show him how he takes the saying of St. Paul amiss, as many others now-a-days do, alleging that they ought not to be compelled to believe, whereas St. Paul speaks of infidels, and not of the faithful. And so St. Augustine, in writing against the Donatists, saith, that the faithful may be compelled to believe.

Phil. St. Bernard, if it please your lordship, takes that sense of St. Paul as I do, saying, that "Faith must be persuaded to a man, and not enjoined." And St. Augustine speaks of such as were first thoroughly persuaded by manifest scriptures, and yet would afterward resist of stubborn wilfulness.

Chich. So Bernard means of infidels also.

Phil. No, my lord, that he does not; for he writes not of the infidels, but of such as were deceived by errors.

Chich. My lord of Durham, I have been so bold as to interrupt your lordship of your tale: I pray you now proceed on.

Dur. Master Philpot, will you be of the same catholic faith and church with us, which you were baptized in, and your godfathers promised for you, and will you hold as we do? and then may you be rid out of trouble. I perceive you are learned, and it is a pity but you should do well.

Phil. I am of the same catholic faith and catholic church I was baptized into, and in that will I live and die.

Dur. That is well said: if you hold there, you cannot but do well.

Chich. Yea, my lord, but he means otherwise than you do. Are you of the same faith your godfathers and godmothers were, or not?

Phil. I cannot certainly tell what faith they were of, but I am of the faith I was baptized into, which is, in the faith of Christ. For I was not baptized in the faith of my godfathers, but in the faith of Christ.

Christo. St. Augustine saith, that infants are baptized " in the faith of their godfathers."

Phil. St. Augustine, in so saying, means the faith of Christ, which the godfathers do or ought to believe, and not otherwise.

Dur. How say you, will you believe as we do, and all the learned of the realm, and be of one church with us, or not?

Phil. My lords, it is not unknown unto you, that there have been always two churches.

Chich. Nay, that is not so: there is but one catholic church.

Phil. I shall desire your lordships to hear out my tale, and to take my meaning. For I know there is but one true church: but always from the beginning there has been joined to the same true church, a false church, adversary to the true; and that was declared at the first in Abel and Cain, who persecuted and slew his brother, in whom, as St. Augustine witnesseth,* is represented the false and true church. And after that, as soon as God had chosen his peculiar people, and showed unto them his sanctuary, holy statutes, and will, soon after arose the false church, and ten of the twelve tribes of Israel divided themselves from the true church of Judah and Benjamin, and made to themselves, and set up, golden calves at Bethel, and yet pretended therewith to serve God, and so abused his word. God was displeased with them, and ceased not his wrath, until he had utterly destroyed them.

Chich. I will grant you, before the coming of Christ, there were two churches in the old law: but in the new

* Aug. de Civit. Dei. lib. 15. c. 15.

law, since Christ's coming, you cannot show it to be so, by scripture.

Phil. Yes my lord that I can, if you will give me leave. After Christ had chosen his twelve apostles, was there not a Judas in the new law, and a Simon Magus? and were not they of the false church?

Chich. Yea, but I mean after the gospel was written, where can you find me two churches after Christ had ascended, and sent the Holy Ghost?

Phil. The gospel was written by St. Matthew within eight years after the ascension, and the writing thereof is not material to the declaration that these two churches have been always from time to time, as by example it may be showed. Yet bad as my memory is, I remember in the New Testament there is mention made of two churches, as appears in the Apocalypse: and also St. Paul to the Thessalonians mentions, that Antichrist with his false generations shall sit in the temple of God.—To this Chichester replied not.

Dur. The church in the scripture is likened to a great fisher's net, which contained in it both good fishes and bad fishes. I trust you will be of the better sort, and lean to the truth.

Phil. My lord it is my whole desire now to follow that which is good, whatsoever I have done in times past, and to cleave to God's truth.

Dur. Do you so, and then shall you do well. It is almost night, my lord of London, I must needs be gone.

Lon. Nay, my lord of Durham, I must desire your lordship, and my lord of Chichester to tarry a little while. ——But before he had so said, the bishop of Bath went his way without saying any word.—What, my lord of Bath will you be gone? I pray you tarry. My lords, I have earnest matters to charge this man with, whereof I would your lordships to be made acquainted, and I have them here written in a libel. I pray you sit down again, or else I will. First I lay to him here, that he has written in a bible, which I took from him, this erroneous saying, " Quod Spiritus est vicarius Christi in terra. The Holy Ghost is Christ's vicar on earth." Wilt thou abide by this saying of thine: that the Spirit is Christ's vicar on earth.

Phil. My lord, it is not my saying, it is a better learned man's than mine. For I use not to write my own sayings, but the notable sayings of ancient writers, as all the others are which you find written. And as I remember, it is the saying of St. Bernard, and a saying that I need not be ashamed of, neither you to be offended at, as my lord of Durham, and my lord of Chichester by their learning can discern, and will not reckon it evil said.

Lon. No? Why, take away the first syllable, and it soundeth like Arius.

Phil. That is far fetched indeed: if your lordship will scan men's sayings in such wise, you may find out what you list.

Lon. But to help this, I find moreover written with his own hand in another book: "In me Joanne Philpotto ubi abundavit peccatum, superabundavit et gratia: that is, in me John Philpot where sin did abound, grace hath superabounded." I pray you what superabundant grace have you more than other men? So said Arius, that he had the abundance of grace above all others.

Phil. My lord you need not be offended with that saying more than the other, for it is the saying of St. Paul himself, and I applied it to myself for my comfort, knowing that though my sins are huge and great in the sight of God, yet is his mercy and grace above them all. And concerning Arius and his adherents, I defy them, as it is well known I have written against them.

Lon. Also I lay to thy charge that thou killedst thy father, and wast accursed of thy mother on her death-bed, as I can bring witnesses to.

Phil. What blasphemy is this! Hath your lordship nothing of truth to charge me with, but, as I may speak it with your honour, such forged blasphemous lies? If any of these can be proved, I will promise here to recant at Paul's cross, what you will have me. I am sure they are as great blasphemies as may be objected against any man. Ha, my lords, I pray you consider how my lord of London has hitherto proceeded against me: for indeed he has no other but such pretended slanderous lies.

Chich. They are Parerga: that is, matters beside the purpose.

Dur. My lord, I must needs bid you farewell.

Lon. Nay, my lord, here is a letter which I shall desire your lordship to hear before you go. This man, being in my keeping, has taken upon him to write letters out of prison, and to pervert a young gentleman called Master Green, in my house, (call him hither) and has made a false report of his examination, as you shall hear, not being content to be evil himself, but to make others as bad as himself. He tore the letter when he saw my man went about to search him, but yet I have pieced it again together, and caused a copy to be written thereof.—And he read the torn letter, bidding Master Christopherson and Morgan to mark the copy thereof.

The contents of the letter was, the examination of Master Green* before the bishop of London in the presence of Master Fecknam dean of Paul's, and of divers others, whose ready answers in the scriptures and in the doctors, was wondered at by the dean himself, and many others, as Master Fecknam reported. And that he was committed to Doctor Chadsey, and to have his meat from the bishop's own table.

Lon. How say you my lords, was this well done of him being my prisoner, to write this? And yet he has written a shameful lie, that he was in Doctor Chadsey's keeping. How say you Master Doctor Chadsey, is it not a shameful lie?

Chad. Yes my lord, he was never in my keeping.

Lon. Art thou not ashamed to write such shameful lies? Come hither Master Green, did not I show you this letter?

Green. Yea my lord, you showed it me.

Lon. How think you, my lords, is not this an honest man to belie me?

Phil. Your lordship mistakes all things. This letter (as your lordship, and all others that have heard the same may perceive) was not written by me, but by a friend of mine, certifying me, at my request, how Master Green sped at the bishop of London's hands: and there is nothing in the letter that either I, or he that wrote it, need to fear, but that might be written as my report.

Lon. Then tell me who wrote it, if you dare.

Phil No, my lord, it is not my duty to accuse my friend, and, specially, seeing you will take all things at the worst. You shall never know of me who wrote it. Your lordship may see in the end of the letter, that my friend wrote unto me upon the occasion of my appeal which I have made to the whole parliament house about such matters as I am wrongfully troubled for.

Lon. I would like to see any so hardy as to put up thine appeal.

* Bartlet Green was a young man of respectable family, a student of the law in the Temple. He was a prisoner at the same time as Philpot, and was burned shortly after. See page 139—142.

Phil. My lord, I cannot tell what God will work, I have written it, speed as it may.

Lon. My lords, I have used him with much gentleness since he came to me. How sayest thou, have I not?

Phil. If to lie in the vilest prison in this town, (being a gentleman, and an archdeacon,) and in a coalhouse, by the space of five or six weeks already, without fire or candle, be counted gentleness at your hands, I must needs say I have found gentleness! But there were never men so cruelly handled as we are at these days.

Lon. Lo, what a varlet is this! Besides this, (my lords,) even yesterday he procured his man to bring a bladder of black powder, I cannot tell for what purpose.

Phil. Your lordship need not mistrust the matter; it is nothing but to make ink with, as I had it before in the King's Bench, when my keeper took away my inkhorn.

Lon. And why shouldest thou go about any such thing unknown to me thy keeper? for I am thy keeper in this house, I tell thee.

Phil. My lord, because though you have caused my pen and inkhorn to be taken from me, yet I would fain that my friends might understand what I lack, not that I intend to write any thing that I would be afraid should come to your sight.

Lon. More than this, my lords, he caused a pig to be roasted, and a knife to be put between the skin and the flesh, for what purpose judge you. How sayest thou, didst thou not so?

Phil. I cannot deny but there was half a pig sent me, and under the same a knife lying in the sauce, but for no ill purpose that I know, your lordship may judge what you will. It was not to kill myself, nor any other, as you would have men to believe; for I was never yet without a knife since I came to prison. Therefore all these are but false surmises, and not worth rehearsal.

Lon. I have here to lay to his charge, (chiefest of all,) his book of the report of the disputation had in the convocation house, which is the rankest heresy that may be, against the blessed sacrament of the altar. How say you, Doctor Weston? did he maintain the same there stubbornly, or not?

West. Yea my lord, that he did, and would never be answered. And it is a pity that the same worshipful congregation should be slandered with such untrue reports.

Phil. You answered me indeed, master doctor, (being then prolocutor,) with "hold thy peace," and " have him to prison," and "put him out of the house." I have read the book, and I find the report of every man's argument is true in all points. And if there is any fault, it is, because it sets forth your doings too favourably, and nothing like to the manner in which you used me, being an archdeacon, and not of the worst of the house.

West. Thou art no archdeacon.

Phil. Indeed, master doctor, you have among you unarchdeaconed me now, (I thank God for it,) and that without any order of law.

Lon. I pray you, my lords hearken what he writes of himself; I read it over this morning, and made a note of it. He saith, that Doctor Weston called him frantic and mad man, and said, he should go to Bedlam.

Phil. Indeed my lord, so it pleased Doctor Weston to taunt at me and say his shameful pleasure, but yet I was no whit the more so for all his sayings, than Christ was when the scribes and the pharisees said likewise he was mad, and that he was possessed of a devil, most blasphemously.

Dur. My lord of London, I can tarry no longer, I must needs bid you farewell. Master Philpot, methinks you have said well, that you will abide in the catholic faith, and in the catholic church. I pray you so do, and you shall do right well.—And so he departed with Master Weston and Master Hussey.

Phil. I have purposed so to do by God's grace, however I speed.

Lon. I pray you my lord of Chichester, and Master Prolocutor and Doctor Morgan, to commune with him whilst I wait upon my lord of Durham.

Christo. Master Philpot, I was acquainted with you at Rome, if you remember, but you have forgotten me, and then talked somewhat with you of these matters, and I find you now the same man as you were then. I wish it were otherwise. For God's sake, be conformable to men that are better learned than you, and stand not in your own conceit.

Phil. Whereas you remind me of acquaintance had at Rome, indeed it was so, though it were but very strange* on your part, toward me being driven to necessity.

Christo. You know the world was dangerous at that time.

Phil. Not so dangerous as it is now: but let that pass. Whereas you say, you find me the same man I was then, I praise God that you see me not like a reed wavering with every wind. And whereas you would have me follow better learned men than myself: indeed I acknowledge that you, with a great many others, are far better learned than I, whose books, in respect of learning, I am not worthy to carry after you. But faith and the wisdom of God consists not in learning only, and therefore St. Paul wills that our faith be not grounded upon the wisdom of man. If you can show out of God's book, by learning, that I ought to be of another faith than I am, I will hear you and any other man, whatsoever he is.

Christo. I marvel why you should dissent from the catholic church, since it has so long been universally received, except within this five or six years here in England.

Phil. I do not dissent from the true catholic church: I only dissent from the bishop of Rome, which if you can prove to be the catholic church of Christ, I will be of the same also with you.

Christo. Will you believe St. Cyprian, if I can show you out of him: "That the church of Rome is such a one, unto the which misbelief cannot approach."

Phil. I am sure you cannot show any such saying out of St. Cyprian.

Christo. What will you lay thereon?

Phil. I will lay as much as I am able.

Morgan. Will you promise to recant, if he show his saying to be true?

Phil. My faith shall not hang upon any doctor's saying, further than he shall be able to prove the same by God's word.

Christo. I will go and fetch the book and show it him. —And therewithal he went into the bishop's study, and brought Cyprian, and pointed out these words in one of his epistles: "But unto the Romans whose faith, by the testimony of the apostle, is praised, misbelief can have no access."

* Distant.

Phil. These words of Cyprian do not prove your pretended assertion, which is, that to the church of Rome there could come no disbelief.

Christo. No? What can be said more plainly?

Phil. He speaks not of the church of Rome absolutely.

Christo. (with an oath,) A child that only knows his grammar, will not deny what you do, the words are so plain.

Phil. Swear not, master doctor, but weigh Cyprian's words with me, and I shall make you to say as I have said.

Christo. I am no doctor, but I perceive it is but labour lost to reason with you.

And with that the bishop of London came in blowing again, and said: "What, is my lord of Chichester gone away also?" (for he even a little before departed also without saying any other word, "but he must needs be gone.") "What is the matter you now stand upon?"

Mor. Master Christopherson hath showed Master Philpot a notable place of the authority of the church of Rome and he makes nothing of it.

Lon. Where is the place? let me see it. By my faith, here is a place quite enough alone. Come hither, sir, what say you to this? Nay tarry a little, I will help this place with St. Paul's own testimony, the first to the Romans, where he saith, that their faith is preached throughout the world: how can you be able to answer to this?

Phil. Yes my lord, it is soon answered, if you wil consider all the words of Cyprian; for he speaks of such as in his time were faithful at Rome, that followed the doctrine of St. Paul as he had taught them, and as it was notified throughout the world, by an epistle which he had written in commendation of their faith. With such as are praised of St. Paul at Rome, for following the true faith, misbelief can have no place. And if you can show, that the faith which the church of Rome now holds, is tha. faith which the apostle praised and allowed in the Romans in his time, then will I say, with you, what St. Cyprian then said, that infidelity can have no place there: but otherwise it makes not absolutely for the authority of the church of Rome, as you mistake it.

Christo. You understand Cyprian well indeed: I think ou never read him in your life.

Phil. Yes, master doctor, that I have, I can show you a copy noted with my own hand : though I have not read so much as you, yet I have read somewhat. It is shame for you to wrest and twist the doctors as you do, to maintain a false religion, when they are altogether against you, if you take them aright. And indeed your false packing of the doctors together, has given me and others occasion to look upon them, whereby we find you shameful liars, and misreporters of the ancient doctors.

Mor. What, will you allow doctors now ? Those of your sect do not so. I marvel therefore, that you will allow them.

Phil. I allow them as far as they agree with the scriptures, and so do all they which are of the truth, however you term us, and I praise God for the good understanding I have received by them.

Christo. What, you understand not the doctors—you may be ashamed to say it.

Phil. I thank God I understand them better than you ; for you have " the blindness of heart," so that you understand not truly what you read, any more than the wall here, as your understanding Cyprian well declares. And, before God, you are but deceivers of the people, for all the brag you make of learning, neither have you scripture or ancient doctrine on your side, if it is truly taken.

Mor. Why, all the doctors are on our side, and against you altogether.

Phil. Yea, so you say when you are in your pulpits alone, and none to answer you. But if you will come to cast accounts with me thereof, I will venture with you a recantation, that I, (as little sight as I have in the doctors,) will bring more authorities of ancient doctors on my side than you shall be able for yours, and he that can bring most, to him let the other side yield. Are you content herewith ?

Christo. It is but folly to reason with you : you will believe no man but yourself.

Phil. I will believe you or any other learned man, if you can bring any thing worthy to be believed. You cannot win me with vain words from my faith. Before God I declare that there is no truth in you.

Mor. What, no truth ? no truth ? ha, ha, ha.

Phil. Except as to the articles of the Trinity—you are corrupt in all other things, and sound in nothing.

Mor. What say you? Do we not believe well respecting the sacrament?

Phil. It is the thing which, (among all others,) you do most abuse.

Mor. Wherein, I pray you? tell us.

Phil. I have told you before, master doctor, in the convocation-house.

Mor. Yea, marry: indeed you told us there very well. For there you fell down upon your knees, and fell to weeping: ha, ha, ha.

Phil. I wept indeed, and so did Christ over Jerusalem, and am not to be blamed, therefore, if you consider the cause of my weeping.

Mor. What, make you yourself Christ? ha, ha, ha.

Phil. No sir, I make not myself Christ: but I am not ashamed to do as my Master and Saviour did; to bewail and lament your infidelity and idolatry, which I there foresaw you would bring again to this realm by tyranny, as this day declares.

Mor. That is your argument.

Christo. Wherein do we abuse the sacrament? tell us.

Phil. That I may touch but one of the least abuses; you minister it not in both kinds as you ought to do, but keep one half from the people, contrary to Christ's institution.

Christo. Why, is there not as much contained in one kind, as in both? And what need is there then to minister in both kinds?

Phil. I believe not so: for if it had, Christ would have given but one kind only: for he instituted nothing superfluous, and therefore you cannot say that the whole effect of the sacrament is in one kind, as well as in both, since the scripture teaches otherwise.

Christo. What, if I can prove by scripture, that we may minister it in one kind? The apostles did so, as appears in the Acts of the Apostles, in one or two places, where it is written that the apostles continued. "In prayers and in breaking of bread," which is meant of the sacrament.

Phil. Why, master doctor, do you not know that St. Luke, by making mention of the breaking of bread, means the whole use of the sacrament, according to Christ's institution, by a figure which you have learned in grammar, called Synecdoche, where part is mentioned, and the whole understood to be done, as Christ commanded it?

Christo. Nay, that is not so. For I can show out of

Eusebius, in his Ecclesiastical History, that there was a man of God, whom he names, that sent the sacrament in one kind by a boy, to one that was sick.

Phil. I have read, indeed, that they used to give what was left of the communion bread to children, to mariners, and to women, and so, peradventure, the boy might carry a piece of what was left to the sick man.*

Christo. Nay, as a sacrament it was purposely sent unto him.

Phil. If it were so, yet can you not precisely say that he had not the cup ministered unto him also by some other sent unto him: but if one man used it thus, does it follow that all men may do the like? St. Cyprian notes many abuses of the sacrament in his time, which rose upon individual men's examples, as using of water instead of wine: therefore he saith: "We must not look what any man hath done before us, but what Christ, first of all men, did and commanded."

Christo. Hath not the church taught us to use the sacrament? And how do we know that Christ is Homousios, that is, "of one substance with the Father," but by the determination of the church? How can you prove that otherwise than by express words of scripture, and where find you Homousios in all the scriptures.

Phil. Yes, that I do, in the first chapter of the epistle to the Hebrews, where it is written that Christ is the express image of God's own substance.

Christo. Nay, that is not so. It is only "The express image of God's substance:" and image is an accident.†

Phil. It is in the text, "Of his substance," or, "Of his own substance," as it may be well interpreted. Besides this, that which Christ spake to himself in St. John manifests the same, saying: "I and the Father are one thing." And whereas you say, image here is only an accident, the ancient fathers use this place for a strong argument, to prove Christ to be God, because he is the very image of God.

* Eusebius has these words. "Parum Eucharistiæ puero dedit. He gave a little of the sacrament to the boy;" which words may very well comprehend both parts: and it seemeth by the words that follow, that part of it was liquor, for it is written in the same place: He commanded that he should pour it, and drop it into the man's mouth, and so he did. Eusebius, Ecclesiastical History, lib. vi. chap. 44.—*Fox.*

† Or mere outward form or appearance

Christo. Do they? Is this a good argument,—because we are the image of God, ergo, we are God?

Phil. We are not called the express image of God, as it is written of Christ. We are the image of God only by participation, and as it is written in Genesis, we are made in the likeness and similitude of God. But you ought to know, Master Christopherson, that there is no accident in God, or outward form, and therefore Christ cannot be the image of God, but he must be of the same substance with God.

Christo. Tush.

Mor. How say you to the presence of the sacrament? will you stand here to the judgment of your book, or not? or will you recant?

Phil. I know you try to catch my words. If you can prove that book is of my setting forth, lay it to my charge when I come to judgment.

Mor. Speak, are you of the same mind as this book is of, or not? Sure I am you were once, unless you have become another manner of man than you were.

Phil. What I was, you know: what I am, I will not tell you now: but this I will say to you by the way, that if you can prove that your sacrament of the mass, as you now use it, is a sacrament, I will then grant you a presence; but first you must prove the same a sacrament, and afterwards treat of the presence.

Mor. Hoo! Do you doubt that it is a sacrament?

Phil. I am past doubting; for I believe you never can be able to prove it a sacrament.

Christo. Doth not St. Augustine call it the sacrament of the altar? How say you to that?

Phil. That makes nothing for the probation of your sacrament. For so he, with other ancient writers, calls the holy communion, or the Supper of the Lord, in respect that it is the sacrament of the sacrifice which Christ offered upon the altar of the cross; which sacrifice all the altars and sacrifices done upon the altars in the old law prefigured and shadowed, which pertains not at all to your sacrament which is hanging over your altars of lime and stone.*

Christo. No? I pray you what signifies altar?

Phil. Not as you falsely take it, materially, but for the sacrifice of the altar of the cross.

* He alludes to the Romish consecrated wafer, which was hung over the altar.

Eleventh examination.

Christo. Where find you it ever so taken?

Phil. In St. Paul to the Hebrews, chapter xiii., where he saith, "We have an altar, of which it is not lawful for them to eat that serve the tabernacle." Is not altar there taken for the sacrifice of the altar, and not for the altar of lime and stone.

Christo. Well, God bless me out of your company.* You are such an obstinate heretic as I have not heard the like.

Phil. I pray God to keep me from such blind doctors, who, when they are not able to prove what they say, fall to blaspheming, as you now do, for lack of better proof.— In the meanwhile, the bishop of London was talking with some others who were by, and at length came in to supply his part, and said:

Lon. I pray you, masters, hearken what I shall say to this man. Come hither, Master Green. And now, sir, pointing to me, you cannot think it sufficient to be naught yourself, but must go about to procure this young gentleman by your letters to do the like.

Phil. My lord, he cannot say, that I ever hitherto wrote unto him concerning any such matter.

Green. No, you never wrote unto me.

Lon. Why, is not this your letter which you wrote concerning him?

Phil. I have showed your lordship my mind concerning that letter already; it was not written to Master Green, neither was he privy to the writing thereof.

Lon. How say you then, if a man be in error, and you know thereof, what are you bound to do in such a case?

Phil. I am bound to do the best I can to bring him out of it.

Lon. If Master Green here is in the like, are you not bound to reform him thereof if you can?

Phil. Yes, that I am, and will do to the uttermost of my power therein.—The bishop remembering himself, and thinking that he would not be helped by me as he expected, but rather confirmed in that which he called an error, ceased to go any further in his demand, and called Master Green aside, and before his registrar read him a

---

* In this and some other places it is unpleasant to record a profane expression; but it is sometimes necessary to do so to give a correct idea of these Romish priests.

letter; (I know not the contents thereof;) and therewithal he gave Master Green the book of my disputation in the convocation-house, and afterwards went aside, communing with Master Christopherson, leaving Master Morgan, Master Harpsfield, and Master Cosins, to reason with me in the hearing of Master Green.

Mor. Master Philpot, I would ask you how old your religion is?

Phil. It is older than yours by a thousand years and more.

Mor. I pray you, where was it fifty years ago?

Phil. It was apparent in Germany by the testimony of Huss, Jerome of Prague, and Wickliff, whose bones your generation, a hundred years ago and more, burnt for his preaching the truth unto you; and before their time and since, it still has continued, although under persecution it has been put to silence.

Mor. That is a marvellous strange religion, which no man can tell certainly where to find.

Phil. It ought to be no marvel unto you to see God's truth oppressed through violence; for so it has been from the beginning, from time to time, as appears by histories; and as Christ's true religion is now to be found here in England, although hypocrisy has by violence the upper hand. And in the Apocalypse you may see it was prophesied, that the true church should be driven into corners and into the wilderness, and suffer great persecution.

Mor. Ah, are you skilled in the Apocalypse? There are many strange things in it.

Phil. If I tell you the truth which you are not able to repel, believe it, and trifle not with such important matters. Methinks you are more like a scoffer in a play, than a reasonable doctor to instruct a man: you dance naked in a net, and yet you see not your own nakedness.

Mor. What, I pray you, be not so quick with me. Let us talk a little more coolly together.

Phil. I will talk with you as mildly as you can desire, if you will speak learnedly and charitably. But if you go about with taunts to delude the truth, I will not hide it from you.

Mor. Why will not you submit your judgment to the learned men of this realm?

Phil. Because I see they can bring no good ground,

whereupon I may with a good conscience settle my faith more surely than on that, on which I am now grounded by God's manifest word.

Mor. No? It is a marvel that so many learned men should be deceived.

Phil. It is no marvel, according to St. Paul; for he saith, "That not many wise, neither many learned after the world, are called to the knowledge of the gospel."

Mor. Have you then alone the Spirit of God, and not we?

Phil. I say not, that I alone have the Spirit of God, but as many as abide in the true faith of Christ, have the Spirit of God as well as I.

Mor. How know you that you have the Spirit of God?

Phil. By the faith of Christ which is in me.

Mor. Ha, by faith do you so? I ween it be the spirit of the buttery,* which your fellows have had that have been burned before you, who were drunk the night before they went to their death, and I ween went drunken unto it.

Phil. It appears by your communication, that you are better acquainted with the spirit of the buttery, than with the Spirit of God. Wherefore, I must now tell thee, thou painted wall and hypocrite, in the name of the living Lord, whose truth I have told thee, that God shall rain fire and brimstone upon such scorners of his word, and blasphemers of his people as thou art.

Mor. What? You rage now!

Phil. Thy foolish blasphemies have compelled the Spirit of God which is in me, to speak that which I have said unto thee, thou enemy of all righteousness.

Mor. Why do you judge me so?

Phil. By thine own wicked words I judge of thee, thou blind and blasphemous doctor. As it is written, "By thy words thou shalt be justified, and by thy words thou shalt be condemned." I have spoken on God's behalf, and now have I done with thee.

Mor. Why then I tell thee, Philpot, that thou art a heretic, and shalt be burned for thine heresy, and afterwards go to hell fire.

Phil. I tell thee, thou hypocrite, that I care not for thy fire and fagots, neither, I thank God my Lord, stand I in fear of the same. My faith in Christ shall overcome them. But the hell fire which thou threatenest me with, 's thy

---

* A fairy or goblin, said to haunt pantries or butteries

portion, and is prepared for thee, unless thou speedily repent, and for such hypocrites as thou art.

Mor. What! Thou speakest upon wine; it seems as if thou hast tippled well to day.

Phil. So the cursed generation said of the apostles, when being replenished with the Holy Ghost, and speaking the wondrous works of God. They said they were drunk, when they had nothing else to say, as thou dost now.

Mor. Why, I am able to answer thee, I think.

Phil. So it seems—with blasphemies and lies.

Mor. Nay, even with learning, say what thou canst.

Phil. That appeared well at my disputation in the convocation-house, when thou tookest upon thee to answer the few arguments I was permitted to make, and yet wast not able to answer one, but in thine answers didst fumble and stammer, so that the whole house was ashamed of thee; and the final conclusion of all thine answers was, that thou couldest answer me if I were in the schools at Oxford.

Mor. What, did I so? Thou beliest me.

Phil. I do not belie thee: the book of the report of the disputation bears record thereto, and all that were present then, can tell, if they list, that thou saidst so. And I tell thee plain, thou art not able to answer that Spirit of truth which speaks in me for the defence of Christ's true religion. I am able, by the might thereof, to drive thee round about this gallery before me; and if it would please the queen's majesty and her council to hear thee and me, I would make thee for shame shrink behind the door.

Mor. Yea, would you so?

Phil. Thou hast the spirit of illusion and sophistry, which is not able to countervail the Spirit of truth. Thou art but an ass in the true understanding of things pertaining unto God. I call thee ass, not in respect of malice, but in that thou kickest against the truth, and art void of all godly understanding, not able to answer that which thou braggest.

Mor. Why, have I not answered thee in all things thou hast said unto me? I take those present to record.

Phil. Ask of my fellow whether I be a thief!

Cosins. Hark, he makes us all thieves.

Phil. You know the proverb, that like will hold with like. And I am sure you will not judge with me against him, speak I ever so true; and in this sense I speak it

The strongest answer that he has made against me is, that you will burn me.

Mor. Why, we do not burn you: it is the temporal men that burn you, and not we.

Phil. Thus you would, as Pilate did, wash your hands of all your wicked doings. But I pray you, do you not call upon the secular power to be executioners of your unrighteous judgments? And have you not a title in your law, " De hæreticis comburendis, Of the burning of heretics ?"

Harps. I have heard you both reason together a good while, and I never heard so stout a heretic as you are, Master Philpot.

Cosins. Neither I in all my life.

Phil. You are not able to prove me a heretic by one jot of God's word.

Harps. You have the spirit of arrogancy. I will reason with you no more.—And so he was departing, and Master Cosins also. And with that the bishop and Christopherson came in again, and said:

Lon. Master doctor, how do this man and you agree?

Mor. My lord, I ask him where his church was fifty years ago.

Lon. Are you not half agreed, as one man said once to two parties, of whom the one was equally disagreeing from the other.

Christo. My lord, it is but folly to reason with him any further; your lordship will but lose time, for he is incurable.

Lon. Well, then, let his keeper have him away.— Doctor Chadsey then led me a way by which we could not pass, and therefore came back again through the bishop's chamber, where all these doctors were clustered together; and as I was passing by, the bishop took me by the gown, and said, " Wot you what Master Christopherson tells me ? I pray you, Master Christopherson, rehearse the sentence in Latin;" and so he did. The contents thereof were, that a heretic would not be won.

Christo. St. Paul saith, " Flee a heretic after once or twice warning."

All the doctors. Yea, my lord, it is best you do so, and trouble your lordship no more with him.

Phil. You must first justly prove me to be a heretic, before you use the judgment of St. Paul against me; for he speaks of such as hold opinions against the manifest word, which you cannot prove against me. And because you want in your proof, and are able to prove nothing against me, therefore you go about falsely to suppose me to be a heretic, for the safeguard of your own counterfeit honesties. But before God, you are the heretics who so stoutly and stubbornly maintain so many things directly against God's word, as God in his time will reveal.

As I went out of his chamber, the bishop called me aside, and said:

Lon. I pray thee, in good sadness,* tell me what meanest thou by writing in the beginning of thy bible, "Spiritus est vicarius Christi in terris," "The Spirit is the vicar of Christ on the earth?" I think that you have some special meaning therein.

Phil. My lord, I have no other meaning than, as I have told you already, that Christ since his ascension works all things in us by his Spirit, and by his Spirit dwells in us. I pray you, my lord, let me have my bible, with other lawful books and writings which you have of mine, whereof many of them are none of mine, but lent to me by my friends.

Lon. Your bible you shall not have; but I will perhaps let you have another; and after I have perused the rest, you shall have such as I think good.

Phil. I pray your lordship then, that you would let me have candle-light.

Lon. To what purpose, I pray you?

Phil. The nights are long, and I would fain occupy myself about somewhat, and not spend my time idly.

Lon. You may pray.

Phil. I cannot well say my prayers without light.

Lon. Can you not say your paternoster without a candle? I tell you, sir, you shall have some meat and drink of me, but candle you get none.

Phil. I had rather have a candle than your meat or drink; but seeing I shall not have my request, the Lord shall be my light.

Lon. Have him down.

Chad. I will bring him to his keeper, my lord. Master Philpot, I wonder that all these learned men whom you have talked with all this day, cannot persuade you.

Phil. Why, master doctor, would you have me to be

* Seriously.

persuaded with nothing? or would you have me build my faith upon sand? What do you all bring whereby I ought, as by any sufficient authority, to be persuaded by you?

Chad. I am sorry you will so wilfully cast away yourself, whereas you might live worshipfully. Do you not think others have souls to save as well as you have?

Phil. Every man shall receive according to his own doings. Sure I am you are deceived, and maintain a false religion; and as for my casting away, I would my burning day were to-morrow, for this delay is to die every day, and yet not to be dead.

Chad. You are not like to die yet, I can tell you.

Phil. I am the more sorry. But the will of God be done of me, to his glory. Amen.

The twelfth Examination of John Philpot, on Wednesday, the fourth of December, before Bonner, bishop of London, the bishop of Worcester, and the bishop of Bangor.

IN the morning I was brought down to the wardrobe adjoining the chapel, and soon after came three of the bishop's chaplains unto me, saying:

"Master Philpot, my lord hath sent us unto you, to desire you to come to mass, certifying you that there is a doctor of divinity, a chaplain of my lord's, a notable learned man, called Doctor Chadsey, going to mass; therefore, we also pray you, good Master Philpot, be content to come: it is close hereby."

Phil. I wonder my lord troubles you in sending you about this matter, seeing he knows I am a man that cannot hear mass by your law, because I stand excommunicated.

Chap. Your excommunication is but upon a contumacy, and my lord will dispense with you, if you will come.

Phil. My lord cannot, for he is not my ordinary, and I will not seek any such thing at his hands.—With this answer they went their way. And after mass the bishop called me before him in his chapel, and there, in the presence of his registrar, after he had said his mind, because I would not come to mass; he recited the articles, which he oftentimes before had done, with the depositions of the witnesses, of whom some were not examined.

Bon. Sir, what can you now say, why I should not proceed to give sentence against you as a heretic?

Phil Why, my lord, will you proceed to give sentence against me before your witnesses are examined? That is plainly against your own law, as all your doings hitherto have been.

Bon. See what a fool thou art in the law. I need not recite the depositions of the witnesses unless I please, for I know them well enough already.

Phil. It appears, indeed, that you may do what you list.

Bon. Tell me, I say, whether thou wilt answer or not, and whether, if thou wert absolved of thine excommunication, thou wouldest come to mass or not?

Phil. I have answered as much as I intend to do, until I am called to lawful judgment; and as concerning my conscience, I will not make you as God to sit there as yet. It is God's part only to be the searcher of my heart.

Bon. Look how foolishly he speaks. Art thou God? and yet dost thou not sit in thine own conscience?

Phil. I sit not in mine own conscience; but I know it, and God only ought to sit there, and no man else.

Bon. Thou art a naughty fellow, and hast done much hurt, and hast seduced other poor fellows here in prison with thee, by thy comforting of them in their errors, and hast made them rejoice and sing with thee.

Phil. Yea, my lord, we shall sing, when you and such other as you are, shall cry "Woe, woe," except you repent.

Bon. What an arrogant fool is this! I will handle thee like a heretic, and that shortly.

Phil. I fear nothing, I thank God, that you can do to me. But God shall destroy such as thou art, and that shortly, as I trust.

Bon. Have him away: this is a knave indeed.

I was had into the wardrobe again by my keeper, and within an hour after was sent for to come before him and the bishops of Worcester and Bangor.

Bon. Sir, I have talked with you many times, and have caused you to be talked with by many learned men, yea and honourable, both temporal and spiritual, and it availeth nothing with you. I am blamed that I have brought thee before so many; for they say, thou gloriest to have many to talk with. Well, now it lies upon thee to look to thyself; for thy time draws near to an end, if thou do not become conformable. And at this present time we are sent from the synod to offer you this grace, that if you will come to the unity of the church of Rome with us, and acknowledge the real presence of Christ in the sacrament of the altar with us, all that is past shall be forgiven, and you shall be received to favour.

Wor. Master Philpot, we are sent, as you have heard, by my lord of London, from the synod to offer you mercy, if you will receive it; and of the good will I bear you, I wish you to take it whilst it is offered, and be not a singular man against a whole multitude of learned men, who now, in fasting and prayer, are gathered together to devise things to do you good. Many learned men have talked with you: why should you think yourself better learned than them all? Be not of such arrogancy, but have humility, and remember there is no salvation but in the church.

Bang. My lord hath said wonderfully well unto you, that you should not think yourself so well learned, but that other men are as well learned as you, neither of so good wit,* but others are as wise as you, neither of such good memory, but others have as good memories as you. Therefore mistrust your own judgment, and come home to us again. I never liked your religion, because it was set forth by violence and tyranny, and that is no token of true religion. And I was the same manner of man then that I am now, and a great many more. Marry, we held our peace for fear, and bare with that time. Wherefore, Master Philpot, I would that you did well, for I love you; and therefore be content to come home with us again into the catholic church of Rome.

Phil. My lord, you say, that religion is to be misliked which is set forth by tyranny: I pray God you give not men occasion to think the same of yours at this day, which has no other argument to stand by but violence. If you can show me by any good sufficient ground, whereby to satisfy my conscience, that the church of Rome, whereunto you call me, is the true catholic church, I will gladly be of the same; otherwise I cannot so soon change the religion I have learned these many years.

Ban. Where was your religion, I pray you, a hundred years ago, that any man knew of it?

Phil. It was in Germany, and in divers other places, apparent.

* Understanding.

Wor. (*with a profane exclamation.*) Will you be still so singular a man? What is Germany compared to the whole world?

Bon. My lords, I pray you give me leave to tell you that I sent for him to hear mass this morning. And will you what excuse he made unto me? forsooth, that he was accursed; alleging his own shame. He playeth as the varlet Latimer did at Cambridge: when the vice-chancellor sent for him (intending to have excommunicated him for some of his heresies), and as the chancellor was coming to his chamber, he hearing that the chancellor was coming, made answer, that he was sick of the plague, and so deluded the chancellor! Even so this man saith, he is accursed, because he will not come to mass.

Wor. My lord here behaves himself like a father unto you; therefore be admonished by him, and by us, who now come friendly unto you, and follow your fathers before you.

Phil. It is forbidden us of God by the prophet Ezekiel, to follow our fathers, or to walk in their commandments.

Wor. It is written also in another place: "Ask of your fathers."

Phil. We ought to ask, indeed, our fathers who have more experience and knowledge than we repecting God's will, but no more to allow them than we perceive they agree with the scripture.

Wor. You will be a contentious man, I see well: and St. Paul saith, that neither we nor the church of God have any such custom.

Phil. I am not contentious but for the verity of my faith, in which I ought to contend with all such as impugn the same without any just objection.

Wor. Let us rise, my lord, for I see we shall do no good.

Bon. Nay, I pray you tarry and hear the articles I lay to his charge.—And after he had recited them, they arose, and after standing, they reasoned with me awhile.

Wor. Master Philpot, I am very sorry that you will be so singular. I never talked with any yet in my diocese, but after once communication had with me, they have been contented to revoke their errors, and to teach the people how they were deceived, and so did much good, as you may, if you list. For, as I understand, you were archdeacon of Winchester, which is the eye of the bishop, and you may do much good in that country if you would forsake your errors, and come to the catholic church.

Phil. How you so soon persuaded them to your will I see not. I hold no error that I know: of the catholic church I am sure I am.

Wor. The catholic church acknowledges a real presence of Christ in the sacrament, and you will not.

Phil. That is not so: for I acknowledge a very essential presence in the duly using of the sacrament.

Wor. What, a real presence?

Phil. Yea, a real presence by the Spirit of God in the right administration.

Wor. That is well said: and do you agree with the catholic church also?

Phil. I agree with the true catholic church.

Wor. My lord of London, this man speaks reasonably now.

Bon. You agree in generalities, but when you shall come to particulars, you will far disagree.

Wor. Well, keep yourself here, and you shall have other learned bishops to commune further with you, as my lord of Durham, and my lord of Chichester, whom (I hear say) you like well.

Phil. I like them as I do all others that speak the truth. I have once already spoken with them, and they found no fault with me.

Wor. Pray in the mean season for grace to God.

Phil. Prayer is the most comfortable exercise I feel in my trouble; and my conscience is quiet, and I have peace of mind, which cannot be the fruits of heresy.

Wor. We will bid you farewell for this time.

After dinner they called for me again, and demanded of me whether I meant as I spake before dinner, and would not go from it. To whom I answered, that I would not go from what I had said.

Wor. You said at my departing from you before dinner, that if we burnt you, we should burn a catholic man. Will you be a catholic man, and stand to the catholic church?

Phil. I will stand to the true catholic church.

Wor. Will you stand to the catholic church of Rome?

Phil. If you can prove the same to be the catholic church, I will be one thereof.

Wor. Did not Christ say unto Peter, and to all his

successors of Rome: "Feed my sheep, feed my lambs?" which signifies that he gave him more authority than to the rest.

Phil. That saying pertains nothing to the authority of Peter above others, but declares what Christ requires of his beloved apostles,—that they should, with all diligence, preach to the flock of Christ the way of salvation, and that the iteration of feeding spoken to Peter, alone signifies. But the bishop of Rome little regards this spiritual feeding, and therefore he has imagined an easier way to make himself lord of the whole world, yea, and of God's word too, and does not feed Christ's flock as Peter did.

Wor. How can you tell that?

Phil. I have been there, and I could not learn from all his countrymen that he ever preaches.

Wor. Though he preaches not one way, he preaches another, by procuring the church to be kept in good order.

Phil. I am sure it will be his damnation before God, that he leaves what he is commanded of Christ, and sets forth his own decrees to deface the gospel.

Wor. It is the evil living that you have seen at Rome that causes you to have this ill judgment of the church of Rome. I cannot tarry now with you to reason further of the matter.

How say you to the real presence of the sacrament, will you stand to that?

Phil. I acknowledge, as I have said, a real presence of the sacrament in the due administration thereof, to the worthy receivers by the Spirit of God.

Wor. You add now a great many more words than you did before: and yet you say more of the sacrament than a great many will do.

Thus they departed, and after them came to me Dr. Chadsey, and Dr. Wright, archdeacon of Oxford, with a great many more.

Chadsey. Master Philpot, here is the archdeacon of Oxford come to you, to give you good counsel, pray hear him.

Phil. I will refuse to hear none that will advise me any good: and if any can bring any matter better than I have, I will stick thereunto.

Wright. I would wish you, Master Philpot, to agree with

the catholic church, and not to stand in your own conceit you see a great many learned men against you.

Phil. Master doctor, I am of the unfeigned catholic church, and will live and die therein: and if you can prove your church to be the true catholic church, I will be one of the same.

Wright. I came not to dispute with you, but to exhort you. Here are better learned than I am who can inform you better than I.

Chad. What proof would you have? I will prove to you our church to have its being and foundation by the scriptures, by the apostles, and by the primitive church; confirmed with the blood of martyrs, and the testimony of all confessors.

Phil. Give me your hand, master doctor; prove that, and I will be with you.

Chad. If I had my books here, I could soon prove it; I will go and fetch some.—And with that he went and brought his book of annotations, saying,—" I cannot bring my books well, therefore I have brought my book of annotations:" and turned there to a common place about the sacrament; asking me whether the catholic church allowed the presence of Christ's body in the sacrament, or not? adding, I hear that you confess a real presence, but I will be hanged if you abide by it. You will deny it by and by.

Phil. What I have said I cannot deny, and intend not, whatever you say.

Chad. If there is a real presence in the sacrament, then evil men receive Christ, which thing you will not grant, I am sure.

Phil. I deny the argument. For I do not grant in the sacrament any real presence by transubstantiation, as you falsely imagine, but in the due administration to the worthy receivers.

Chad. I will prove that evil and wicked men eat the body of Christ as well as the good men, by St. Austin here.

In the beginning of his text St. Austin seemed to approve this assertion: but I bade him read out to the end, and said,

Phil. There St. Augustine declares, that it was " after a certain manner the evil men received the body of Christ," only sacramentally in the outer signs, and not really, or indeed, as the good. And thus all the doctors that you seem to bring in for your purpose are quite against you, if you rightly weigh them.

Chad. (*with an oath.*) You are a subtle fellow. See how he would writhe St. Augustine's words.

Phil. See which of us writhes St. Austin the most, you, or I who take his meaning by his own express words. And seeing you charge me with subtlety, what subtlety is this of you to say, that you will prove your matter of the church, even from the beginning, promising to show your books therein; and when it comes to the showing, you are able to show none, and for want of proof slip into a bye matter, and yet faint in the proof thereof. In the sight of God, I declare you have not a pretence for your religion.

Chad. You shall be constrained to come to us at length whether you will or not.

Phil. Hold that argument fast; for it is the best you have, for you have nothing but violence.

The thirteenth Examination of Master Philpot, before the archbishop of York, and divers other bishops.

THE Thursday after, I was called, in the morning, before the archbishop of York, the bishop of Chichester, the bishop of Bath, and the bishop of London. The bishop of Chichester being first come, began to talk with me.

Chich. I am come of good will to talk with you; to instruct you what I can, to come to the catholic church; and to will you to mistrust your own judgment, and to learn first to have humility, and by the same to learn of others that are better learned than you, as they learned of such as were their betters before them.

Phil. We must all be taught of God, and I will with all humility learn of them that will inform me by God's word, what I have to do. I confess I have but little learning in respect of you, who both from your years and great exercise excel therein: but faith consists not only in learning, but in simplicity of believing that which God's word teaches. Therefore I shall be glad to hear both of your lordship, and of any other that God hath revealed unto by his word the true doctrine thereof, and to thank you, that it pleases you to take pains herein.

Chich. You take the first allegation amiss, as though all men should be taught by inspiration, and not by learning. How do we believe the gospel, but by the authority of the church, and because the same has allowed it?

Phil. St. Paul saith, " He learned not the gospel by men, neither of men, but by the revelation of Jesus Christ." Which is a sufficient proof that the gospel takes not its authority of man, but of God only.

Chich. St. Paul speaks but of his own knowledge how he came thereto.

Phil. Nay, he speaks of the gospel generally, " Which cometh not from man but from God," and that the church must only teach that which comes from God, and not man's precepts.

Chich. Doth not St. Augustine say: " I would not believe the gospel, if the authority of the church did not move me thereto?"

Phil. I grant that the authority of the church moves the unbelievers to believe, but yet the church gives not the word its authority: for the word hath its authority only from God, and not of men: men are but disposers thereof. For first the word has its being before the church, and the word is the foundation of the church, and the foundation first is sure, before the building thereon can be stedfast.

Chich. I perceive you mistake me. I speak of the knowledge of the gospel, and not of the authority: for by the church we have all knowledge of the gospel.

Phil. I confess that. " For faith cometh by hearing, and hearing by the word." And I acknowledge that God now appoints ordinary means for men to come to knowledge, and not miraculously, as in times past, yet we that are taught by men, must take heed that we learn nothing but that which was taught in the primitive church by revelation.

Here came in the archbishop of York, and the bishop of Bath, and after they had saluted one another, and communed awhile together, the archbishop of York called me unto them, saying:

York. Sir, we hearing that you are out of the way, are come of charity to inform you, and to bring you into the true faith, and to the catholic church again,—willing you first to have humility, and to be humble and willing to learn of your betters: for else we can do no good with you And God saith by his prophet, " On whom shall I rest but on the humble and meek, and such as tremble at my word." Now, if you will be so, we shall be glad to travail* with you.

Phil. I know that humility is the door whereby we enter unto Christ, and I thank his goodness I have entered in at the same door unto him; and with all humility I will hear whatsoever truth you shall speak unto me.

York. What are the matters you stand on, and require to be satisfied in?

Phil. My lord, and it shall please your grace, we were entered into a good matter before you came, of the church and how we should know the truth except by the church?

York. Indeed that is the head, we need to begin at. For the church being truly known, we shall sooner agree in the particular things.

Phil. If your lordships can prove the church of Rome to be the true catholic church, it will do much to persuade me toward that which you would have me incline unto.

York. Why, let us go to the definition of the church. What is it?

Phil. It is a congregation of people, dispersed through the world, agreeing together in the word of God, using the sacraments and all other things according to the same.

York. Your definition is of many words to no purpose.

Phil. I do not precisely define the church, but declare unto you what I think the church is.

York. Is the church visible or invisible?

Phil. It is both visible and invisible. The invisible church is of all the elect of God only: the visible consists of both good and bad, using all things in faith, according to God's word.

York. The church is a universal congregation of faithful people in Christ throughout the world: which this word catholic well expresses: for what is Catholic else? does it not signify Universal?

Phil. The church is defined by St. Austin to be called catholic for this cause: " The church is called catholic because it is thoroughly perfect, and halteth in nothing."

York. Nay, it is called catholic, because it is universally received of all christian nations for the most part.

Phil. The church was catholic in the apostles' time, yet

* Labour.

it was not universally received of the world; but because their doctrine which they had received of Christ was perfect; and appointed to be preached and received of the whole world. Therefore it is called the catholic faith, and all persons receiving the same, are to be counted the catholic church. And St. Austin, in another place, writes that the catholic church is that which believes aright.

York. If you will learn, I will show you by St. Austin writing against the Donatists, that he proves the catholic church by two principal points, which are, universality and succession of bishops in one apostolical see from time to time. Now thus I will make mine argument:

The church of Rome is univeral, and hath her succession of bishops from time to time. Ergo, it is the catholic church. How answer you to this argument?

Phil. I deny the antecedent, that the catholic church is only known by universality and succession of bishops.

York. I will prove it.—And with that he brought forth a book in which he had noted passages out of the doctors, and turned to his common-places therein "of the church," and recited one or two out of St. Austin, and specially out of his epistle written against the Donatists, adding, St. Austin manifestly proves that the Donatists were not the catholic church, because they had no succession of bishops in their opinion, neither universality: and the same force has St. Austin's argument against you.

Phil. My lord, I have weighed the force of that argument before now, and I perceive it makes nothing against me, neither does it come to your purpose. For I will stand to the trial of St. Austin for the approbation of the catholic church, whereof I am. For St. Austin speaks of universality joined with verity, and of faithful successors of Peter, before corruption came into the church. And so if you can deduce your argument to apply to the see of Rome now, as St. Austin might do in his time, I would say it might be of some force: otherwise not.

York. St. Austin proves the catholic church principally by succession of bishops, and therefore you understand not St. Austin. For what, I pray you, was the opinion of the Donatists against whom he wrote? Can you tell? What country were they of?

Phil. They were a certain sect of men, affirming among other heresies, that the dignity of the sacraments depended upon the worthiness of the minister: so that if the minister were good, the sacraments which he ministered were available, or else not.

Chich. That was their error, and they had none other but that.—And he read another authority of St. Austin out of a book which he brought, even to the same purpose that the other was.

Phil. I challenge St. Austin to be with me, thoroughly in this point, and will stand to his judgment, taking one place with another.

Chich. If you will not have the church to be certain: I pray you by whom will you be judged in matters of controversy.

Phil. I do not deny the church to be certain: but I deny that it is necessarily tied to any place, longer than that place abides in the word: and for all controversies the word ought to be judge.

Chich. But what if I take it one way, and you another, how then?

Phil. St. Austin shows a remedy for that: "That one place of the scripture ought to be understood by the more numerous."

York. How answer you to this argument?

Rome has a known succession of bishops: which your church has not. Ergo, It is the catholic church, and yours is not; because no such succession can be proved for your church.

Phil. I deny, my lord, that succession of bishops is an infallible point to know the church by: for there may be a succession of bishops known in a place, and yet there be no church, as at Antioch and at Jerusalem, and in other places, where the apostles abode as well as at Rome. But if you put to the succession of bishops, succession of doctrine also, as St. Austin does, I will grant it to be a good proof for the catholic church; but a local succession alone is not available.

York. You will have no church then, I see well.

Phil. Yes, my lord, I acknowledge the catholic church, as I am bound by my creed: but I cannot acknowledge a false church for the true.

Chich. Why, are there two catholic churches then?

Phil. No, I know there is but one catholic church, but there have been, and are at this present, those that take upon them the name of Christ and of his church, which are not so indeed, as it is written: "There are

Thirteenth examination.

that call themselves apostles, and are not so indeed, but the synagogue of Satan and liars." And now it is with us, as it was with the two women in Solomon's time, which lived together, and the one suppressed her child, and afterwards went about to challenge the true mother's child.

Chich. What a babbling is here with you now! I see you lack humility. You will go about to teach, and not to learn.

Phil. My lords, I must desire you to bear with my hasty speech: it is my infirmity of nature. All that I speak is from desire to learn, I would you understood all my mind, that I might be satisfied by you through better authority.

Chich. My lord, and it please your grace, turn the argument upon him, which you have made, and let him show the succession of the bishops of his church, as we can do. How say you, can you show the succession of bishops in your church from time to time? I tell you, this argument troubled Doctor Ridley so sorely, that he could never answer it: yet he was a man well learned, I dare say you will say so.*

Phil. He was a man so learned, that I was not worthy to carry his books.

Chich. I promise you he was never able to answer that. He was a man that I loved well, and he me: for he came unto me divers times being in prison, and conferred with me.

Phil. I wonder, my lord, you should make this argument which you would turn upon me, for the trial of my church whereof I am, or that you would make bishop Ridley so ignorant, that he was not able to answer it, since it is of no force. For behold, first I denied you, that local succession of bishops in one place, is a necessary point alone to prove the catholic church by, and that which I have denied, you cannot prove: and is it then reasonable that you should put me to the trial of that, which by you is unproved, and of no force to conclude against me?

Chich. I see, my lords, we do but lose our labours to reason with him: he takes himself to be better learned than we are.

Phil. I take upon me the name of no learning. I boast of no knowledge, but of faith and of Christ, and that I am bound undoubtedly to know as I am sure I do.

* "So ye say now, when ye would give him no leave nor time when he was alive to make his answers."—*Fox.*

Chich. These heretics take upon them to be sure of all things they stand in. You should say rather with humility, " I trust I know Christ," than that you are sure thereof.

Phil. Let him doubt of his faith that listeth. God give me always grace to believe that I am sure of true faith and favour in Christ.

Bath. How will you be able to answer heretics, but by the determination of the known catholic church?

Phil. I am able to answer all heretics by the word of God, and convince them by the same.

Chich. How arrogantly is that spoken? I dare not say so.

Phil. My lord, I pray you bear with me: for I am bold on the truth's side, and I speak somewhat by experience that I have had with heretics. I know the Arians are the subtlest that ever were, and yet I have manifest scriptures to beat them down with.

Chich. I perceive now you are the same manner of man I have heard of, who will not be satisfied by learning.

Phil. Alas, my lord, why do you say so? I do desire most humbly to be taught, if there is any better way that I should learn, and hitherto you have showed me no better: therefore I pray your lordship not to misjudge without a cause.

Bath. If you are the true catholic church, then will you hold the real presence of Christ in the sacrament, which the true church hath ever maintained.

Phil. And I my lord, with the true church hold the same in the due ministration of the sacrament: but I desire you, my lord, that there may be made a better conclusion, in our first matter, before we enter into any other: for if the church is proved, we shall soon agree in the rest. —In the meanwhile my lord of York was turning his book for more places to help forth his cause.

York. I have found at length a very notable place, which I have looked for all this while, of St. Augustine.

Chich. It is but folly, my lord, that your grace do read him any more places, for he esteems them not.

Phil. I esteem them, for as much as they are of force. As your lordship hears me deny no doctors you bring, but only require the true application of them, according to the writer's meaning, and as by his own words may be proved.

York. I will read him the place, and so make an end. —After he had read the senten he said,-- that by four

Thirteenth examination.

special points here St. Augustine proved the catholic church. The first is, by the consent of all nations; the second, by the apostolic see; the third, by universality; and the fourth, by this word catholic.

Chich. That is a notable place indeed, and it please your grace.

Phil. I pray you, my lord, of what church does St. Augustine write the same, of Rome, or not?

York. Yea, he writes it of the church of Rome.

Phil. I will lay with your lordship as much as I can make, it is not so: and let the book be seen.

Bath. What art thou able to lay, that hast nothing.

York. Doth he not make mention here of the apostolic see, whereby he means Rome?

Phil. That is very straitly interpreted my lord, as though the apostolic see had been nowhere else but at Rome. But let it be Rome, and yet shall you never verify the same, unless all the other conditions go therewith, which St. Augustine proceeds to show; whereof none except that of the apostolic see can now be verified of the church of Rome. For the faith which that see now maintains hath not the consent of all nations, neither hath had. Besides that, it cannot have the name of catholic, because it differeth from the catholic churches which the apostles planted, almost in all things.

York. Nay, he here proves the catholic church by universality: and how can you show your church to be universal fifty, or an hundred years ago?*

Phil. That is not material, neither any thing against St. Augustine. For my church, whereof I am, should be counted universal, though it were but in ten persons, because it agrees with the same that the apostles universally did plant.

York. I perceive you are an obstinate man in your opinion, and will not be taught: wherefore it is but lost labour to talk with you any longer: you are a member to be cut off.

Chich. I have heard of you before, how you troubled the good bishop of Winchester, and now I see in you what I have heard.

Phil. I trust you see no evil in me by this; I desire of you a sure ground to build my faith on, and if you show

---

* Christ's church ceaseth not to be his church, albeit in time of persecution it be hid sometimes in corners.—*Fox.*

me none, I pray you speak not ill of him that means well.

Chich. Thou art as impudent a fellow as I have communed withal.

Phil. That is spoken uncharitably my lord, to blaspheme him whom you cannot justly reprove.

Chich. Why you are not God. Blasphemy is counted a rebuke towards God, and not to man.

Phil. Yes, it may be as well verified of an infamy laid to the charge of a man speaking in God's cause; as you now lay it unto me for speaking freely the truth before God, to maintain your vain religion. You are void of all good ground. I perceive you are blind guides, and leaders of the blind, and therefore, as I am bound to tell you, very hypocrites, tyrannously persecuting the truth, which otherwise by just order you are able by no means to convince. Your own doctors and testimonies which you bring, are evidently against you, and yet you will not see the truth.

Chich. Have we this thanks for our good will in coming to instruct thee?

Phil. My lords, you must bear with me, since I speak in Christ's cause: and because his glory is defaced, and his people cruelly and wrongfully slain by you, because they will not consent to the dishonour of God, and to hypocrisy with you. If I told you not your fault, it should be required at my hands in the day of judgment. Therefore know you, ye hypocrites indeed, that it is the Spirit of God that tells you your sin, and not I. I care not, I thank God, for all your cruelty. God forgive it you, and give you grace to repent.—And so they departed.

Another talk the same day.

The same day at night before supper, the bishop sent for me into his chapel in presence of the archdeacon Harpsfield, Doctor Chadsey, and other his chaplains, and his servants; and said:

Lon. Master Philpot, I have by sundry means gone about to do you good, and I marvel you so little consider it: by my truth I cannot tell what to say to you. Tell me directly, whether you will be a conformable man or not, and whereupon you chiefly stand?

Phil. I have told your lordship oftentimes plain enough,

whereon I stand chiefly, requiring a sure probation of the church whereunto you call me.

Harps. St. Augustine writing against the Donatists, declares four special notes to know the church by: the consent of many nations, the faith of the sacraments confirmed by antiquity, succession of bishops, and universality.

Lon. I pray you, master archdeacon, bring the book hither, it is a notable place, let him see it. The book was brought and the bishop read it, demanding how I could answer the same.

Phil. My lord, I like St. Augustine's four points for the trial of the catholic church, whereof I am: for it can abide every point thereof, which yours cannot do.

Harps. Have not we succession of bishops in the see and church of Rome? Wherefore then do you deny our church to be the catholic church?

Phil. St. Augustine does not put succession of bishops alone, to be sufficient, but he adds the use of the sacraments according to antiquity, and doctrine universally taught and received of most nations, from the beginning of the primitive church, which your church is far from. But my church can avouch all these better than yours: therefore, by St. Augustine's judgment which you here bring, mine is the catholic church, and not yours.

Harps. Chad. It is but folly, my lord, for you to reason with him, for he is irrecoverable.

Phil. That is a good shift for you to run unto, when you are confounded in your own sayings, and have nothing else to say: you are evidently deceived, and yet will not see it when it is laid to your face.

Thus have I at large set forth as many of John Philpot's examinations and privy conferences, as are yet come to light, *being faithfully written with his own hand*. And although he was divers other times after this examined, both openly in the consistory at Paul's, and also secretly in the bishop's house: yet, what was there said, is not sufficiently known, either because Master Philpot was not himself suffered to write, or else for that his writings are by some kept close, and not brought forth otherwise than as the bishop's registrar has noted, whose handling of such matters, because, either for fear or for favour of his lord and master, it is but very slender; little light of any true and right meaning can be gathered, especially in behalf of the answerer. Howbeit, such as it is, such I thought good to put it forth, requiring the reader to judge thereof according to his answers in his former examinations.—*Fox.*

The last examinations of Master Philpot in open judgment, with his final condemnation, by bishop Bonner in the consistory at Paul's.

THE bishop having sufficiently taken his pleasure with Master Philpot in his private talks, and seeing his zealous, learned, and immutable constancy, thought it now high time to rid his hands of him, and therefore, on the thirteenth and fourteenth days of December, sitting judicially in the consistory at Paul's, he caused him to be brought thither before him and others, as it seemed, more for order's sake, than for any good affection to justice and right judgment. The effect as well of which two proceedings, as also of one other, had the eleventh day of the same month in his chapel, appears to be nearly the same. The bishop therefore first speaking to Philpot, said:

Lon. Master Philpot, amongst other things that were laid and objected unto you, these three things you were especially charged with.

The first is, That you being fallen from the unity of Christ's catholic church, refuse and will not come and be reconciled thereunto.

The second is, That you have blasphemously spoken against the sacrifice of the mass, calling it idolatry.

And the third is, That you have spoken against the sacrament of the altar, denying the real presence of Christ's body and blood to be in the same.

And, according to the will and pleasure of the synod legatine, you have been many times invited and required by me, to go from your errors and heresies, and to return to the unity of the catholic church, which if you will now willingly do, you shall be mercifully and gladly received, charitably used, and have all the favour I can show you. And now, to tell you true, it is assigned and appointed to give sentence against you, if you stand herein, and will not return. Wherefore, if you so refuse, I ask of you whether you have any cause that you can show, why I should not now give sentence against you?

Phil. Under protestation, and not to go from my appeal that I have made, and also not to consent to you as my competent judge, I say—Touching your first objection concerning the catholic church, I neither was nor am out of the same. And as touching the sacrifice of the mass, and the sacrament of the altar, I never spake against the same.*
And as concerning the pleasure of the synod, I say: that these twenty years I have been brought up in the faith of the true catholic church, which is contrary to your church, whereunto ye would have me come. And in that time I have been many times sworn, as well in the reign of king Henry the eighth, as in the reign of good king Edward his son, against the usurped power of the bishop of Rome, which oath I think that I am bound in my conscience to keep. But if you or any of the synod can, by God's word, persuade me that my said oath was unlawful, and that I am bound by God's law to come to your church, faith and religion, whereof you now are, I will gladly yield, agree, and be conformable unto you: otherwise not.

Bonner not being able with the help of all his learned doctors to accomplish this his offered condition, fell to persuading of him, as well by his accustomed vain promises, as also by bloody threatnings, to return to their church: to which he answered.

Phil. You and all others of your sort are hypocrites, and I would that all the world knew your hypocrisy, your tyranny, ignorance, and idolatry.

Upon these words, the bishop for that time dismissed him, commanding that on Monday the sixteenth day of the same month, between the hours of one and three in the afternoon, he should again be brought thither, there to have the definitive sentence of condemnation pronounced against him, if he remained then in his former constancy.

The last examination of Master John Philpot.

At which day and time, Master Philpot being there presented before the bishops of London, Bath, Worcester, and

* Here either the registrar belieth Master Philpot, or else he meant as not offending the law, thereby to be accused, for otherwise all his former examinations show that he spake against the sacrament of the altar.—*Fox.*

Lichfield, Bonner, bishop of London, began his talk in this manner.

Lon. My lords, Stokesley, my predecessor, when he gave sentence against a heretic, used to make this prayer which I will follow. And so he read it with a loud voice in Latin. To which Master Philpot said:

Phil. I would you would speak in English, that all men might hear and understand you: for Paul willeth that all things spoken in the congregation to edify, should be spoken in a tongue that all men might understand.

Whereupon the bishop did read it in English.

" O God, who showest the light of thy truth to them that are in error, to the intent that they may return into the way of righteousness. Grant unto all them that are admitted into the fellowship of Christ's religion, that they may refuse those things that are contrary to this name, and follow all such things as are agreeable to the same, through our Lord Jesus Christ.*

When he came to these words: " refuse those things that are contrary to this name," Philpot said:

Phil. Then they all must turn away from you: for you are enemies to that name, meaning Christ's name; and God save us from such hypocrites as would have things in a tongue that men cannot understand.

Lon. Whom do you mean?

Phil. You and all others that are of your generation and sect. And I am sorry to see you sit in the place that you now sit in, pretending to execute justice, and doing nothing but deceiving all men in this realm.

And then turning himself unto the people, he farther said: " Oh all you gentlemen, beware of these men (meaning the bishops) and all their doings, which are contrary unto the primitive church. And I would know of you, my lord, by what authority you do proceed against me?"

Lon. Because I am bishop of London.

Phil. Well, then you are not my bishop, nor have I offended in your diocese. And, moreover, I have appealed from you, and therefore, by your own law, you ought not to proceed against me, especially being brought hither from another place by violence.

Lon. Why, who sent you hither to me?

Phil. Doctor Story and Doctor Cooke, with others, the king and queen's commissioners. And, my lord, is it not

* The Collect for the third Sunday after Easter.

enough for you to worry your own sheep, but you must also meddle with other men's sheep?

Then the bishop delivered unto Philpot two books, one of the civil law, and the other of the canon, out of the which, he would have proved that he had authority to proceed against him as he did. Master Philpot then perusing the same, and seeing the small and slender proof that was there alleged, said unto the bishop.

Phil. I perceive your law and divinity is all one; for you have knowledge in neither of them: and I would that you knew your own ignorance: but you dance in a net, and think that no man sees you.—Hereupon they had much talk, but what it was, it is not yet known. At last Bonner spake unto him and said:

Lon. Philpot, as concerning your objections against my jurisdiction, you shall understand that both the civil and canon laws make against you. And as for your appeal, it is not allowed in this case. For so it is written in the law.

Phil. My lord, it appears by your interpretation of the law, that you have no knowledge therein, nor that you understand the law.

Hereupon the bishop recited a law of the Romans, that it was not lawful for a Jew to keep a christian man in captivity, and to use him as his slave, laying then to the said Philpot's charge, that he did not understand the law, but did like a Jew. Whereunto Philpot answered:

Phil. No, I am no Jew: but you my lord are a Jew. For you profess Christ and maintain antichrist: you profess the gospel, and maintain superstition, and you are able to charge me with nothing.

Lon. and other bishops. With what can you charge us?

Phil. You are enemies to all truth, and all your doings are naught, full of idolatry, except in the article of the Trinity.

Whilst they were thus debating the matter, there came thither Sir William Garret, knight, then mayor of London, Sir Martin Bowes, knight, and Thomas Leigh, then sheriffs of the same city, and sat down with the said bishops in the said consistory, where and what time bishop Bonner spake these words.

Lon. Philpot, before the coming of my lord mayor, because I would not enter with you into the matter wherewith I have heretofore, and now intend to charge you withal; until his coming, I did rehearse unto you a prayer both in English and in Latin, which bishop Stokesley, my predecessor, used when he intended to proceed to give sentence against a heretic.

And then Bonner again read the said prayer, both in English and also in Latin; which being ended, he spake again unto him, and said:

Lon. Philpot, amongst other I have to charge you specially with three things.

First, whereas you have fallen from the unity of Christ's catholic church, you have thereon been invited and required, not only by me, but also by many and divers other catholic bishops, and other learned men, to return and come again to the same; and also you have been offered by me, that if you would return and confess your errors and heresies, you should be mercifully received, and have as much favour as I could show unto you.

The second is, that you have blasphemously spoken against the sacrifice of the mass, calling it idolatry and abomination.

And thirdly, that you have spoken and holden against the sacrament of the altar, denying the real presence of Christ's body and blood to be in the same.

This being spoken, the bishop recited unto him an exhortation in English, the tenour and form whereof is this:

" Master Philpot, this is to be told you, that if you, not being yet reconciled to the unity of the catholic church, from whence you did fall in the time of the late schism here in this realm of England, against the apostolic see of Rome; will now heartily and obediently be reconciled to the unity of the same catholic church, professing and promising to observe and keep to the best of your power the faith and christian religion observed and kept of all faithful people of the same;—and, moreover, if you, who heretofore, especially in the years of our Lord 1553, 1554, 1555, or in one of them, have offended and trespassed grievously against the sacrifice of the mass, calling it idolatry and abominable, and likewise have offended and trespassed against the sacrament of the altar, denying the real presence of Christ's body and blood to be there in the sacrament of the altar; affirming also, material bread and material wine to be in the sacrament of the altar, and not the substance of the body and blood of Christ: if you, I say, will be reconciled, and will forsake your heresies and errors, being heretical and damnable, and will allow also the sacrament of the mass, you shall be mercifully received and charitably used, with as much favour as may be. If not, you shall be reputed, taken, and judged for a heretic (as you are indeed). Now choose what you will do: you are counselled herein friendly and favourably."

The bishop's exhortation being ended, Philpot turned himself unto the lord-mayor, and said:

Phil. To you, my lord mayor, bearing the sword, I speak. I am glad now to stand before that authority which has defended the gospel and the truth of God's word; but I am sorry to see that the authority which represents the king and queen's persons should now be changed, and be at the commandment of antichrist. And you, speaking to the bishops, pretend to be the fellows of the apostles of Christ, and yet are very antichrists and deceivers of the people; and I am glad that God has given me power to stand here this day, and to declare and defend my faith, which is founded on Christ.

Therefore, as touching your first objection, I say that I am of the catholic church, which I never was out of, and that your church (which you pretend to be the catholic church) is the church of Rome, and so the Babylonian and not the catholic church—of that church I am not.

As touching your second objection, which is, that I spake against the sacrifice of the mass, I say, that I have not spoken against the true sacrifice, but I have spoken against your private masses which you use in corners, which is blasphemy to the true sacrifice; for your sacrifice daily reiterated, is a blasphemy against Christ's death, and it is a lie of your own invention. And that abominable sacrifice which ye set upon the altar, and use in your private masses instead of the living sacrifice, is idolatry, and ye shall never prove it by God's word; therefore ye have deceived the people with that your sacrifice of the mass, which ye make a masking.*

Thirdly, where you lay to my charge that I deny the body and blood of Christ to be in the sacrament of the altar—I cannot tell what altar ye mean, whether it be the altar of the cross, or the altar of stone. And if ye call it the sacrament of the altar in respect of the altar of stone, then I defy your Christ: for it is a rotten Christ.†

* A pretence or feigned show   † A piece of bread

And as touching your transubstantiation, I utterly deny it; for it was brought up first by a pope. Now as concerning your offer made from the synod, which is gathered together in antichrist's name, prove to me that it is of the catholic church, which you shall never do, and I will follow you, and do as you would have me. But ye are idolaters, and daily commit idolatry. Ye are also traitors; for in your pulpits you rail upon good kings, as king Henry, and king Edward his son, who have stood against the usurped power of the bishop of Rome; against whom also I have taken an oath, which if you can show me by God's law that I have taken unjustly, I will then yield unto you. But I pray God to turn the king and queen's hearts from your synagogue and church, for you do abuse that good queen.

Here the bishop of Coventry and Lichfield began to show where the true church was, saying:

Cov. The true catholic church is set upon a high hill.

Phil. Yea, at Rome, which is the Babylonian church.

Cov. No: in our true catholic church are the apostles, evangelists, and martyrs; but before Martin Luther, there was no apostle, evangelist, or martyr of your church.

Phil. Will you know the cause why? Christ prophesied that in the latter days there should come false prophets and hypocrites as you are.

Cov. Your church of Geneva, which you call the catholic church, is that which Christ prophesied of.

Phil. I allow the church of Geneva, and the doctrine of the same; for it is catholic and apostolic, and follows the doctrine which the apostles preached; and the doctrine taught and preached in king Edward's days, was also according to the same. And are you not ashamed to persecute me and others for your church's sake, which is Babylonian, and contrary to the **true** catholic church?

After this, they had great conference together out of the scriptures, and also out of the doctors. But when Bonner saw that by learning they were not able to convince Master Philpot, he thought then by his defamations to bring him out of credit; and therefore, turning himself unto the lord mayor of London, he brought forth a knife, and a bladder full of powder, and said

Lon. My lord, this man had a roasted pig brought unto him, and this knife was put secretly between the skin and the flesh thereof, and so was it sent him, being in prison.

And also this powder was sent unto him, under pretence that it was good and comfortable for him to eat or drink; which powder was only to make ink to write with. For when his keeper perceived it, he took it, and brought it unto me. Which when I saw, I thought it had been gunpowder, and thereupon I put fire to it, but it would not burn. Then I took it for poison, and so gave it to a dog, but it was not so. Then I took a little water, and it made as fair ink as ever I wrote with. Therefore, my lord, you may understand what a naughty fellow this is.

Phil. Ah, my lord, have you nothing else to charge me withal but these trifles, seeing I stand upon life and death? Doth the knife in the pig prove the church of Rome to be a catholic church?

Then the bishop brought forth a certain instrument containing articles and questions, agreed upon both in Oxford and Cambridge. Also he exhibited two books in print; the one was the catechism made in king Edward's days, anno 1552; the other, concerning the true report of the disputation in the convocation-house, mention whereof is before made.

Moreover, he brought forth and laid to Master Philpot's charge two letters; the one touching Bartlet Green, the other containing godly exhortations and comforts; both which were written unto him by some of his godly friends.

A letter exhibited by Bonner, written by some friend of Master Philpot, and sent to him concerning the handling of Master Green in Bonner's house at London.

You shall understand that Master Green came unto the bishop of London on Sunday last, where he was courteously received; for what policy the sequel declareth. His entertainment for a day or two, was to dine at my lord's own table, or else to have his meat from thence. During those days he lay in Doctor Chadsey's chamber, and was examined, although the bishop had earnestly and faithfully promised many right worshipful men, who were suitors for him, but to him unknown, that he in no case should be examined; and before which, Master Fecknam would have had him in his friendly custody, if he would have desired to have conferred with him, which he utterly refused. And when the bishop objected against him singularity and obstinacy, his answer thereunto was: "To avoid all suspicion thereof, although I myself am young, and utterly unlearned in respect of the learned, (and yet I understand, I thank my Lord), yet let me have such books as I shall require; and if I, by God's Spirit, do not thereby answer all your books and objections contrary thereto, I will assent to you." Whereunto the bishop and his clergy assented, permitting him at first to have such books; they at sundry times have reasoned with him, and have found him so strong in the scripture and godly fathers, that since then they have not only taken from him such liberty of books, but all other books, not leaving him so much as the New Testament. Since then they have baited and used him most cruelly. This Master Fecknam reported; saying further, that he never heard the like young man, and so perfect. What shall become further of him God knows; but death, I think, for he remains more and more willing to die, as I understand. Concerning your bill, I shall confer with others therein, knowing that the same court is able to redress the same.* And yet I think it will not be reformed, for I know few or none that dare or will speak therein, or prefer the same, because it concerns spiritual things. Notwithstanding, I will ascertain you thereof: committing you to the Holy Ghost, and may he keep you, and us all, as his.

Your own, &c.

The copy of another letter, written by the faithful and christian-hearted lady, the lady Vane, to Master Philpot, exhibited likewise by bishop Bonner.

HEARTY thanks rendered unto you, my well beloved in Christ, for the books you sent me, wherein I find great consolations; and according to the doctrine thereof, do prepare my cheeks to the strikers, and my womanish back to their burdens of reproof, and so, in the strength of my God, I trust to leap over the wall. For his sweetness overcometh me daily, and maketh all these apothecary drugs of the world, even medicine-like in my mouth. For the continuance whereof, I beseech thee, my dear fellow soldier, make thy faithful prayer for me, that I may with a

* This bill was the supplication, to be offered up in the parliament in behalf of Philpot.—*Fox.*

strong and gladsome conscience finish my course, and obtain the reward, though it is not at all due to my work. I am not content that you so often gratify me with thanks for that which is none worthy—but duty on my part, and small relief to you. But if you would love me so much, that I might supply your lacks, then would I think you believed my offers to be such as agreed with my heart. And for the short charges you speak of, the means are not so pleasant, if God (in whom my trust is) will otherwise prepare; but Solomon saith, "All things here have their time:" you to-day, and I to-morrow, and so the end of Adam's line is soon run out: the mighty God give us his grace, that during this time his glory be not defaced through our weakness. Because you desire to show yourself a worthy soldier, if need so require, I will supply your request for the scarf you wrote of,* that you may present my handy-work before your Captain, that I be not forgotten in the odours of incense, which our beloved Christ offereth for his own; to whom I bequeath both our bodies and souls.

Your own in the Lord.

The bishops also brought forth a supplication made by Philpot unto the high court of parliament, mentioned in the first of these letters, the copy whereof here follows.

To the king and queen's majesties' highness, the lords spiritual and temporal, and the commons of this present parliament assembled.

In most humble wise complains unto this honourable court of parliament John Philpot, clerk, that whereas there was by the queen's highness a parliament called in the first year of her gracious reign, and after the old custom, a convocation of the clergy, your suppliant then being one of the said convocation-house, and matters there rising upon the using of the sacraments, did dispute in the same, knowing that there all men had and have had free speech, and ought not to be afterwards troubled for anything there spoken. And yet, notwithstanding, not long after the said parliament, your said suppliant, without any act or matter,

* Some clothes for his burning.

was commanded to prison to the King's Bench by the late lord-chancellor, where he hath remained ever since, until now of late that my lord, the bishop of London, hath sent for your said suppliant to examine him (being none of his diocese) upon certain matters, wherein they would have your orator to declare his conscience; which the said bishop saith he hath authority to do, by reason of an act of parliament made in the first and second years of the king and queen's majesties' reigns, for the reviving of three statutes made against them that hold any opinion against the catholic faith; whereby he affirms that every ordinary may, by virtue of his office, examine every man's conscience. And as your said orator hath and doth refuse that the said bishop of London has any authority over your said orator, for that he is not his diocesan, nor hath he published, preached, or held any opinion against the catholic faith, notwithstanding which, the said bishop of London detains him in the coalhouse, in the stocks, without either bed, or any other thing to lie upon, but straw. And as your said orator cannot appeal for relief from the said bishop to any other judge, but the same bishop may refuse the same by their law, and therefore has no succour and help, but by this high court of parliament, for the explanation of the said act. Therefore may it please you, that it may be enacted by the king and queen's majesties, the lords spiritual and temporal, and the commons of this present parliament assembled, and by the authority of the same, that no bishop or ordinary shall commit or detain in prison any person or persons suspected as opposers of the catholic faith, except he or they have spoken, written, or done some manifest act against the catholic faith, and the same be lawfully proved against every such person and persons, by the testimony of two lawful witnesses, to be brought before the said person or persons so accused, before he or they shall either be committed to prison, or convicted for any such offence or offences; the said former statute, made in the said first and second year of our said sovereign lord and lady, notwithstanding. Whereby your said orator shall not only be set at liberty, and divers others now remaining in prison, but also the blood of divers of the queen's majesty's true and faithful subjects preserved.*

* This supplication, and the two letters which precede it, have been referred to in the eleventh examination.

The Condemnation of the worthy martyr of God, John Philpot.

THESE books, letters, supplications, and other matters being thus read, the bishop demanded of him, if the book intituled, " The true report of the disputation, &c." were his penning or not? Whereunto Philpot answered, that it was a good and true book, and of his own penning and setting forth.

The bishops waxing now weary, and being not able to convince and overcome him, by any sufficient ground, either of God's word or of the true ancient catholic fathers, fell to fair and flattering speech, to persuade him; promising that if he would revoke his opinions, and come home again to their Romish and Babylonian church, he should not only be pardoned that which was past, but also they would, with all favour and cheerfulness of heart, receive him again as a true member thereof. Which words, when Bonner saw they would take no effect, he demanded of Master Philpot, whether he had any just cause to allege why he should not condemn him as a heretic. " Well," quoth Master Philpot: " your idolatrous sacrament which you have found out, ye would fain defend, but ye cannot, nor ever shall."

In the end, the bishop, seeing his immovable stedfastness in the truth, pronounced openly the sentence of condemnation against him. While he was reading whereof, Philpot said, I thank God that I am a heretic out of your cursed church: I am no heretic before God. But may God bless you, and give you grace to repent your wicked doings; and let all men beware of your bloody church.

Moreover, whilst Bonner was about the middle of the sentence, the bishop of Bath pulled him by the sleeve and said: " My lord, my lord, know of him first, whether he will recant or not?" Then Bonner said, full like himself. " Oh let me alone:" and so read forth the sentence.

And when he had done, he delivered Philpot to the sheriffs: and so two officers brought him through the bishop's house into Paternoster-row, and there his servant met him, and when he saw him, he said, " Ah, dear master!"

Then Master Philpot said to his man; " Content

thyself I shall do well enough: for thou shalt see me again."

And so the officers thrust him away, and took his master to Newgate: and as he went, he said to the people; " Ah, good people, blessed be God for this day." And so the officers delivered him to the keeper. Then his man tried to go in after his master, and one of the officers said unto him: " Hence, fellow, what wouldst thou have?" And he said, " I would go speak with my master." Master Philpot then turned about, and said to him, " To-morrow you shall speak with me."

Then the under keeper said to Master Philpot: " Is this your man? And he said, " Yea." So he allowed his man to go in with him, and Master Philpot and his man were turned into a little chamber on the right hand, and there remained a little time, until Alexander, the chief keeper, came unto him: who, at his entrance, greeted him with these words: " Ah," said he, " hast not thou done well to bring thyself hither?" Well, said Master Philpot, I must be content, for it is God's appointment; and I shall desire you to let me have your gentle favour; for you and I have been of old acquaintance. " Well," said Alexander, " I will show thee gentleness and favour, so thou wilt be ruled by me." Then said Master Philpot, " I pray you show me what you would have me do."

He said, " If you would recant, I will show you any pleasure I can." " Nay," said Philpot, " I will never recant that which I have spoken whilst I have my life, for it is most certain truth: and in witness hereof, I will seal it with my blood." Then Alexander said; " This is the saying of the whole pack of you heretics." Whereupon he commanded him to be set upon the block, and as many irons fastened upon his legs as he might bear, because he would not follow his wicked mind.

Then the clerk told Alexander, that Master Philpot had given his man money. And Alexander said to his man: " What money hath thy master given thee?" His man said: " My master hath given me none" " No," said Alexander: " hath he given thee none? that will I know, for I will search thee." " Do with me what you 'ist, and search me all you can," said his servant: " he has given me a token or two, to send to his friends, as to his brother and sisters." " Ah," said Alexander, to Master Philpot, " Thou art a maintainer of heretics: thy man should have gone to some of thine affinity, but he shall be known well enough." "Nay," said Master Philpot, " I send it to my friends; there he is, let him make answer to it. But, good Master Alexander, be so much my friend that these irons may be taken off." "Well," said Alexander, " give me my fee, and I will take them off: if not, thou shalt wear them still."

Then said Master Philpot, " Sir, what is your fee? he said four pounds was his fee. " Ah," said Master Philpot, " I have not so much: I am but a poor man, and I have been long in prison." " What wilt thou give me then?" said Alexander. " Sir," said he, " I will give you twenty shillings, and that I will send my man for, or else I will pawn my gown: for the time is not long, I am sure, that I shall be with you; for the bishop said to me that I should be soon despatched."

Then said Alexander unto him, " What is that to me?" and with that he departed from him, and commanded him to be had into limbo;* and so his commandment was fulfilled: but before he could be taken from the block, the clerk would have a groat.

Then one Witterenee, steward of the house, took Master Philpot on his back, and carried him down, his man knew not whither. Wherefore Master Philpot said to his man; " Go to master sheriff, and show him how I am used, and desire master sheriff to be good unto me:" and so his servant went straightway, and took an honest man with him.

And when they came to the sheriff, which was Master Macham, and showed him how Master Philpot was handled in Newgate, the sheriff hearing this, took his ring off from his finger, and delivered it unto that honest man which came with Master Philpot's man, and bade him go unto Alexander, the keeper, and command him to take off his irons, and to handle him more gently, and to give his man again that which he had taken from him. And when they came again to the said Alexander, and told their message from the sheriff, Alexander took the ring, and said: " Ah, I perceive that master sheriff is a bearer with him, and all such heretics as he is, therefore, to-morrow, I will show it to his betters." Yet, at ten of the clock, he went to Master Philpot where he lay, and took

* A dungeon.

off his irons, and gave him such things as he had taken before from his servant.

Upon Tuesday, at supper, being the 17th day of December, there came a messenger from the sheriffs, and bade Master Philpot make himself ready; for the next day he should suffer, and be burned at a stake with fire. Master Philpot answered and said, " I am ready: God grant me strength, and a joyful resurrection." And so he went into his chamber, and poured out his spirit unto the Lord God, giving him most hearty thanks that he of his mercy had made him worthy to suffer for his truth.

In the morning the sheriffs came according to the order, about eight o'clock, and called for him, and he most joyfully came down unto them. And there his man met him, and said : " Ah, dear master, farewell." His master said unto him, " Serve God, and he will help thee." And so Master Philpot went with the sheriffs unto the place of execution ; and when he was entering into Smithfield, the way was foul, and two officers took him up to bear him to the stake. Then he said merrily, " What, will you make me a pope? I am content to go to my journey's end on foot." But, at first coming into Smithfield, he kneeled down there, saying these words: " I will pay my vows in thee, O Smithfield !"

And when he was come to the place of suffering, he kissed the stake, and said: " Shall I disdain to suffer at this stake, seeing my Redeemer did not refuse to suffer a most vile death upon the cross for me ?" And then, with an obedient heart, full meekly he said the cvi. cvii. and cviii. psalms: and when he had made an end of all his prayers, he said to the officers: " What have you done for me ?" and every one of them declared what they had done: and he gave to each of them money.

Then they bound him to the stake, and set fire to that constant martyr; who, the 18th day of December, in the midst of the fiery flames, yielded his soul into the hands of the almighty God, and like a lamb gave up his breath, his body being consumed into ashes.

Thus hast thou, gentle reader, the life and doings of this learned and worthy soldier of the Lord, JOHN PHILPOT: with all his examinations that came to our hands: first penned and written with his own hand, being marvellously preserved from the sight and hands of his enemies: who, by all means sought not only to stop him from all writing, but also to spoil and deprive him of that which he had written. For which cause he was many times stripped and searched in the prison by his keeper: but yet so happily these his writings were conveyed, and hid in places about him, or else his keeper's eyes so blinded, that, notwithstanding all this malicious purpose of the bishops, they are yet remaining, and are come to light.

A prayer to be said at the stake by all them that God shall account worthy to suffer for his sake.

Merciful God and Father, to whom our Saviour Christ approached in his fear and need by reason of death, and found comfort: Gracious God, and most bounteous Christ, on whom Stephen called in his extreme need, and received strength: most benign Holy Spirit, who, in the midst of all crosses and death, didst comfort the apostle St. Paul, with more consolations in Christ, than he felt sorrows and terrors: have mercy upon me, miserable, vile, and wretched sinner, who now draw near the gates of death, deserved both in soul and body eternally, by reason of manifold, horrible, old and new transgressions, which to thine eyes, O Lord, are open and known. O be merciful unto me, for the bitter death and bloodshedding of thine own only Son Jesus Christ. And though thy justice requires, in respect of my sins, that now thou shouldst not hear me, but measure me with the same measure with which I have measured thy Majesty, and contemned thy daily calls; yet let thy mercy, which is over all thy works, and wherewith the earth is filled; let thy mercy, prevail toward me, through and for the mediation of Christ our Saviour. And for whose sake since it hath pleased thee to bring me forth now as one of his witnesses, and a record-bearer of thy verity and truth taught by him, to give my life therefore; to which dignity I do acknowledge, O God, that there was never any so unworthy and so unmeet, no not the thief that hanged with Christ on the cross: I most humbly, therefore, pray thee that thou wouldst accordingly, aid, help, and assist me with thy strength and heavenly grace; that with

Christ thy Son I may find comfort; with Stephen I may see thy presence, and gracious power; and with Paul and all others, who for thy name sake have suffered affliction and death, I may find thy gracious consolations so present with me, that I may, by my death, glorify thy holy name, propagate and ratify thy verity, comfort the hearts of the heavy, confirm thy church in thy verity, convert some that are to be converted, and so depart forth out of this miserable world, where I do nothing but daily heap sin upon sin, and so enter into the fruition of thy blessed mercy: whereof now give and increase in me a lively trust, sense, and feeling, whereby the terrors of death, the torments of fire, the pangs of sin, the darts of satan, and the dolours of hell may never depress me, but may be driven away through the working of that most gracious Spirit: which now plenteously endue me withal, that through the same Spirit I may offer, as I now desire to do in Christ and by him, myself wholly, soul and body, to be a lively sacrifice, holy and acceptable in thy sight. Dear Father, whose I am, and always have been, even from my mother's womb, yea even before the world was made, to whom I commend myself, soul and body, family, and friends, country and all the whole church, yea even my very enemies, according to thy good pleasure, beseeching thee entirely to give once more to this realm of England, the blessing of thy word again, with godly peace, to the teaching and setting forth of the same. O dear Father, now give me grace to come unto thee. Purge and so purify me by this fire in Christ's death and passion through thy Spirit, that I may be a burnt offering of a sweet smell in thy sight, who livest and reignest with the Son and the Holy Ghost, now and evermore world without end. Amen.

LETTERS

OF

THAT HEARTY AND ZEALOUS MAN OF GOD,

JOHN PHILPOT,

ARCHDEACON OF WINCHESTER;

Who, besides the great tyranny and torments which he suffered
in Bonner's blind Coalhouse, and his other painful
imprisonments, was also most cruelly
martyred for the testimony
of the Lord Jesus,
The 18th day of December, 1555.

LETTERS.

LETTER I.

A letter sent to the christian congregation, exhorting them to refrain from the idolatrous service of the papists, and to serve God with a pure and undefiled conscience after his word.

It is a lamentable thing to behold at this present time in England, the faithless departing both of men and women from the true knowledge and use of Christ's sincere religion, which they have been taught so plentifully, and do know; their own consciences bearing witness to the verity thereof.

If that earth is cursed of God, which, receiving moisture and pleasant dews from heaven, brings not forth fruit accordingly, how much more grievous judgment shall such persons receive, who, having received from the Father of heaven the perfect knowledge of his word by the ministry thereof, do not show forth God's worship according to the same!

If the Lord will require in the day of judgment a godly usury of all manner of talents, which he lendeth unto men and women, how much more will he require the same for his pure religion revealed unto us, which is of all other talents the chiefest, and most pertaining to our exercise in this life, if we hide the same in a napkin, and set it not forth to the usury of God's glory, and edifying of his church by true confession! God has kindled the bright light of his gospel, which in times past was suppressed and hid under the vile ashes of man's traditions; and has caused the brightness thereof to shine in our hearts, to the end that the same might shine before men to the honour of his name.

It is not only given us to believe, but also to confess and declare what we believe, by our outward conversation. For, as St. Paul writes to the Romans, "The belief of the heart justifieth, and to acknowledge with the mouth maketh a man safe." It is all one before God, not to believe at all, and not to show forth the lively works of our belief. For Christ saith, "Either make the tree good and its fruits good, or else make the tree evil and its fruits evil, because a good tree bringeth forth good fruits, as an evil tree doth evil fruits." So that the person which knoweth his master's will and doth it not, shall be beaten with many stripes. And, "not all they which say, Lord, Lord, shall enter into the kingdom of God, but he that doeth the will of the Father." And, "Whosoever in the time of trial is ashamed of me, saith Christ, and of my words, of him the Son of man will be ashamed before his Father."

After we have built ourselves into the true church of God, it has pleased him, by giving us over into the hands of the wicked synagogues, to prove our building, and to have it known, as well to the world as to ourselves, that we have been wise builders into the true church of God upon the rock, and not on the sand; and, therefore, now the tempest is risen, and the storms do mightily blow against us, that we might, notwithstanding, stand upright, and be firm in the Lord, to his honour and glory, and to our eternal felicity. There is no new thing happened unto us; for with such tempests and dangerous weather the church of God has continually been exercised. Now once again, as the prophet Haggai tells us, "The Lord shaketh the earth, that those might abide for ever which are not overthrown."

Therefore, my dearly beloved, be stable and unmoveable in the word of God, and in the faithful observation thereof, and let no man deceive you with vain words, saying, that "you may keep your faith to yourselves, and dissemble with antichrist, and so live at rest and quietness in the world, as most men do, yielding to necessity." This is the wisdom of the flesh; but the wisdom of the flesh is death and enmity to God, as our Saviour for example aptly did declare in Peter, who exhorted Christ not to go to Jerusalem to celebrate the passover, and there to be slain, but counselled him to look better to himself.

Likewise, the world would not have us forsake it, nor associate ourselves to the true church, which is the body of Christ, whereof we are lively members, and use the sacraments after God's word with the danger of our lives. But we must learn to answer the world, as Christ did

Peter, and say, "Go behind me, Satan, thou savourest no the things of God. Shall I not drink of the cup which the Father giveth me?" For it is better to be afflicted and slain in the church of God, than to be counted the son of the king in the synagogue of false religion. Death for righteousness is not to be abhorred, but rather to be desired, for it assuredly brings with it the crown of everlasting glory. These bloody executioners do not persecute Christ's martyrs, but crown them with everlasting felicity; we were born into this world to be witnesses unto the truth, both learned and unlearned.

Now, since the time is come that we must show our faith, and declare whether we will be God's servants in righteousness and holiness, as we have been taught and are bound to follow, or else with hypocrisy serve unrighteousness, let us take good heed, that we are found faithful in the Lord's covenant, and true members of his church, in the which through knowledge we are ingrafted; from the which if we fall by transgression with the common sort of people, it will more straitly be required of us, than many yet make account of. We cannot serve two masters; we may not halt on both sides, and think to please God; we must be fervent in God's cause, or else he will cast us out from him. For, by the first commandment, we are commanded to love God with all our heart, with all our mind, with all our power and strength; but they are manifest transgressors of this commandment, who with their heart, mind, or bodily power communicate with a strange religion, contrary to the word of God, in the papistical synagogue, which calls itself the church, and is not. As greatly do they offend God now who so do, as the Israelites did in times past by forsaking Jerusalem, the true church of God, and by going to Bethel to serve God in a congregation of their own setting up, and after their own imaginations and traditions; for doing which God utterly destroyed all Israel, as almost all the prophets do testify. This happened unto them for our ensample, that we might beware not to have any fellowship with any like congregation to our destruction.

God hath one catholic church dispersed throughout the world, and, therefore, we are taught in our creed to believe one catholic church, and to have communion therewith which catholic church is grounded upon the foundation of the prophets and of the apostles, and upon none other, as

St. Paul witnesses to the Ephesians. Therefore, wheresoever we perceive any people worship God truly after his word, there we may be certain the church of Christ to be; unto which we ought to associate ourselves, and to desire, with the prophet David, to praise God in the midst of his church. But if we behold, through the iniquity of the times, segregations* to be made with counterfeit religion, otherwise than the word of God teaches, we ought then, if we are required to be companions thereof, to say again with David, "I have hated the synagogue of the malignant, and will not sit with the wicked." In the Revelation, the church of Ephesus is highly commended, because she tried such as said they were apostles, and were not indeed, and therefore would not abide the company of them. Further, God commanded his people, by the mouth of his prophet Amos, that they should not seek Bethel, neither enter into Gilgal, where idolatry was used. Also, we must consider that our bodies are the temple of God, and whosoever, as St. Paul teaches, profanes the temple of God, him the Lord will destroy. May we then take the temple of Christ, and make it the member of an harlot? All strange religion and idolatry is counted as whoredom by the prophets, and more detestable in the sight of God, than the adultery of the body.

Therefore, the princes of the earth, in the Revelation of John, are said to commit fornication when they are in love with false religion, and follow the same. How then, by any means, may a christian man think it tolerable to be present at the popish private mass, which is the very profanation of the sacrament of the body and blood of Christ, and at other idolatrous worshippings and rites, which are not after the word of God, but rather to the derogation thereof, by setting man's traditions above God's precepts; since God by his word judges all strange religion, which is not according to his institution, as fornication and adultery?

Some fondly think that the presence of the body is not material, so that the heart does not consent to their wicked doings. But such persons little consider what St. Paul wrote to the Corinthians, commanding them to glorify God in body as well as in soul.

Moreover, we can do no greater injury to the true church of Christ, than to seem to have forsaken her, and

* Separations.

to disallow her, by cleaving to her adversary; whereby it appears to others who are weak, that we allow the same; and so, contrary to the word, give a great offence to the church of God, and outwardly slander, as much as men may, the truth of Christ. But woe be unto him by whom any such offence cometh. Better it were for him to have a millstone tied about his neck, and to be cast into the bottom of the sea. Such are traitors to the truth, like unto Judas, who with a kiss betrayed Christ.

Our God is a jealous God, and cannot be content that we should be of any other than of that unspotted church, whereof he alone is the head, and wherein he has planted us by baptism. This jealousy which God has towards us, will cry for vengeance in the day of vengeance, against all such as now have such large consciences, as to do that which is contrary to God's glory, and the sincerity of his word; except they do repent in time, and cleave inseparably to the gospel of Christ, how much soever at this present time both men and women in their own corrupt judgment do flatter themselves otherwise. God willeth us to judge uprightly, and to allow and follow that which is holy and acceptable in his sight, and to abstain from all manner of evil; and, therefore, Christ commands us, in the gospel, to beware of the leaven of the Pharisees, which is hypocrisy.

St. Paul, in his epistle to the Hebrews, saith, "If any man withdraw himself from the faith, his soul shall have no pleasure in him;" therefore he saith also, "that we are not such as withdraw ourselves unto perdition, but we belong unto faith, for the attainment of life." St. John, in the Revelation, tells us plainly, that "none of those who are written in the book of life receive the mark of the beast," which is the mark of the papistical synagogue; either in their foreheads, or else in their hands, that is, apparently or obediently.

St. Paul, to the Philippians, affirms, that "we may not have any fellowship with the works of darkness, but, in the midst of this wicked and froward generation, we ought to shine like lights, upholding the word of truth." Further, he says, that we may "not touch any unclean thing;" which signifies that our outward conversation in foreign* things ought to be pure and undefiled, as well as the inward, that with a clean spirit and rectified body we

* Strange, unusual.

might serve God justly in holiness and righteousness all the days of our life.

Finally, in the eighteenth chapter of the Revelation, God biddeth us plainly to " depart from the Babylonical synagogue, and not to be partakers of her trespass." St. Paul. to the Thessalonians, commands us in the name of the Lord Jesus Christ to withdraw ourselves from every brother that walketh inordinately, and not according to the institution which he received of him.

Ponder, therefore, well, good brethren and sisters, these scriptures, which are written for your erudition and reformation, whereof one jot is not written in vain They are utterly against all counterfeit collusion to be used by us with the papists in their fantastical religion, and are adversaries to all them that have such light consciences in so doing. And if they do not agree with this adversary, I mean the word of God, which is contrary to their attempts, he will, as it is signified in the gospel, deliver them to the Judge, which is Christ; and the Judge will deliver them to the executioner, that is, to the devil; and the devil will commit them to the horrible prison of hell-fire, where is the portion of all hypocrites, with sulphur and brimstone, with wailing and gnashing of teeth, world without end.

But yet many will say, for their vain excuse, God is merciful, and his mercy is over all. But the scripture teaches us, that cursed is he that sinneth upon hope of forgiveness. Truth it is that the mercy of God is over all his works, and yet only upon such as fear him; for it is written in the psalms, "The mercy of God is on them that fear him, and on such as put their trust in him." Where we may learn, that they only put their trust in God that fear him; and that to fear God is to turn from evil and do that which is good. So that such as look to be partakers of God's mercy, may not abide in that which is known to be manifest evil and detestable in the sight of God.

Another sort of persons make themselves a cloak for the rain, under the pretence of obedience to the magistrates, whom we ought to obey, although they be wicked. But such must learn of Christ to give to Cæsar what is Cæsar's, and to God what is due to God. and, with St. Peter, to obey the higher powers in the Lord, although they are evil if they command nothing contrary to God's word; otherwise we ought not to obey their commandments, although we should suffer death therefore; as we have the apostles for our example herein to follow, who answered the magistrates as we ought to do in this case, not obeying their wicked precepts, but saying, "Judge you whether it is more righteous that we should obey man rather than God."

Also, Daniel chose rather to be cast into the den of lions to be devoured, than to obey the king's wicked commandments. "If the blind lead the blind, both fall into the ditch." There is no excuse for the transgression of God's word, whether a man do it voluntarily or at commandment, although great damnation is to them by whom the offence cometh. Some others there are, who, for an extreme refuge in their evil doings, do run to God's predestination and election, saying, "If I am elected of God to salvation, I shall be saved, whatsoever I do." But such are great tempters of God, and abominable blasphemers of God's holy election, and cast themselves down from the pinnacle of the temple, in presumption that God may preserve them by his angels through predestination. Such as will do evil that good may ensue, verily, may reckon themselves to be none of God's elect children; whose damnation is just, as St. Paul saith. God's predestination and election ought to be considered with a simple eye, to make us walk more warily in good and godly conversation, according to God's word, and not live presumptuously, and put all on God, that we may do wickedly at large. For the elect children of God must walk in righteousness and holiness, after they are once called to true knowledge. For so saith St. Paul to the Ephesians; that "God hath chosen us before the foundations of the world were laid, that we should be holy and blameless in his sight."

Therefore St. Peter willeth us, through good works, to make our vocation and election certain to ourselves, which we know not but by the good working of God's Spirit in us, according to the rule of the gospel. And he that transforms not himself to the same in godly conversation, may justly tremble and doubt that he is none of the elect children of God, but of the viperous generation, and a child of darkness. For the children of light will walk in the works of light and not of darkness; though they fall, they do not lie still.

Let all vain excuses be set apart, and while you have

light, as Christ commandeth, believe the light, and abide in the same, lest eternal darkness overtake you unawares. The light is come into the world, but, alas! men love darkness more than the light. May God give us his pure eye-salve, to heal our blindness in this respect. O that men and women would be healed, and not seek to be wilfully blinded. May the Lord open their eyes, that they may see how dangerous a thing it is to decline from the knowledge of truth, contrary to their conscience.

But what said I—Conscience? Many affirm their conscience will bear them well enough to do all that they do, and to go to the idolatrous church to service. Their conscience is very large to satisfy man more than God. And although their conscience can bear them so to do, yet I am sure a good conscience will not permit them so to do; which cannot be good, unless it is directed after the knowledge of God's word; and, therefore, in Latin this feeling mind is called *conscientia*, which, by interpretation, is as much as to say, " with knowledge."

And, therefore, if our conscience is led of herself, and not after true knowledge, yet are we not so to be excused, as St. Paul bears witness, saying, " Although my conscience accuses me not, yet in this I am not justified." And he joins a good conscience with these three sisters, charity, and a pure heart, and unfeigned faith. Charity keeps God's commandments; a pure heart loves and fears God above all; and unfeigned faith is never ashamed of the profession of the gospel, whatsoever damage shall be suffered in body thereby.

The Lord who hath revealed his holy will unto us by his word, grant us never to be ashamed of it, and give us grace so earnestly to cleave to his holy word and true church, that for no manner of worldly respect we may become partakers of the works of hypocrisy, which God doth abhor; so that we may be found faithful in the Lord's testament to the end, both in heart, word, and deed, to the glory of God and our everlasting salvation. Amen.

JOHN PHILPOT,

Prisoner in the King's Bench, for the testimony of the truth, 1555.

LETTER II.

To Mistress Ann Hartpole, who was fallen from the sincerity of the gospel, which she had before long known and professed, to the pope and his idolatrous religion.

The grace of God and true light, wherewith he enlighteneth the hearts of all the true and faithful believers, lovers, and followers of his holy gospel, lighten your heart by the mighty operation of his Holy Spirit. Amen.

I have not hitherto been accustomed to write unto you in the matters of our common faith, which is now dangerously assaulted, especially, as by mutual conference we have had consolation in the same, as the times did require. In which I perceived your judgment and constancy to be so much, that I received by your good and godly example strength in the same, even from the beginning, before I was called unto the light of the gospel, in the which you went before me, and ministered occasion to me to follow, at such time as that blessed woman, Ann Askew,* now a glorious martyr in the sight of Jesus Christ, was harboured in your house: so that I thought it superfluous and not needful to write thereof unto you, who so long have been instructed, and by so many learned books confirmed.

But now, hearing that the old serpent, our ancient enemy, who lies in continual wait for our steps, hath bitten you by the heel, and given you a foul fall, I cannot but be heartily sorry; and, as brotherly charity moves me, I testify the same unto you by writing, as I may not at present otherwise open myself in this matter. Alas! sister, that so sincere a profession should receive so gross an infection, to the dishonour of God and of his church. What means it that you are so suddenly departed from Jerusalem unto Jericho, to be a companion of thieves and idolaters, to the utter overthrowing of that good which you have professed? For, as St. James teaches us, "He that offendeth in one, is guilty in all;" and to come to idolatry and strange worshipping of God, forbidden by his word, is, of all transgressions, the most detestable.

Therefore I cannot cease to wonder how you could so soon be allured or drawn thereto. I had thought that the

* Ann Askew was burned in the year 1546.

love of the truth had been so grafted in your heart, that neither persecution, sword, fire, nor gallows, could have brought this to pass, that at the voice of a handmaid, in the first temptation, you should have denied Christ. For not to walk after the sincerity of his gospel, indeed is to deny him; and none can be partakers of the Lord's table and of the table of devils, which is the popish mass, and the malignant synagogue using the same.

Methinks I hear your excuse, pretending your conscience is sound before God notwithstanding, and that your conscience will give you leave thus to do with the common sort of dissemblers both with God and man. But I must tell you plainly, in God's cause, that your conscience so affected,* is a sickly and unsound conscience, and craftily blinded; for before God there is no such conscience allowed, which allows your body to do that which it condemns. "We shall receive all according to that which we do in our bodies, whether it be good or evil;" and it is commanded us, as well to "glorify God in our bodies as in our souls." We must show our faith by our outward conversation, that "men seeing our good works, might glorify our Father which is in heaven."

Will you now with your presence go about to beautify that which hitherto you have justly destroyed? What do you else in so doing, but notify yourself to be an infidel to the church of Christ, who are content to associate yourself with her enemy, for the contentation of man? Has ever any person of God so done, that was allowed therein? Be not deceived, good sister, with the persuasible words of man, neither be afraid of his threats. Follow the gospel of Christ according to true knowledge, and fear to do that which thereby is straitly forbidden you. Tempt not God any longer by this evil doing, for you can do nothing more heinous in his sight. Let this halting be healed up, and turn not from the right ways of the Lord.

Be not ashamed of his gospel, neither of his cross, with the badge of the true and unfeigned professors thereof, which you see now his faithful (praised be his name therefore) are so well content and so willing to bear. But rather, as you are called, take up your cross, and be assured thereby to enter into Christ's glory: for unless we suffer with him, we shall not reign with him, and if we die not with Christ, we shall not live with Christ. The cross now

* Inclined.

is the ready way to heaven, therefore I wish you would choose to be afflicted with the people of God, rather than to live in the tabernacles of the wicked.

Do not any more that which of all things you have now most cause to repent; neither lay daily the foundation of repentance; but let this fall be a teaching unto you of the want of faith which is in you, and so become more fervent in prayer and godly exercises, that, with this new year, you may become a new woman in a godly and new perfection, which God for his mercy sake in Christ, work both in you and me to the end. Amen.

Written in haste by your brother in captivity,
JOHN PHILPOT.

LETTER III.

To certain godly Women, forsaking their own country and going beyond the seas, in the time of persecution, for the testimony of the gospel. Full of fruitful precepts and lessons for all good women.

MAY the Spirit of truth, revealed unto you, my dearly beloved, by the gospel of our Saviour Jesus Christ, be continually abiding with you, and augmented into a perfect building of you into the lively temple of God, through the mighty operation of his holy power. Amen.

I read in the evangelists of certain godly women, who ministered unto Christ, following him in the days of his passion, and never forsook him, but, he being dead and in his grave, they brought oil to anoint him, until he had shown himself unto them after his resurrection, and bidden them show unto his disciples, who were dispersed at his passion, and tell them that he was risen, and that they should see him in Galilee. To them I may justly compare you, my loving sisters in Christ, who of late have seen him suffer in his members, and have ministered to their necessity, anointing them with the comfortable oil of your charitable assistance, even to the death. And now, since you have seen Christ live in the ashes of them whom the tyrants have slain, he willeth you to go away upon just occasion offered you, and to declare to our dispersed brethren and sisters, that he is risen, and liveth in his elect members in England, and by death doth overcome infidelity;* and that they shall see him in Galilee,—which is, by forsaking this world, and by a faithful desire to pass out of this world, by those ways, which he with his holy martyrs has gone on before.

God therefore, entier sisters,† direct your way, as he did Abraham, unto a strange land. God give you health, both of body and soul, that ye may go from virtue to virtue, and grow from strength to strength, until you may see face to face the God of Sion in his holy hill, with the innumerable company of his blessed martyrs and saints. Let there be continual ascensions unto heaven in your hearts.

Let there be no decrease of any virtue, which is already planted in you. Be as the light of the just, which, as Solomon saith, increaseth to the perfect day of the Lord. Let the strength of God be commended in your weak vessels, as it is. Be examples of faith and sobriety, to all that you shall come in company with. Let your godly conversation speak, where your tongue may not, in the congregation. Be swift to hear, and slow to speak, after the counsel of St. James. Be not curious about other men's doings, but be occupied in prayer and continual meditation, with reverend talking of the word of God, without contention among the saints. Let your faith shine in a strange country, as it has done in your own, that your Father which is in heaven may be glorified by you unto the end.

This farewell I send unto you, not as a thing needful, for you know already what your duty is, and are desirous to perform the same, but as one who would have you understand that he is mindful of your godly conversation, whereof he has had good experience, and therefore writes this to be a perpetual memorial betwixt you and him, until our meeting together before God, where we shall rejoice that we have here lovingly put one another in memory of our duty to perform it.

Farewell again, mine own beloved in Christ, and take me with you wheresoever you go, and leave yourself with me, that in spirit we may be present one with another. Commend me to the whole congregation of Christ, willing them not to leave their country without witnesses of the gospel, after that we are all slain, who already are stalled

* Unbelief.   † Faithful sisters.

up and appointed to the slaughter, and in the mean season to pray earnestly for our constancy, that Christ may be glorified in us and in them, both by life and death. Farewell in the Lord.

Yours for ever,
JOHN PHILPOT.

LETTER IV.

To Master Robert Glover, prisoner in Coventry, for the maintenance of God's gospel.*

THE knowledge of God, which hath enlightened your mind with the true religion of Christ, and now, in the beginning of darkness, shines in you to the commendation of your true faith, and to the strength of many weak brethren, remain with you to the end, through the mighty operation of the Holy Ghost. Amen.

It is a singular comfort to the afflicted flock of Christ, to behold such as have been ministers and professors of his truth in religion, stand in the same, and that in the time of persecution, when the same may not be abided by before the face of the rich and mighty in this world, to be preached without present danger. So Paul willeth Timothy, both in season and out of season, to be earnest in sowing the word. And praised be God that we, who are here in prison for the testimony thereof, hear of your diligence in this behalf, who cease not to do the office of an evangelist, although it is with danger of affliction.

Such faithful ministers are to be honoured who submit their own heads to peril for the love of the gospel. Such Christ will acknowledge and confess before his Father in heaven, that they are those which have abode with him in temptations, and therefore shall eat and drink with him at his table in the kingdom of heaven. I thought it, therefore, my duty, at the motion of this bearer, although I have no bodily acquaintance with you ; to exhort you, as St. Paul willeth us to exhort one another as long as we are in this life, boldly to continue in this good and necessary work of the Lord, especially in these evil days, in which Satan

---

* Robert Glover was burned at Coventry, 20th September, 1555. His two brothers died from the effects of the hardships they suffered while secreting themselves from the papists.

rages against the church of Christ, and daily imprisons and robs the members thereof for their faithful testimony.

And be you assured he will not leave you untouched; for above all others he seeks to suppress the good ministers of the word, for they are such as have destroyed his kingdom: but you must not, for fear of his odious and tedious assaults, withdraw yourself from your vocation, but rather provoke him by your constant profession to do his worst, knowing that the same shall turn unto you to the best, even to the crown of your glory. There is none crowned but such as hold out to the goal end, and therefore our Saviour Christ saith in the gospel, " Blessed is he that endureth unto the end." You run well, God is praised therein, and the afflicted church much comforted by so faithful a captain; run out, therefore, as I doubt not you will, and fear nothing of what you shall suffer for your labour; for, if you are faithful unto death, you shall assuredly have the reward of eternal life.

Many go on well till they come to the pikes,* and then they turn their backs, and give over in the plain field, to the shame of Christ and his church, who has such faint-hearted soldiers in his host at the time of need, in which his glory ought most manfully to be showed. I doubt not but you have already cast the price of this your building of the house of God, and know that it is like to be no less than your life: for I believe (as St. Paul saith) that " God hath appointed us in these latter days like sheep to the slaughter." Antichrist is come again, and he must make a feast for Beelzebub his father, of many christian bodies for the restoring again of his kingdom. Let us watch and pray that the same day may not find us unready. The peace of God be with you, and remain with you for ever. Your loving brother in Christ, and in spirit your familiar friend, captive in the King's Bench,

JOHN PHILPOT.

LETTER V.

To certain godly Brethren.

THE grace of God the Father, and the peace of our Saviour Jesus Christ, his eternal Son, and the consolation

* Extreme danger

of the Holy Ghost, our Comforter, strengthen your hearts, and comfort your minds, that you may rejoice, and live in the truth of Christ's gospel to the end. Amen.

I do much rejoice, dearly beloved in the Lord, to hear of your constant faith in the word of God, which you have so purely received; and that you do not, with the worldlings, decline from the purity thereof, although you suffer grief and trouble thereby; for which I praise God most heartily: and the Lord of all strength, who hath begun this good work in you, make it perfect to the end, as I doubt not but he will, for the faithful zeal you have to his truth and to his afflicted church. Therefore, that you may the better stand and bear the brunt of many temptations, which you are likely to be assaulted with in these wicked and stormy days, I thought it good, as it is the duty of one christian man to exhort another in the time of trouble, to put you in remembrance thereof, and to will you with the wise man to prepare yourselves for temptations, and to beware that ye, who yet do stand by the goodness of God, may not fall from your lively knowledge and hope. It is an easy thing to begin to do well, but to continue to the end in well doing, is only the property of the children of God, and such as assuredly shall be saved. For, so saith our Saviour in his gospel, " Blessed are they that persevere to the end."

Let not, therefore, this certainty of your salvation, which is continuance in the sincerity of faith, slide from you. Esteem it more than all the riches and pleasures of this world; for it is the most acceptable treasure of eternal life. This is that precious stone, for which the wise merchantman, according to the gospel, sells all that he hath, and buyeth the same. God, in the third of the Revelation, signifies to the church, that there shall come a time of temptation upon the whole world, to try the dwellers on the earth. From the danger of which temptation all such shall be delivered as observe his word; which word there, is called the word of patience, to give us to understand that we must be ready to suffer all kind of injuries and slanders for the profession thereof.

Therefore God commands us there, to hold it fast, that no man may bereave us of our crown of glory; and St. Peter tells us, " now we are afflicted with divers trials, as it is needful it should so be; that the trial of our faith, being much more precious than gold that perisheth, and yet is tried by fire, might redound to the laud, glory, and honour of Jesus Christ." St. Paul to the Hebrews shows us, that " Christ our Saviour was in his humanity* made perfect by suffering, that we, being called to perfection in him, might more willingly sustain the troubles of the world, by which God gives his holiness to all them that are exercised in the same for his sake. And in the twelfth chapter of the said epistle is written, " My son, refuse not the correction of the Lord, nor shrink when thou art rebuked of him: for the Lord doth chastise every son whom he receiveth, &c." Christ, in the gospel of St. John, bade his disciples to look for affliction, saying, " In the world ye shall have trouble, but in me ye shall have joy." And therefore in the midst of their trouble, in the 21st of St. Luke, he bids them " look up and lift up their heads, for your redemption," saith he, " is at hand." And in the 22d he saith to all such as are afflicted for him, " You are those that have abode with me in my temptation, and therefore I appoint unto you a kingdom, as my Father hath appointed for me, to eat and drink upon my table in my kingdom."

Oh how glorious are the crosses of Christ, which bring the bearers of them unto so blessed an end! Shall we not be glad to be partakers of such shame, as may bring us to so high a dignity? God open our eyes to see all things as they are, and to judge uprightly. Then, doubtless, we should think with Moses, that it is better to be afflicted with the people of God, than to be counted the king of Egypt's son. Then should we joyfully say with David in all our adversities and troubles, " It is good, O Lord, that thou hast brought me low, to the end I might learn thy righteousness." Therefore St. Paul would not glory in any other thing in the world, but in the cross of Christ, and in his infirmities. We have the commandment of Christ, daily to take up his cross and follow him. We have the godly examples of all his apostles, and holy martyrs, who with great joy and exultation have suffered the loss of lands, goods, and life, for the hope of a better reward, which is laid up for all those in heaven, that unfeignedly cleave to the gospel, and never are ashamed thereof.

Great is the felicity of the world to the outward man, and very pleasant are the transitory delights thereof: but

* Human nature.

according to the word of God, the reward of the righteous incomparably excels them all, insomuch that St. Paul, in his epistle to the Romans, plainly affirms, that all the tribulations of this world cannot deserve that glory which shall be showed unto us.

Let us, therefore, good brethren and sisters, be joyful and glad in these troublesome days, which are sent of God to declare our faith, and to bring us to the end and fruition of that which we hope for. If we would enter into the Lord's sanctuary, and behold what is prepared for us, we could not but desire the Lord to hasten the day of our death, in which we might set forth, by true confession, his glory. Neither should we be afraid to meet our adversaries, who so earnestly seek our spoil and death, as Christ met Judas and that wicked rout which came to apprehend him, saying, " I am he whom ye seek." It is commanded us by the gospel, not to fear them that kill the body, but to fear God, who can cast both body and soul into hell fire. We are as much bound to observe this commandment as any other which God hath given us. The Lord increase our faith, that we may fear God more than man. The Lord give us such love towards him and his truth, that we may be content to forsake all and follow him. Now will it appear what we love best; for to that which we love, we will stick.

There is none worthy to be counted a christian, except he can find in his heart, for Christ's sake, if the confession of his truth requires it, to renounce all which he hath, and follow him. And in so doing he gains a hundred fold more in this life, as our Saviour said to Peter, and hereafter is assured of eternal life. Behold, I pray you, what he loses, who in this life receives a hundred for one, with assurance of eternal life. O happy exchange! perchance your outward man will say; if I were sure of this great recompense here, I would be glad to forsake all. But where is this hundred fold in this life to be found? Yes truly; for instead of worldly riches which thou dost forsake, which are but temporal, thou hast found the everlasting riches of heaven, which are glory, honour, and praise before God, angels, and men; and, for an earthly habitation, thou hast an eternal mansion with Christ in heaven; for even now thou art of the city and household of the saints with God, as is verified in the fourth to the Philippians. For worldly peace, which can last but a while, thou dost possess the peace of God, which passeth all understanding; and, for the loss of a few friends, thou art made a fellow of the innumerable company of heaven, and a perpetual friend of all those that died in the Lord, from the beginning of the world. Is not this more than a hundred fold? Is not the peace of God, which in this world we have through faithful imitation of Christ (which the world cannot take from us), ten thousand fold more than those things that are most highly esteemed in this world, without the peace of God? All the peace of the world is no peace, but mere anguish and a gnawing fury of hell: as God of late has set examples before our eyes, to teach us how horrible an evil it is to forsake the peace of Christ's truth, which breedeth a worm in the conscience that never shall rest.

O that we would weigh this with indifferent* balances! Then should we not be dismayed at this troublesome time, neither sorrow in a worldly manner for the loss which we now are like to sustain, as the weak faithless persons do, who love their goods more than God, and the visible things above those which are invisible. But we rather should heartily rejoice and be thankful, that it pleased God to call us to be soldiers in his cause against the works of hypocrisy, and to make us like unto our Saviour Christ in suffering, whereby we may assure ourselves of his eternal glory: for blessed are they, saith Christ, that suffer persecution for righteousness sake. And as St. Paul witnesses to Timothy; "If we die with Christ, we shall live with Christ; and if we deny him, he will deny us."

O that we would enter into the veil of God's promises! Then should we, with St. Paul to the Philippians, reject all, and count all things but dross, so that we may gain Christ. May God who is the lightener of darkness, and putter away of all blindness, anoint our eyes with the true eye-salve, that we may behold his glory, and our eternal felicity, which is hid with Christ, and prepared for us who abide in his testament. For blessed is that servant, whom the master when he cometh, as Christ said, finds faithful. Let us, therefore, watch and pray, one for another, that we yield not in any point of our religion to the antichristian synagogue, and that we are not overthrown by these temptations.

* Impartial.

Stand, therefore, and be not cowards in the cause of your salvation; for his Spirit that is in us, is stronger than he which now rages in the world against us. Let us not put out the Spirit of God from us, by whose might we shall overcome our enemies, and then death shall be as great a gain to us as it was to the blessed apostle Paul. Why then do ye mourn? Why do ye weep? Why are ye so careful, as though God had forsaken you? He is never more present with us, than when we are in trouble, if we do not forsake him. We are in his hands, and nobody can do us any injury or wrong without his good will and pleasure. He has commanded his angels to keep us, that we stumble not at a stone without his divine providence. The devil cannot hurt any of us, and much less any of his ministers, without the good will of our eternal Father.

Therefore, let us be of good comfort, and continually give thanks unto God for our state, whatsoever it be: for if we murmur against the same, we murmur against God, who sendeth the same; which, if we do, we kick but against the pricks, and provoke the wrath of God more against us, who, by our patient suffering, otherwise would sooner be turned in our favour through faithful prayer.

I beseech you, with St. Paul, to give your bodies pure and holy sacrifices unto God. He has given us bodies to bestow unto his glory, and not after our own concupiscence. If for many years God has suffered us to use our bodies, which are his temple, after the lust of the flesh, in vain delights, not according to his glory,—is it not our duty in the latter end of our life, the more willingly to yield our bodies unto God's glory with all that we have, in demonstration of true repentance of that which we have evil spent before? Cannot the examples of the blessed man Job when so horribly afflicted, cause us to say, "The Lord hath given it, the Lord hath taken it. Blessed be the name of the Lord." Even as it pleased the Lord, so it came to pass: if we cast our whole care likewise upon God, he will turn our misery into felicity, as well as he did to Job. God tempteth us now, as he did our forefather Abraham, commanding him to slay his son Isaac in sacrifice to him; which name Isaac, by interpretation, signifies mirth and joy; who by his obedience preserved Isaac unto long life, and offered instead, a ram that was tied by the horns in the brambles. In like manner we are commanded to sacrifice unto God, our Isaac, which is our joy and consolation; which, if we are ready to do, as Abraham was, our joy shall not perish, but live and be increased, although our ram be sacrificed for our Isaac; which signifies that the pride and concupiscence of our flesh, entangled through sin with the cares of this world, must be mortified for the preservation and perfect augmentation of our mirth and joy, which is sealed up for us in Christ.

And to withstand these present temptations wherewith we now are incumbered, you cannot have a better remedy than to set before your eyes how our Saviour Christ overcame them in the desert; and to follow his example, that if the devil himself, or any other by him, willeth you to make stones bread, that is, to take such a worldly-wise way, that you still may have your fair houses, lands, and goods, to live on, you must say, that " a man liveth not only by bread, but by every word that proceedeth out of the mouth of God."

Again, if the devil counsels you to cast yourselves down to the earth, to revoke your sincere belief and godly conversation, and to be conformable to the learned men of the world, pretending that Christ will be well enough content therewith, you must answer that it is written, that " a man shall not tempt his Lord God."

Further, if the devil offer you large promises of honour, dignity, and possessions, if you will but worship idols in his synagogue, you must say, " Go behind me, Satan, for it is otherwise written, that a man must worship his Lord God, and serve him only."

Finally, if your mother, brother, sister, wife, child, kinsman, or friend, seek of you to do otherwise than the word of God has taught you, you must say with Christ, that " they are your mothers, brothers, sisters, wives, children, and kinsmen, which do the will of God the Father." To the which will, may the Lord for his mercy conform us all unfeignedly to the end. Amen.

Your loving and faithful brother in Christ, in captivity
JOHN PHILPOT, Anno 1555.

LETTER VI.

Written to the lady Vane, who was a great supporter of him.

I CANNOT but most heartily give God thanks for these his gifts in you, whose brightness many beholding that are weak, are much encouraged to seek God likewise, and to cleave to him, having the example of so faithful and constant a gentlewoman before their eyes. If the queen of the south shall rise with the men of Christ's generation, and condemn them, for she came from the ends of the world to hear the wisdom of Solomon, then shall your sincere and godly conversation, thus shining in this dangerous time of the trial of Christ's people (you being a woman of right worshipful estate and wealthy condition), condemn in the latter day a great many of these fainthearted gospellers, who so soon are gone back and turned from the truth, at the voice of a hand-maiden.* For neither the fear of imprisonment, nor the possessions of the world, wherewith you are sufficiently endued above a great many, can separate you from the love of the truth, which God has revealed unto you. Whereby it appears that the seed of God's word, which was sown in you, fell neither in the highway, nor among the thorns, nor upon the stones, but upon a good ground, which is blessed of God, and brings forth fruit with great affliction, an hundred fold, to the glory of God, and the increase of his church, &c.

In consideration whereof St. James bids us highly rejoice, whenever we fall into many temptations, knowing that it is but the trial of our faith, that we might bring forth that excellent virtue patience, by which we are made like unto our Redeemer Christ, with whom we here being like in suffering, assuredly shall hereafter be partakers of his eternal glory. Therefore, St. Paul saith, "God forbid that I should glory in any thing but in the cross of our Lord Jesus Christ." I that am under the cross with you (thanks be given to God therefore), have felt in the same more true joy and consolation than ever I felt any benefit that God has given me in my life before. For the more the world hates us, the nearer God is unto us, and there is no perfect

* Queen Mary.

joy but in God. Wherefore Christ said, "In me ye shall have joy, but in the world affliction." Blessed be God that sends us this affliction, that we might perfectly joy in him. For this cause, in the ripest time of iniquity, and in the most fervent season of persecution of the true church, which Christ in the twenty-first of Luke prophesied to come, he tells us to be of good cheer, and to lift up our heads, for our redemption is at hand.

Oh! that the Lord would come and deliver us from this world, which is a vale of misery, unto his own kingdom, where flow perpetual joy and consolation. And, verily, that is the true and only joy which is conceived, not of the creature, but of the Creator, and which, when we possess, nobody can take it from us. To which joy all other joys being compared, are but mournings; all delights sorrow; all sweetness sour; all beauty filth; and, finally, all other things that are counted pleasant, are tediousness. Your own self is a better witness of this than I am. Ask yourself, with whom you are best acquainted. Does not the Holy Ghost speak the same in your heart? Have you not persuaded yourself that this is true, before I wrote thereof? For how should you, being a woman and a young gentlewoman, beautiful, and at your own liberty, have overcome this your frail kind and age, and have despised your excellent beauty and estate, unless all those things which are subject to the senses had been counted of you vile, and little to be esteemed, in comparison of those things which inwardly do comfort you, to overcome the flesh, the world, and the devil?

God increase your joy in all spiritual things, and stablish your hope to the day of eternal rest. You have forsaken darkness, and entered into light: God grant the same may shine still in you, until the perfect day of the Lord come, in which is all our consolation. Here we must be darkened, that there we may appear as bright as the sun in the face of the whole world, and of all them that now condemn us for our well-doing; whose judges then we shall be, to their horrible grief, though now they judge us wrongfully. Pray heartily, and that often, that God once again for his Christ's sake, would be merciful to his afflicted church in England. Faithful prayer is the only remedy that we have against the fiery darts of the devil, that are kindled against us. By prayer the Amalekites shall be overcome, and the roarings of the lion, which seeketh still to devour us, shall be stopped and put to silence. The Lord stop leviathan's mouth, that he swallow not up God's simple people, according to his expectation.

Praise the Lord for the faithful testimony and sacrifice which two of our brethren of late have, through fire, rendered to the truth of the gospel, which now triumphs by the death of godly martyrs.* The Lord is at hand, therefore watch and pray. The last of May, 1555, captive in the King's Bench.

Yours, with heart in Christ,
JOHN PHILPOT.

LETTER VII.

An exhortation to his own dear Sister, constantly and cheerfully to cleave to the truth, and to abide the trial of that doctrine which she had fruitfully professed.

MAY God, the eternal Father, who hath justified you by the blood of his Son Jesus Christ, and called you to hallow his name, through a good conversation and profession of life, sanctify you with daily increase of virtue and faith by his Holy Spirit, that you may appear a vessel of sanctification, in the midst of this wicked and perverse generation, to the laud and praise of the gospel. Amen.

I have occasion, mine own dear sister, to praise God in you for two causes; the one, that according to your ability you are ready to show yourself a natural loving sister to me, your poor afflicted brother, as by your gentle tokens you have testified when absent, and also by your speedy visiting me, which well declares that you are a very natural† sister indeed, and to be praised in this respect.

But the other is, that you are also a sister to me in faith, according to Christ's gospel. I am occasioned to thank God so much the more, by how much the one excels the other. And the spiritual consanguinity is more perdurable‡ than that which is of flesh and blood, and is a worker of that which is by nature; for, commonly

---

* These were John Cardmaker, prebendary of Wells, and John Warne, an upholsterer of Walbrook. They were burned in Smithfield, on the 30th of May, 1555.
† Naturally affectionate.
‡ Lasting.

such as are ungodly, are unnatural, and only lovers of themselves, as daily experience teaches us. The living Lord, who, through the incorruptible seed of his word, hath begotten you to be my liege* sister, give you grace so to grow in that generation, that you may increase to a perfect age in the Lord, to be my sister with Christ for ever.

Look, therefore, that you continue a faithful sister as you are called and are godly entered, not only to me, but to all the church of Christ, yea, to Christ himself, who vouchsafes you, in this your unfeigned faith, worthy to be his sister. Consider this dignity surmounts all the vain dignities of the world, and let it accordingly prevail more with you than all earthly delights. For thereby you are called to an equal portion of the everlasting inheritance of Christ, if now in nowise you show yourself an unnatural sister to him, by forsaking him in trouble, which I trust you will never do for any kind of worldly respect. You are under dangerous temptations to be turned from that natural love which you owe unto Christ, and you shall be tried with God's people through a sieve of great affliction; for so satan desires us to be sifted, that through fear of sharp troubles, we might fall from the stableness of our faith, and so be deprived of that honour, joy, and reward, which is prepared for such as continue faithful brothers and sisters in the Lord's covenant to the end. Therefore the wise man in the book of Ecclesiasticus bids them that come to the service of the Lord, to prepare themselves to suffer temptations.

Since then, for the glory of God and our faith, we now are called to abide the brunt of them—and that when our adversary has done all that he can, we may yet be stable and stand, Christ, our first begotten brother, looks for this at our hands, and all our brethren and sisters in heaven desire to see our faith to be perfect through afflictions, that we might fulfil their number. And the universal church, here militant, rejoices at our constancy, all whom, by the contrary, we should make sorry, to the danger of the loss both of body and soul. Fear not, therefore, whatsoever is threatened by the wicked world—prepare your back, and see that it is ready to carry Christ's cross. And if you see any untowardness in you, as the flesh is continually repugnant to the will of God, ask with faithful prayer, that the good Spirit of God may lead your

* Lawful.

sinful flesh whither it would not. For if we will dwell in the flesh and follow the counsel thereof, we never shall do the will of God, nor work that which tendeth to our salvation.

You are at present in the confines and borders of Babylon, where you are in danger of drinking of the harlot's cup, unless you are vigilant in prayer. Take heed the serpent seduce you not from the simplicity of your faith, as he did our first mother Eve. Let no worldly fellowship make you a partaker of iniquity. He that touches tar, cannot but be defiled thereby; and with such as are perverse, a man shall soon be perverted; with the holy you shall be holy. Therefore, say continually with the prophet David, Psalm xxvi. "Unto the saints that are on the earth, all my will is on them." You have been sanctified and made pure through the truth; take heed you are not made unholy and defiled, lest the last be worse than the first.

I write not this because I stand in any doubt of your sincere continuance, of which I have such good experience; but because the days are evil, and in them it is the duty of every one of us to exhort and stir up one another. I am bold, therefore, to put you, my good sister, in remembrance of that which it does not a little comfort me to remember in my troubles and daily temptations. Wherefore, I doubt not, you will take that in good part which comes from your brother both in spirit and body, who tenders* your salvation as earnestly as his own, that we might joy together eternally with such joy as the world shall never be able to take from us. Thanks be unto God, you have begun to run a good and great time well in the ways of the Lord. Run out the race to the end, which you have begun, and then you shall receive the crown of glory. None shall be crowned, but such as strive lawfully. Be not overcome of evil, but overcome evil with good, and the Lord shall make you one of those faithful virgins, that shall follow the Lamb wheresoever he goeth, the which Christ grant both you and me. Amen.

Commend me to all them that love me in the Lord unfeignedly. May God increase our faith, and give us grace never to be ashamed of his gospel. That same request which I have made to my brother Thomas, I make also to you, desiring you by all means you can, to accomplish my request, that my sureties may be satisfied with that which

* Cares for.

is mine own, to the contentation of my mind, which cannot be quiet until they are discharged.* Therefore, I pray you to help to purchase quietness, that I might depart out of this world in peace. My dissolution I look for daily, but the Lord knoweth how unworthy I am of so high an honour, as to die for the testimony of his truth. Pray that God would vouchsafe to make me worthy thereof, as he has done of long imprisonment, for which his name be praised for ever. Pray and look for the coming of the Lord, whose wrath is great over us, and I will pray for you as long as I live. The 9th of July, in the King's Bench.

Your own loving brother, as well in faith as in body,
JOHN PHILPOT.

LETTER VIII.

To the godly lady Vane.

GOD, the Father of our Lord Jesus Christ, increase in your godly heart the faith of the gospel, which is your eternal inheritance; and the Holy Ghost comfort your spirit with all spiritual consolation, to the day of the Lord. Amen.

I cannot but praise God most highly and earnestly, my dear and faithful lady, for the great and unfeigned love which you bear unto me in Christ, declared oftentimes, as well now as of late, by manifest and liberal tokens. Blessed be God that has made you so worthy a member in his kingdom. For such shall reap with abundance in time of reward, that here sow so plenteously in welldoing; although I am most unworthy to receive any such benefit at your hands, as if I were a pillar of Christ's church, who am scarce a shadow thereof. But the zeal of Christ's church in you wishes me to be such a one as the time requires. God fulfil your desire of me, that I may be found constant, and no wandering star. I am not worthy of the name of a prophet, or of a minister of God's word, for that I, being hindered by the iniquity of the time, have little or nothing laboured therein. I am a friend of our common spouse Jesus, and do rejoice in the

* This was for the first-fruits of his archdeaconry, which his sureties were compelled to pay, although during the time of his imprisonment he had no advantage from it.—*Letters of the Martyrs.*

verity of his word, for which, praised be his name, he has counted me worthy to suffer; and, indeed, "He that giveth a draught of water in the name of a disciple (as Christ hath promised), shall not lose his reward." Therefore, what your gentleness does in his name, the Lord recompense unto you, in all his blessings which he is accustomed to pour on those who love his flock unfeignedly.

Good lady, you have cause to joy that the kingdom of God is thus continually before your eyes, and that you are not ashamed of the bands of Christ, which you with his people in part do suffer. They may be assured of everlasting glory, who are not ashamed here to take up the cross of Christ, and to follow him. Here we must weep and lament, while the world laughs and triumphs over us; but our tears shall shortly be turned into unspeakable joy, and we shall eternally be joyful together, when the world shall lament their infidelity without end.

I would that I were able to do anything that might show condign thanks for that sincere love which you bear unto me in Christ. You adjure me in Christ, as it were, by your gentle letters to be bold on you in all my need. I thank God, who ceases not to provide for his, I lack nothing at present, but only ability to thank your faithful heart for your goodness toward me. I love you and not yours, as it is meet for christians to love one another in God; and your faith which I behold in you, is worth more unto me than all your possessions. And I think I shall not need to be chargeable unto you long, for this week I look for commissioners to sit on me and my fellow prisoners in prison, lest the spirit of our breath might blow further abroad. The will of God be done. We are not so good as John the Baptist, who was beheaded in prison. Darkness cannot abide the light. Therefore their doings must declare what they are.

We are as sheep appointed as a sacrifice to the Lord. We must not fear the fire, for our Lord is a consuming fire, who will put out the fierceness of raging torments for us. Be not afraid of them that can kill the body, but fear him who can cast both body and soul into hell-fire. God forbid that we should rejoice otherwise than in the cross of Christ, and pray that he would make us worthy to suffer for his sake. God will have our faith tried and known, and, therefore, let us willingly humble ourselves under the mighty hand of God, that he may gloriously lift us up in his good time. There is none perfectly faithful indeed, till he can say with St. Paul, " I am persuaded that neither death, nor life, nor angels, nor princes, nor powers, nor things present, nor things to come, nor highness, nor owness, nor any other creature, is able to separate me rom the love of God, which is in Christ Jesus our Lord." This faith God plant both in you and me immoveably. In this faith we have to rejoice, and in no other.

All the tribulations of the world are not worthy of the eternal weight of glory which is prepared for those who here with patience abide the cross. Wherefore, let us be strong with the strength of him that is able to make us strong, and lament the weakness, I might say the infidelity, of our faint gospellers. Christ, whom we would pretend to have put upon us, is the strength of God, and how then may they be weak where Christ is? We have more cause to be glad, touching ourselves, at this time, than we have had at any time before, in which we have so ready a way to go unto God, and so good an occasion to show our duty in glorifying his holy name. For if we are imprisoned in this cause, we are blessed. If we lose all that we have, we are blessed a hundred fold. If we die, we are blessed eternally; so that in suffering persecutions, all is full of blessings.

O, elect lady, be blessed therefore of God, with the blessed of God, and flee, as you do, the concupiscence of the world. Embrace that which is perfect, joyfully looking for the coming and the cross of our Lord Jesus Christ. Thus desiring God to preserve you to his true peace, and to give you victory over that temptation which is come to try our faith. Christ be with you, and bless you both in body and soul; and my prayer shall follow you wheresoever you go, as I desire you may be with me. The last week I sent your beneficence to Oxford: I could not before have a convenient messenger. As soon as I have word, you shall be satisfied of your request. Love me as you do, and the God of love be with you. The 20th day of August.

By yours, with all his power in the Lord,

JOHN PHILPOT.

LETTER IX.

A letter written to certain of his faithful Friends, as his last farewell, a little before he suffered.

THE knowledge of God, which hath enlightened you with true understanding of the gospel of Christ, be remaining with you still to the end, and be augmented in your hearts and doings, through the operations of the Holy Spirit, to the glory of God, and your eternal salvation. Amen.

A man that is passing into far countries, before his departure, commits such goods as God has endued him with to his dearest friends, that they might be the better by them, if he returns not again. Even so, dearly beloved, and right worshipful, my good friends, I, having shortly to pass unto my heavenly inheritance which is hid with Christ, and to our common country and eternal dwelling-place, which we shall have with God, never to return before the latter day, in which our souls shall come to judgment, and receive their bodies to be glorified, according to their doings; have thought it my duty to communicate something unto you (with whom I have found great humanity), something of the few heavenly treasures with which God, among others, has endued me in Christ, whereby he has made me his child, and assuredly the inheritor of the kingdom of heaven, with all those who unfeignedly love him, and constantly cleave to his holy gospel. And that is, by the renovation of his image, whereunto man was first created like unto God, which is, to be in the favour of God, to know God truly, to live justly, to delight fervently in the contemplation of God, to be continually happy, to be immortal, void of all corruption and sin; which blessed image, through sin, is deformed in us, and in a manner lost, saving that it hath pleased God of his mercy, who willeth not the death of a sinner, to restore that image by grace, through knowledge and belief of the gospel, which otherwise is entirely suppressed and extinguished in our nature.

Therefore, we, knowing the great and lamentable loss which we sustain in Adam, ought most earnestly to seek the recovery thereof, that we might eternally live like unto God in immortality and felicity; which we shall never recover, unless we go about to mortify our outward man all the days of our lives more and more, and are renewed in spirit, according to the true knowledge of God. Which if we are, then may we be assured that we have found that joy, felicity, and eternal life, which Adam had in paradise; yea, and more than that, ten thousand fold, for it is such as the eye hath not seen, the ear hath not heard, neither the heart can conceive, which Christ has prepared for us. This image of God, whosoever by faith does find, he has found the most precious treasure that any man can find, for he is even here a citizen of heaven and in possession of eternal life.

Therefore, I commit unto you principally a daily care of the renovation of this image, as the chiefest jewel you can desire in this world. And thereof now I am the more moved to put you in remembrance, because I love you entirely in the Lord, and desire your fellowship, which the iniquity of our time will not permit me to enjoy here. And forasmuch as we have a better life to come than this present is, an eternal society with Christ, which neither the malice of time, nor the distance of place can dissolve or separate, I exhort you now, as one that has obtained mercy of God in the reparation of his image in me, to embrace the care thereof, with earnest desire to attain the same; whereby we shall all have a perfect fruition of our love and friendship, which already we have here begun, and with God in heaven shall be, without all doubt, made joyfully perfect.

Let this be a perpetual remembrance of your poor afflicted friend, who daily looks, through fire, to enter into that eternal life; where he trusts assuredly to enjoy your fellowship, if the image of God is renewed in you, through the knowledge of Christ, which you have received and do know. Look whose image the coin bears, his it is. Semblably,* if your conversation be after the gospel, verily, you are the elect of Christ; but if it is according to the world, his servants you are whom your life doth express.

We have all in baptism put on Christ, whom if we endeavour to represent, we are, indeed, the sons of God and inheritors with Christ. One good rule, St. Paul to the Romans, in the twelfth chapter, appoints for the restoration of this our image of God: "Fashion not yourselves, saith he, unto this world, but be ye changed in

* In like manner

your shape, by the renewing of your mind, that ye may prove what is the will of God, which is good, acceptable and perfect." God grant that this rule may take place with you, and then, doubtless, our company shall be inseparable with all the saints of God in eternal bliss.

Be you not deceived by the vain possessions and uncertain pleasures of this world, which serve to no other purpose than to blind your eyes, that they might not behold the things which are glorious and permanent for ever. The things which we see are mortal; but the things which we see not, but certainly hope for, are immortal. For " all flesh," as the prophet Isaiah saith, " is but grass, and the glory thereof as the flower of the field." Oh that you, who have the possessions of this world, would so account them, and not sell your eternal inheritance for a mess of porridge, as Esau did! God open your eyes, that you may see the glory of Christ in the mount, with Peter, John, and James. Then I doubt not, you would say with Peter, " Lord, it is good for us to abide here: let us here make our dwelling-places."

We have in this world no firm mansion, but we seek after that which is to come: which, if we seek now where it may be found, we shall surely find. If we mortify the image of Adam, which, through sin, reigns in our flesh, then shall the image of Christ revive in us to our eternal glory. We are all baptized to die with Christ, to the end we should walk in newness of life, as persons dead to the world, and living to God. And if we die with him by crucifying our concupiscence and lusts, we shall eternally live. Infidelity* is the cause of all our misery: which causes us to fear man more than God, and to esteem the things present more than the things to come. God enlighten our eyes, that we may understand how precious an inheritance Christ has prepared for such as hunger and thirst thereafter. Then, I doubt not, we would say with St. Paul, " I am surely persuaded that neither death nor life, neither angels, nor rule, neither power, neither things present, neither things to come, neither any other treasure or creature, shall separate us from the love which is in Christ Jesus."

The Lord increase our faith, and give us his Holy Spirit to discern with ourselves, how much we are grown in

* Unbelief.

his image, and are like unto him; for how much we are unlike to the world, so much more are we like unto God, and so much the more do we approach unto him. The Lord draw you by his Holy Spirit, and fashion you unto his likeness, that we may eternally live together. The means to come thereunto, is diligent exercise in God's word; continual and faithful prayer; a desire and love to God; the fear of God; the contempt of the world; and a constant faith in the knowledge of his word, joined with the works of righteousness.

This is the sum of all our christian religion which we do profess, which, if we follow, happy are we that ever we were born. But if we are negligent in this, it had been better for us never to have been born: for cursed are they that decline from the Lord and his holy commandments, and have their delights in the vanities of this world. Cease not to follow the image of God, and to express the same in yourselves to the glory of God, and then God will glorify you for his image sake, which he makes to live in you. We are all weak in transforming the same in us at the beginning, for our flesh is quite contrary to it.

But we must not give over by lawful striving, till we may say with St. Paul, "Now live I, but not I, but Christ in me." The Lord grant that Christ, who, by the gospel, is planted in us, may be fashioned in our godly conversation, to the glory of God, and to the good example of our brethren, that our temporal life may be changed into eternal life, and our friendship in God, eternally endure. Amen.

This last farewell I send unto you to be a token of my love, until we shall meet in the kingdom of Christ, there to rejoice perfectly of that godly fellowship which here we have had on the earth. God hasten that meeting, and deliver you from the temptation which is now come upon the church of England, for the trial of such as are faithful in the Lord's testament, to the crown of their glory, if they are found faithful to the end.

Let us watch and pray one for another, that these evil days do not overwhelm us, in which our adversary the devil goeth about like a roaring lion seeking whom he may devour. The peace of God remain with you for ever.

Written in the King's Bench by one of the poor captive sheep of Christ, appointed to the slaughter for the testi mony of the truth, where he doth joy, and wishes you to joy, praising God with him. Amen.

JOHN PHILPOT.

LETTER X.

To a faithful Woman, and late wife to one of the bishops, which gave their lives in the Lord's quarrel.

REMEMBER, dear sister, that your life in this world is a continual warfare, to fight against the world, the flesh, and the devil, in which you are appointed, for the trial of your faith and love to God, to fight manfully to overcome. For the Spirit of God which is in you, is stronger than he which is in the world, and by this you may know that you are the child of God, even by the Spirit which striveth in you against the flesh and sin, and will not suffer sin to reign in you. This Spirit is obtained by often and daily reading and hearing the word of God, joined with faithful and hearty prayer: for diligent reading of God's word planteth the Holy Spirit in you, and earnest prayer increases the same. Read, therefore, the word studiously; and pray heartily that the same good gift of faith which you have learned of your faithful husband and good bishop in the Lord, who has gloriously yielded his life for the same, may be confirmed in you even unto death, that you may receive the same crown of glory which he now has. For precious is the death of the faithful in the Lord's sight; therefore, desire still to die to the Lord, and be glad to be poor both in body and spirit, and thus assure yourself that the kingdom of heaven is yours.

Your own in the Lord,
JOHN PHILPOT.

LETTER XI.

To his dear friend in the Lord, John Careless, prisoner in the King's Bench.

MY dearly beloved brother Careless, I have received your loving letters full of love and compassion, insomuch that they made my hard heart to weep, to see you so careful for one who has been so unprofitable a member as I have been, and am, in Christ's church. God make me worthy of that which I am called unto, and I pray you cease not to pray for me, but cease to weep for him who has not deserved such gentle tears: and praise God with me, for I now approach to the company of those whose want you may worthily lament. May God give your pitiful* heart his inward consolation. Indeed, my dear Careless, I am in this world in hell, and in the shadow of death; but He that, for my deserts, has brought me down into hell, shall shortly lift me up to heaven, where I shall look continually for your coming, and others, my faithful brethren, in the King's Bench. And though I tell you that I am in hell in the judgment of this world, yet assuredly I feel in the same the consolation of heaven, I praise God; and this loathsome and horrible prison is as pleasant to me as the walk in the garden of the King's Bench.

You know, brother Careless, you know that the way to heaven out of this life is very narrow, and we must strive to enter in at a narrow gate. If God mitigates the ugliness of mine imprisonment, what will he not do in the rage of the fire whereunto I am appointed? And this has happened to me, that hereafter I might be an example of comfort, if the like happen unto you, or to any other of my dear brethren with you, in these cruel days, in which the devil so rages at the faithful flock of Christ; —but in vain, I trust, against any of us; who are persuaded that neither life, nor death, is able to separate us from the love of Christ's gospel, which is God's high treasure committed to our brittle vessels to glorify us by the same. May God of his mercy make us faithful stewards to the end, and give us grace to fear nothing, whatsoever in his good pleasure we shall suffer for the same. The cause that I have not written unto you is our strait keeping, and the want of light by night; for the day serves us but a little while in our dark closet. This is the first letter that I have written since I came to prison, besides the report of mine examinations, and I am fain to scribble it out in haste.

Commend me to all our faithful brethren, and bid them with a good courage look for their redemption, and frame themselves to be hearty soldiers in Christ. They have

* Full of pity, compassionate.

taken his prest-money* a great while, and now let them show themselves ready to serve him faithfully, and not fly out of the Lord's camp into the world, as many do. Let them remember that, in the Apocalypse, the fearful are excluded the kingdom. Let us be of good cheer, for our Lord overcame the world, that we should do the same. Blessed is the servant whom, when the Lord cometh, he findeth watching. O let us watch and pray earnestly, one for another, that we be not led into temptation. Be joyful under the cross, and praise the Lord continually, for this is the whole burnt sacrifice which the Lord delighteth in. Commend me to my father Hunt, and desire him to love and continue in the unity of Christ's true church, which he hath begun; and then shall he make me more and more joyful under my cross with him. Tell my brother, Clement, that he has comforted me much by his loving token in signification of an unfeigned unity with us; let him increase my joy unto the end perfectly. The Lord of peace be with you all. Salute all my loving friends, M. Mering, M. Crooch, with the rest, and, specially, M. Marshall and his wife, with great thanks for his kindness showed unto me. Farewell, my dear Careless. I have dallied with the devil awhile, but now I am over the shoes :† God send me well out.

Out of the Coalhouse, by your brother,
John Philpot.

LETTER XII.

A letter, full of spiritual consolation, to the lady Vane.

The mercy of God the Father, and the consolation of the Holy Ghost through Jesus Christ, be with you and strengthen you, my dear mother and sister in the Lord, in these dangerous days, to the crown of eternal glory, which is now offered to all faithful soldiers in the gospel Amen.

As your good ladyship desires to hear from me, so am I desirous to write, as your gentleness and daily goodness binds me. But satan of late hath hindered me, who, envying all good exercises which I have had and received by mine easy imprisonment in times past, has brought me out

* Bounty money. † Psalm lxix. 2, 14.

of the King's Bench into the bishop of London's Coalhouse, as dark and as ugly a prison as any about London. But my dark body of sin has well deserved the same, and the Lord has now brought me into outward darkness, that I might the more be enlightened by him, as he is most present with his children in the midst of darkness. Here I cannot be suffered to have any candle-light, neither ink nor paper, but by stealth. Wherefore I cannot write to you as I would, neither as my duty is. As Christ, my master, was sent from Annas to Caiaphas, so am I sent from Winchester diocese to that of London. I trust to make a speedy end of my course. God give me grace and patience to be a faithful follower of my Master. I have already been this sevennight in his Coalhouse, and have of late been four times called to my answer, but hitherto am not called to judgment, which I daily look for; but I fear they will prolong me, and try me by strait imprisonment awhile, in the which God's will be done.

Pray, dear lady, that my faith faint not, which, I praise God, is at present more lively with me than it has been in times past.* I taste and feel the faithfulness of God in his promise, who has promised to be with his in their trouble, and to deliver them. I thank the Lord, I am not alone, but I have six other faithful companions, who, in our darkness, do cheerfully sing hymns and praises unto God for his great goodness.

We are so joyful, that I wish you to partake of my joy. For you that are so careful of my bodily relief, how can I but wish you spiritual consolation, and that abundantly? Let not, dear heart, my strait imprisonment any thing molest you: for it has added, and daily does add, unto my joy; but rather be glad, and thankful unto God with me, that it has pleased him to make me, most wretched sinner, worthy to suffer any thing for his sake. Hitherto we have not resisted unto blood. God make us never to count our blood more precious in our eyes than his truth.

Ah, my dear sister, I thank you again for your last letter you sent me; it is a singular comfort unto me, as often as I read the same. I have it in my bosom, and will carry the same even to the stake with me, in witness that Christ has so constant and faithful a lady in England. God succour and keep that spirit in you; for it is the very

* "As thy days, so shall thy strength be!"

spirit of adoption of the child of God. Such cheerful and holy spirits under the cross are acceptable sacrifices in the sight of God; for Christ came to cast fire into the earth, and looks that it should be kindled. Be you fervent in spirit in our Christ's cause, as you have begun, for that is the principal spirit wherewith David desired to be confirmed. O how I rejoice that your ladyship goes arm in arm with me unto Christ, or rather before me. I cannot but joy of such a worshipful fellow.* Methinks I see you mourn, and desire to be loosed out of the earthly and frail habitation of this body.

O how amiable and pleasant is it to dwell in the Lord's tabernacle! Our Christ and his heavenly company look for us; let us haste and run thereto, for, behold, the Lord is ready to embrace us. Mine own beloved in the Lord, be joyful in the Lord with your afflicted brother, who daily offers your merciful alms, which most unworthily I still receive of you, unto the Lord. But now, dear mother, you need not burden yourself so much, as my last letter did signify, for that chargeable imprisonment is cut off, and a little now serves me; wherefore I pray you send no more until I send to you, for I have sufficient and abound. God's peace be with you for ever.

Out of my lord of London's Coalhouse, the last of October.

Your own,
JOHN PHILPOT.

LETTER XIII.

To my brother, John Careless, prisoner in the King's Bench.

THE grace of God the Father, through his dear Son, Christ our Saviour, with perseverance in all godly verity, be with thee, my dear brother Careless, and with all my prison-fellows. Amen.

Ah, my own love in Christ, I am sorry to hear of the great troubles which these schismatics* do daily put thee to. I would that I were with thee, in part to relieve thy grief; but since it has pleased God otherwise, take my

* Companion.
† These were certain freewill men.—*Letters of the Martyrs.*

advice in this your conflict, and be patient whatsoever your adversaries can say or do against you. Know that you are appointed for the defence of the gospel, for which you, God be praised, do suffer: yet you must understand that you are but a voice in the wilderness, and a planter, and that it is God who must give the increase. And, therefore, if there come not such fruit of your good labours as you would wish, be content, and know that a stony ground cannot fructify, yet God will not forget your labour, but you shall reap as plenteously in the day of reward as though it increased after your expectation.

Have patience, therefore, in your labour, and let not care eat out your heart. Commit the success to God, and cease not with charity to be earnest in the defence of the truth, against these arrogant and self-will blinded scatterers. These sects are necessary for the trial of our faith, and for the beautifying thereof. Be not perverted by them that are perverse and intractable. They resist not you, they resist Christ, and are workers against their own salvation. Show as much modesty and humility as you possibly may. So shall your labour best please God, and your adversaries receive the more shame, and others seeing your modest conversation amongst these contentious babblers, shall glorify God in his truth by you, and the more abhor them, as you see it has come to pass in times past.

Be content that Shimei rail at David and cast stones awhile; be sure that his railing judgment will fall upon his own pate. Have always that notable rule of Christ's church before your eyes, which St. Paul writes, that " if any body be contentious, neither we, neither the church of God, have any such custom."

Desire all our brethren in the bowels of Jesus Christ to keep the bond of peace, which is the unity of Christ's church, where are all the treasures of spiritual consolation in heavenly things. Let no root of bitterness spring up, which the devil, with all diligence, seeks to thrust in amongst the children of God. Kiss one another with the kiss of unfeigned brotherly love, and take one another by the hand cheerfully, and say, " Let us take up our cross together, and go to the mount of Calvary, and there be willing to suffer whatsoever it pleases God we shall." Hitherto we have not resisted to blood-shedding. Our blood must not be too dear for the Lord, and then his kingdom shall not be too dear for us. Thus exhort one another to offer yourselves a joyful sacrifice unto God, for this is that pleasant sacrifice wherewith his wrath shall be pacified, which is now kindled most justly against us.

Be thankful unto God that it has pleased him to make you worthy of this glorious affliction: yea, and I pray you give thanks unto God for me, that it has been his good will to take me, most filthy and unthankful sinner, to be one of this number. My joy of the love of God towards me in this behalf is such, that it makes all my strait imprisonment to seem pleasure. God be praised, I cannot be sorry, though I would. O how great is the love of God towards us!

Be merry, brethren, and rejoice continually in the Lord, for the victory is ours; yea, heaven is ours, and all the glory thereof. Faint not, but run on; for we are near at the end. Be glad of nothing so much as the mortification of the old Adam: murmur in no case, whatsoever necessity you are in. Communicate your necessities to me and to others of his people, and God will make us divide stakes. Be always praising God, talking, comforting, teaching, and exhorting in God, and he will not see you utterly destitute. I commend me to all your faithful prayers. And you, Careless, see that you are in my dungeon with me, as I am in spirit with you in the King's Bench, and with you all.

Thine own brother, JOHN PHILPOT.

LETTER XIV.

To his friend and faithful brother in the Lord, Master Robert Harrington.

GENTLE Master Harrington, I cannot tell what condign* thanks I may give unto God for you, in respect of the great gentleness and the pains which you have taken for the relief of me and of our other afflicted brethren in Christ. God be praised for his mercy, whose loving providence towards us we have seen by such faithful stewards as you have been towards a great many. Blessed be you of God for the loving care which you have taken for his poor flock. God has reserved your reward of thanks in heaven, and therefore I go not about to render you any,

* Suitable, deserved.

lest I might seem to judge that you looked for that here, which is reserved to a better place.

I thank God for what I have obtained by your faithful and diligent industry, and God forgive me my unworthiness for such great benefits. God give me grace to serve him faithfully, and to run out my race with joy. Glorious is the course of the martyrs of Christ at this day. Never had the elect of God a better time for their glory than this is. Now may they be assured under the cross, that they are Christ's disciples for ever.

Methinks I see you desiring to be under the same. The flesh draws back, but the spirit saith it must be brought whither it would not. Here is the victory of the world— here is the true faith and everlasting glory. Who is he that desires not to be found faithful to his Master? And now is the time that every faithful servant of Christ has a just opportunity to show himself a glorious soldier in the Lord's sight. Now do the Amalekites invade the true Israelites, that the Israelites might speedily be glorified! I need not, for want of understanding, admonish you hereof, but, as a willing soldier of Christ, I would exhort so to run that you may get the victory speedily with us. A man who is bid to a glorious feast wishes his friend to go with him, and to be a partaker thereof. God calls me, most unworthy, among others, to drink of the bride-cup of his Son, whereby we shall be made worthy, as many of our brethren have been before us, to sit at the right hand and at the left hand of Christ. O what an unspeakable condition is that! May any worldly thing stop us from the desire thereof? Since we seek the kingdom of God, why do we not take hold upon it, being so near offered unto us?

Let us approach near unto God, and God will draw near unto us. God draw us after him, that we all may run after the savour of his sweet ointments. Christ anoint us, that we may be suppled in these evil days to run lightly unto the glory of the Lord. Shame, imprisonment, loss of goods, and shedding of our blood, are the just price which we must willingly bestow for the same. Wherefore, dearly beloved in the Lord, let not the great charges keep you back from buying this glory; for the reward is ten thousand fold greater than the price.

Because you have married a wife, whom God bless, I can not excuse you from this mart,* but you must bring your

* Bargain, matter of loss or gain.

wife for a usury to the Lord, whose pleasure is in godly yoke-fellows. I wish you to be as I am, except these horrible bonds, but yet they are most comfortable to the spirit, assuring us that we are made worthy through Christ of the kingdom for which we suffer. Praised be the Lord for the affliction which we suffer, and may he give us strength to continue to the end!

Commend me to Master Heath, and tell him that I would wish him to be with me, to prove how apt he is to carry the cross of Christ. I pray for his continuance in Christ, as for my own. Commend me to his wife, and to Mistress Hall, certifying them that I am brought to the gates of hell, that I might never enter into the same, but be raised up from hell to heaven, through the word that sanctifies us. Commend me to Master Elsing and his wife, and thank them that they remembered to provide me some ease in prison; and tell them, that though my lord's Coalhouse is but very black, yet it is more to be desired by the faithful, than the queen's palace. May God make her a joyful mother, and preserve them both to the comfort of God's people. Thus, for this time, farewell, dear brother. Written in post haste because of strait keeping.

This day I look to be called before the commissioners again. Pray, dear brother, for the Spirit of wisdom to remain with me. Commend me to your wife, and I thank you both for your tokens. Your token I have sent to your wife; and my token unto you, is my faithful heart with this letter. Commend me to all my friends, and tell them I thank God I am cheerful in Christ, wishing them to fear God more than man, and to learn to despise earnestly the vanities of this world, desiring you all to pray for me, that I may end my journey with fidelity. Amen.

JOHN PHILPOT.

LETTER XV.

To my dearly beloved sister in the Lord, Mistress Heath.

THE light of the gospel of Christ, which has enlightened you with the true understanding of faith, be daily increased in you, my dearly beloved sister, unto the perfect day of the Lord, through the mighty operation of his Spirit. Amen

To Mistress Heath.

Whereas you have required of me a token at your departing, that might be a remembrance with you of my brotherly love towards you, I mused of divers things what I might best commend to you; and among all others, I found none so certain a token either of the love of God towards us, or else of our love one to another, as to bear the cross together with Christ. To bear the cross is to be partaker of the afflictions of Christ, which he now suffers in his members for the accomplishment of his body, the church, which we are who believe in him sincerely, which is the surest token of God's love towards us that we can have in this world. "For whom God loveth he chasteneth:" and as it is written, "He chasteneth every son whom he receiveth." Wherefore, above all things, love the cross of Christ, under which all the church of Christ in England now is, and be content to have your faith tried every day by some cross or other, as it pleases God to put on you; and if God puts no grievous cross upon you, let your brethren's cross be your cross, which is a certain token of true brotherly love.

If the church in England had learned with the gospel to have borne the cross of Christ, as all that are professors of the gospel are called thereunto, they would not so lightly, at the commandment of man, have turned from the ways of salvation to their old ways again, contrary to their conscience, and all to avoid the cross, the merciful sign of God's love towards us! If the cross were not, the faithful could not be known. If the cross were not, God should not so manifestly appear to be our deliverer and comforter, as he shows himself in the midst thereof unto all who put their trust in him. Therefore, believe them verily to be in a most happy state that are under the cross: and such as utterly abhor the same, are cowards, and not fit soldiers for the Lord.

We all have received the credit of faith from God in Christ, that we should beautify the same, or rather God in the same. We have this treasure in brittle vessels: let us take heed that the brittleness of the vessel shed not our precious treasure on the earth, as it is lamentable to see, at this day, many have most unfaithfully done. Are they worthy of the heavenly kingdom, who here esteem earth more than heaven? O palpable infidelity! Will not God require the credit of faith which he has committed unto us? Yea, verily, is this the usury of faith, to love the world more than the gospel, and to fear man more than God? If men who count themselves stronger and worthier vessels have thus unfaithfully dealt in the things of God, let the weakness of women be more firm in their faith to the glory of God, whose might appears in weakness There is no exception of persons before God: both man and woman are one in God: and that person who strives to do his will, of all sorts of people is acceptable to him.

Wherefore contend in these cross days, which are the love days of God towards us, to show yourselves faithful to Him that calleth you, and be ready to do his will according to true knowledge, and that under the cross. God has given you a faithful guide, whom see that you love with all humility, patience, and obedience, as it becomes a holy woman to be subject to a faithful head in the Lord: and comfort him in our common cross, and bid him cheerfully take up the one end, and you will bear the other, a double string knit together. As you, in your godly matrimony, represent the mystery of Christ and his church; so continue lively members by faith in the same, and learn daily more and more to bear the cross of Christ, that others, seeing your strength, may be comforted, and be ashamed of their weakness in their Master's cause.

The Lord loveth the faithful servant who brings his talent to his table, with increase. Now is the time to increase to the Lord, and not to decrease; to multiply our faith under the cross, and not to diminish it. "The ways of the just do increase as the dawning of the day:" embrace, therefore, the cross, as the rainbow of God's merciful covenant: pray that we may together end our course therein with joy. Take my token in good worth until we are made partakers of the glory of the cross. Out of my lord of London's Coalhouse. The 11th of November.

Yours, JOHN PHILPOT.

LETTER XVI.

To lady Vane, encouraging her under the present evil times.

THE Spirit of joy and rejoicing be with you, and be you comforted through his loving and comfortable leading and governance, and make your unfeigned heart, my dearest sister in the Lord, continually joyful against all the fiery temptations of the enemy in these our days, by Jesus Christ our Saviour. Amen.

Praised and exalted be the name of our living God for the truth of his faithful promises, which he makes his people to feel in the time of extremity, when they seem to the world to be forlorn and most miserable; such is the goodness of the omnipotence of our God, that he can and does make to his elect, sour sweet, and misery felicity. Wherefore it was not without cause that the wise man in his Proverbs wrote, "Whatsoever happeneth to a just person, it cannot make him sorrowful." All things work to good unto them which be good. Unrighteous we are, and wicked of ourselves, yea, when we have our gayest peacock's feathers on; but through Christ, on whom we believe, we are just, and in his goodness we are good, and hereby have daily experience of his mercy and loving kindness towards us in our afflictions and miseries, contrary to man's judgment.

Therefore, let us always, as David did, put the Lord before us, and then we shall find, as he said, that " He is on my right hand, and I shall not be moved." Sure it is, as St. Paul said, " If God be with us, who shall be against us?" as though he would say that all that our enemies can do maketh for our glory, so long as we abide in God. What hurt had Shadrach, Meshach, and Abednego by the fire, whilst the Lord walked with them? What annoyance had Daniel by the fierce lions in the dungeon, the Lord being with him? So mighty is our Lord, and able, yea, and ready, to comfort such as put their whole trust in him.

Therefore, mine own heart, be of good cheer in these cruel days, for these are to the increase of our glory. They that bring us low, do exalt us, and they that kill us do open the gates of eternal life. You, by the Spirit of God, wherewith your mind is endowed, do see what I say, and I by experience do feel it, praise be to God therefore. I cannot but lament the blindness, or rather madness, of the world, to see how they abhor the prison of the body, in a most righteous cause, and little or nothing at all regard the prison of infidelity,* in which their soul is fettered most miserably, which is more horrible than all the pri-

* Unbelief.

sons of the world. How much the soul is more precious than the body, so much is the captivity and misery of the soul to be lamented more than that of the body. God, therefore, be blessed, who hath given your tender person to understand that the liberty of the soul surmounteth all the treasures of the world, and that the soul being free, nothing can be hurtful to the body. Hold fast this liberty, for this is the freedom of the children of God, by the which we pass, without fear, both through fire and water. And where those are terrible to the world, to the elect they are joyous and full of glory.

God spake to Moses on the mount, in fire, thunder, and storms, and the voice was so terrible to the people, that they trembled thereat, and wished that God would not speak unto them in such wise; but Moses' face, coming out of the same, was so bright that the children of Israel could not behold his face. Even so shall our faces be in the midst of our fiery forms, and our enemies shall hereafter never be able to behold the brightness of our countenance. And although we are made as black as the bottom of the pot that hangs over the fire, yet sure I am that we shall be made whiter than snow, and purer than silver or fine gold.

If we have to joy in any thing in this world, it is in tribulations, by which we are certified to be the children of God, and inheritors of his everlasting kingdom. By this, saith St. John, we know the love of Christ towards us, that he gave his life for us. And by this we know we love him, that we are ready at his calling to yield our life, for the testimony of his truth to our brothers, that they might have occasion to learn, by our faithful example, to esteem the things of God more than those of the world.

O may God increase this true faith in you! for I see hereby you are in possession of heaven. Continually, through hope, behold the things that are not seen, but yet are hidden for our greater reward: and then this noble faith shall not perish, but grow to perfection and fruition of God. What, though this sack of dung, which we carry about us pinches, and repines at this our pure faith, shall it discomfort us? No, truly, but make us more circumspect and vigilant, that we are not overthrown in our right ways, since we have so familiar an enemy.

By faith we overcome, and he that overcometh shall be crowned. Therefore the assaults of the flesh and of the world, wherewith we are to be pressed as long as we live, ought to make us more diligent in spiritual things, and more desirous to be delivered out of this body of corruption. Happy are we that see the danger of our conflict, whereby we are admonished to beware, and to run to the strong hold of the name of the Lord our defence, to which in all your temptations I do most heartily commit your faithful heart for ever.

As concerning mine own affairs, since I came to the bishop's Coalhouse, I have now been six times in examination, twice before the spiritual bishops, and once of late before a great many of the lords of the council, before whom I have more frankly, I thank God, uttered my mind than I did any time before. The matter laid against me was, the disputation in the convocation-house two years past, concerning their idol, the mass, which, by all means, they would have me recant; and I have answered, that if the clergy, that now rule the roast, can prove either their sacrament of the altar to be a sacrament, or else themselves to be of the true church of Christ, that I would be as conformable to their doings as they could desire. I look daily for my final judgment, which was promised me ere this, but I think now they will defer it till the end of the parliament. God, in whose hands my life is, hasten the time in his good pleasure, and make me worthy of that great glory. You are as present with me, as I am with you. Christ give us a perfect fruition one of another in his kingdom. Our brethren, that are gone before us, look for us. Hasten, O Lord, our redemption, and suffer us not to be overcome of evil. Amen.

Out of the bishop's Coalhouse, whereof one Eleyny, dwelling in Paternoster-row, gaoler of Lollards' tower; and another, named Fountain, are keepers, the 13th of November.

Your own in Jesus Christ, JOHN PHILPOT.

To my right well beloved, and the very elect lady of God, which hath chosen the better part, this be delivered.

LETTER XVII.

A letter of Master Philpot to the lady Vane, wherein he complains of the dissimulation and perjury of Englishmen, falling again to the Pope, and expresses his joy in his afflictions.

I CANNOT but joy with you, my heartily beloved in Christ, at the fall of Sennacherib;* since it is to the glory of God, and to the consolation of his church, to see the fall of their enemies before their face, according as it is written; "The just shall rejoice, when he seeth the vengeance of the wicked." God make this your joy perfect; for, as concerning myself, I count not to see those good days whereof you have a glimmering in this life; for although the cockatrice is dead, yet his pestilent chickens, with the harlot of Babylon,† still live. But there is a great hope of their confusion shortly, because God does not prosper their doings according to their expectation. Most happy shall he be, whom the Lord shall soonest take out of this life, that he may not see the plagues which the manifest perjury, and the manifold idolatry, and detestable dissimulation, and that of such as know the truth, threaten to come upon us.

The Lord is just, and all unrighteousness displeases him, and here, or else in another world, he will punish this gross infidelity of the world. But his elect, and such as he loves, he will punish here, that they should not be condemned hereafter with the world eternally: we have nothing so much to rejoice in as in the cross of Jesus Christ, and that we are partakers of his afflictions, which are the earnest-penny of that eternal kingdom, which he, upon the cross, hath purchased for us. For as St. Paul, his faithful witness, saith, "If we suffer with him, we shall reign with him. If we die with him, we shall live with him."

Wherefore, mine own dearly beloved, praise God with me most entirely, that it has pleased him now most mercifully to visit the sins of my youth, and my great unthankfulness, and by the same gives me such consolation, that he assures me of his great goodness and mercy, and

* The death of Gardiner, bishop of Winchester, a most decided enemy to the truth, and a persecutor of God's people.
† The Romish bishops and the popedom. Rev. xvii.

turns his fatherly castigation into my crown of glory. O good God! what am I on whom he should show this great mercy! To Him that is immortal, invisible, and only wise, be all honour, praise, and glory therefore. Amen.

"This is the day that the Lord hath made, let us rejoice and be glad in the same." This is the way, though it be narrow, which is full of the peace of God, and leadeth to eternal bliss. O how my heart leaps for joy, that I am so near the apprehension* thereof! God forgive me mine unthankfulness and unworthiness of so great glory. The swords which pierced Mary's heart in the passion of our Saviour, which daily also go through your faithful heart, are more glorious and to be desired than the golden sceptres of this world. O blessed are they that mourn in this world toward God, for they shall be eternally comforted. God make my stony heart mourn more than it does. I have so much joy of the reward that is prepared for me, most wretched sinner, that though I am in a place of darkness and mourning, yet I cannot lament, but both night and day am joyful, as though I were under no cross at all. Yea, in all the days of my life I never was so joyful; the name of the Lord be praised for ever and ever, and may he pardon mine unthankfulness. Our enemies fret, fume, and gnash their teeth, to see and hear that we, under this grievous affliction in the world, can be so joyful. We are by them counted as desperate persons, for the certain hope and feeling which we have of our everlasting salvation: and it is no marvel, for the worldly men cannot perceive the things of God, it is mere foolishness and abomination to them.

Be thankful unto our God, mine own dear helper, for his wondrous working in his chosen people. Pray instantly that this joy may never be taken from us, for it passes all the delights of this world. This is the peace of God which surmounteth all understanding—this peace, the more his chosen are afflicted, the more they feel; and therefore cannot faint, neither for fire, neither for water. Let us pray for our weak brethren and sisters' sake, that it may please God to alleviate the grievous and intolerable burdens of these cruel days. But touching ourselves, let us heartily beseech our Saviour to vouchsafe to give us this glorious gift to suffer for his gospel's sake, and that we may think the shame of the world to be our glory, as

* Attainment.

it is indeed. God increase our faith, and open our eyes to behold what is prepared for us. I lack nothing, praised be God. I trust, my marriage garment is ready. I will send you my examinations as soon as I can get them written, if you are desirous of them.

God of his mercy fill your merciful heart with all joy and consolation of the hope to come.

Out of the Coalhouse, the 19th of November.

Your own lover, JOHN PHILPOT.

LETTER XVIII.

A letter written to John Careless out of the Coalhouse of darkness, whereby he gives light and heavenly comfort to his heavy and troubled mind. Profitable to be read by all who mourn in repentance for their sins.

THE God of all comfort, and the Father of our Lord Jesus Christ, send unto thee, my dear brother Careless, the inward consolations of his Holy Spirit, in all the malicious assaults and troublous temptations of our common adversary the devil. Amen.

I cannot but rejoice to behold that God gives you a heart so contrite for your sins. It is the lively mark of the children of God, whose property is to think more lowly and vilely of themselves than of any others, and oftentimes to set their sins before them, that they might be the more stirred to bring forth the fruits of repentance; and learn to mourn in this world, that in another they might be glad and rejoice. Such a broken heart is a pleasant sacrifice unto God. O that I had the like contrite heart! May God mollify my stony heart, which laments not in such wise my former detestable iniquities. Praised be God that he has given you this sorrowful heart in respect of righteousness, and I pray you let me partake of these godly sorrows for sin, which are the testimony of the presence of the Holy Ghost. Did not the sword of sorrow pierce the heart of the elect and blessed mother of our Lord? Did not Peter, who was so beloved of Christ, weep bitterly for his sins? Did not Mary Magdalen wash the feet of our Saviour with her tears, and receive remission of her sevenfold sins?

Be of good comfort therefore, mine own dear heart, in

this thy sorrow, for it is the earnest of eternal consolation
In thy sorrow laugh, for the Spirit of God is with thee.
Blessed are they, saith Christ, that mourn, for they shall
be comforted. They went forth and wept, saith the prophet; such shall come again, having their hands full of
gladness. And although a heart sorrowful in consideration
of his sin, be an acceptable sacrifice before God, whereby
we are stirred up to more thankfulness unto God, knowing
that much is forgiven us that we might love the more, yet
the man of God must keep a measure in the same, lest
he be swallowed up by too much sorrow. St. Paul would
not that the Thessalonians should be sorry as other men
which have no hope. Such a sorrow is not commendable,
but worketh damnation, and is far from the children of
God, who are continually sorrowful in God when they look
upon their own unworthiness, with hope of forgiveness.
For God to this end by his Spirit setteth the sins of his
elect still before them, that where they perceive sin to
abound, there they might be assured that grace shall su-
perabound, and he brings them down into hell, that he
might lift them up with greater joy unto heaven. Wherefore, my own beloved in Christ, as long as you are not
void altogether of hope, be not dismayed through your
heart pensive for your sins, how huge soever they have
been, for God is able to forgive more than you are able to
sin: yea, and he will forgive him, who with hope is sorry
for his sins.

But know, brother, that as oft as we go about, by the
help of God's Spirit, to do that which is good, the evil
spirit satan, lieth hard in wait to turn the good unto evil,
and goes about to mix the detestable darnel* of desperation with the godly sorrow of a pure penitent heart. You
are not ignorant of his malicious subtlety, and how that
continually he assaults the good which the grace of God
planteth. I see the battle betwixt you and him, but the
victory is yours, yea, and that daily: for you have laid
hold upon the anchor of salvation, which is hope in Christ,
who will not suffer you to be made ashamed.

Be not discomforted that you have this conflict: but be
glad that God has given you the same to try your faith,
and that you might daily appear worthy of the kingdom of
God, for which you strive. God beholds your faith striving against satan, and is pleased with your mighty resist-

* Weed.

ance. The Spirit which is in you is mightier than all the adversary's power. Tempt he may, and lying await at your heels, he may give you a fall unawares; but overcome he shall not; yea, he cannot, for you are sealed up already with a lively faith to be the child of God for ever: and whom God hath once sealed for his own, him he never utterly forsaketh. "The just falleth seven times, but he riseth again." It is man's frailty to fall, but it is the property of the devil's child to lie still.

This strife against sin is a sufficient testimony that you are the child of God: for if you were not, you would feel no such malice as he now troubles you withal. When this strong Goliah hath the hold, all things are in peace which he possesses: and because he has you not, he will not suffer you to be unassaulted. But stand fast, and hold out the buckler of faith, and with the sword of God's promises smite him on the scalp; that he may receive a deadly wound, and never be able to stand against you any more. St. James tells you he is but a coward, saying, "Resist the devil, and he will flee from thee." It is the will of God that he should thus long tempt you and not go away as yet, or else he had done with you long ere this. He knows already that he shall receive the foil at your hands, and increase the crown of your glory; for he that overcometh shall be crowned. Therefore, glory in your temptations, since they shall turn to your felicity. Be not afraid of your continual assaults, which are occasions of your daily victory. The word of God abideth for ever. In what hour soever a sinner repenteth him of his sins, they are forgiven. Who can lay any thing to the charge of God's elect? Do you not perceive the manifest tokens of your election? First, your vocation to the gospel,—and after your vocation, the manifest gifts of the Spirit of God given unto you above many others of your condition, with godliness which believeth, and yields to the authority of the Scripture, and is zealous for the same. Seeing you are God's own darling, who can hurt you? Be not of a dejected mind for these temptations, neither make your unfeigned friends more sorrowful for you than need requires.

Since God has willed you at your baptism in Christ to be " Careless,"* why do you make yourself careful? Cast all your care upon him. Set the Lord always before your

* Without anxious care.

eyes, for he is on your right side, that you shall not be moved. Behold the goodness of God towards me. I am careless,* being fast closed in a pair of stocks, which pinch me for very straitness; and will you be careful? I will not have that unseemly addition to your name. Be as your name pretendeth, for doubtless you have no other cause but to be so. Pray, I beseech you, that I may still be careless* in my careful estate, as you have cause to be careless in your easier condition. Be thankful, and put away all care, and then I shall be joyful in my present care.

Commend me to all our brethren, and desire them to pray for me, that I may overcome my temptations; for the devil rages against me. I am put in the stocks in a place alone, because I would not answer to such articles, as they charged me with in a corner, at the bishop's appointment, and because I did not come to mass when the bishop sent for me. I will lie all the days of my life in the stocks, by God's grace, rather than I will consent to the wicked generation. Praise God, and be joyful, that it has pleased him to make us worthy to suffer somewhat for his name sake. The devil must rage for ten days. Commend me to Master Fokes, and thank him for his law books;† but neither law nor equity will take any place among these bloodthirsty ones. I would for your sake their unjust dealings were noted unto the parliament-house, if it might avail. God shorten these evil days! I have answered the bishop sufficiently plain already, and I said unto him, if he will call me in open judgment, I will answer him as plainly as he will require: otherwise I have refused, because I fear they will condemn me in hugger-mugger.‡ The peace of God be with you, my dear brother. I can write no more for lack of light, and what I have written I cannot read myself, and God knows it is written uneasily. I pray God you may pick out some understanding of my mind towards you. Written in a Coalhouse of darkness, out of a pair of painful stocks, by thine own in Christ,

JOHN PHILPOT.

* Without anxious care.   † See the examinations.
‡ It is evident that Bonner wished to avoid bringing Philpot to be examined publicly.
§ A reply to this letter will be found in the letters of Careless.

LETTER XIX.

*To the lady Vane.**

THE principal Spirit of God the Father, given unto us by Christ our merciful Saviour, confirm, strengthen, and stablish you in the true knowledge of the gospel, that your faithful heart, worshipful and dear sister in the Lord, may attain and taste with all the saints, what is the height, the depth, the length, and the breadth, of the sweet cross of Christ. Amen, &c.

Oh! happy are you amongst all other women, who have found this precious stone which is hid in the gospel; for which we ought to sell all other things, and purchase the same. O happy woman! whose heart God has moved and enlarged to be in the profession thereof. Others seek worldly goods, honours, and delights; but you seek with good understanding to serve God in spirit and verity. This is the gate that leads to heaven; this is your portion for ever. By this you shall see God face to face, which sight is unspeakable joy; and by this shall you see whatever your heart can desire. By this shall you have a full sight of all the beautiful powers, and of all the celestial paradise. By this shall you know those whom you never knew, and be joyous and glad with those whom you have known here in God, world without end.

Ah! I lament the infidelity of England, which after such great light is stept into such great darkness again. The servant that knoweth his master's will and doth it not, shall be beaten with many stripes. Ah! great are the plagues that hang over England, yea, though the gospel should be restored again. Happy shall that person be whom the Lord shall take out of this world, not to see them. Ah! the great perjury which men have so willingly run into against God, by receiving antichrist again and his wicked laws, which do threaten a great ruin unto England. Oh! that the Lord would turn his just judgments upon the authors of the truce-breaking between God and us, that they might be brought low as Nebuchadnezzar was, that his people might be delivered, and his glory exalted. God grant that the good luck which you hope may shortly come upon the house of God, may be a true

---

* Here follows a letter of Master Philpot to the Lady Vane, which because I could not wholly insert for the length, I have excerpted certain specialities thereout.—*Fox.*

prophecy, and not a well-wishing only. Ah! Lord, take away thy heavy hand from us, and stretch it out upon thine enemies, these hypocrites, as thou hast begun, that they may be confounded. O! let not the weak perish for want of knowledge through our sins. Although thou kill us, yet will we put our trust in thee.

Thus, dear heart, you teach me to pray with you in writing. God hear our prayers, and give us the Spirit of effectual prayer, to pour out our hearts continually together before God, that we may find mercy both for ourselves and for our afflicted brethren and sisters. I cannot but praise God in you, for that pitiful heart which takes other folk's calamities to heart, as your own. Blessed are they that mourn, for such shall be comforted. God wipe away all tears from your pitiful eyes, and sorrow from your merciful heart, that you may, as doubtless you shall do shortly, rejoice with his elect for ever.

You have so armed me to the Lord's battle both inwardly and outwardly, that except I am a very coward, I cannot faint, but shall overcome by death. You have appointed me to so good and gracious a general of the field, to so victorious a captain, and to so favourable a marshal, that if I should not go on lustily,* there were no sparkle of heavenly manhood in me. I will present your coat armour before my captain, and in the same I trust by him to overcome. The scarf† I desire as an outward sign to show our enemies, who see not our glorious end, neither what God works inwardly in us, through the blindness of their hearts, that they persecute Christ's cross in us, whereby he has sealed up the truth of his gospel by his death unto us, that we, by our death, if need be, might confirm the same, and never be ashamed whatsoever torment we suffer for his name's sake; and our weak brethren seeing the same might be more encouraged to take up Christ's cross, and follow him. God give us grace to do all things to his glory. Amen.

The world wonders how we can be joyful in such extreme misery, but our God is omnipotent, who turns misery into felicity. Believe me, dear sister, there is no such joy in the world as the people of Christ have under the cross. I speak by experience; therefore believe me, and fear nothing that the world can do unto you. For when they imprison our bodies, they set our souls at liberty

* Courageously.
† Some apparel he had requested to be prepared for his burning.

with God. When they cast us down, they lift us up; yea, when they kill us, then do they bring us to everlasting life And what greater glory can there be, than to be at conformity with Christ; which afflictions work in us.

God open our eyes to see more and more the glory of God in the cross of Jesus Christ, and make us worthy partakers of the same. Let us with St. Paul, rejoice in nothing but in the cross of Jesus Christ, by whom the world is crucified unto us, and we to the world. The cross of Christ be our standard to fight under for ever. While I am thus talking with you of our common consolation, I forget how I trouble you with my rude and inordinate tediousness; but you must impute it to love, which cannot quickly depart from those whom He loveth, and that desireth to pour himself into their bosoms.

Therefore, though your flesh would be offended, as it might justly be at such rudeness, yet your spirit which taketh all things in good part that come of love, will say nay. And now I am departing; yet I will take my leave ere I go, and would fain speak somewhat that might declare my sincere love to you for ever. Farewell, O elect vessel of the Lord, to the comfort of his afflicted flock; farewell on earth, whom in heaven I am sure I shall not forget. Farewell most joyfully under the cross, and until we meet, always remember what Christ saith; "Be of good cheer, for I have overcome the world."

God pour his Spirit abundantly upon you, mine own dearly beloved in Christ, until you come to see the God of all gods with his elect in the everlasting Sion. I send to you the kiss of peace, with which I take my leave of you at this present. It is necessary we depart hence, or else we could not be glorified. Your heart is heavy, because I say I must depart from you. It is the calling of the merciful Father, wherewithal you are content, and so am I. Be of good comfort, hold out your buckler of faith; for by the strength thereof we shall shortly meet in eternal glory: to which Christ bring us both. Amen. Amen. The 10th of December, 1555.

Death, why should I fear thee,
Since thou canst not hurt me,
But rid me from misery
Unto eternal glory.

Dead to the world, and living to Christ, your own brother, sealed up in the verity of the gospel for ever,

JOHN PHILPOT.

THE END

www.ingramcontent.com/pod-product-compliance
Lightning Source LLC
Chambersburg PA
CBHW062037220426
43662CB00010B/1532